THE ESSENTIAL OYSTER

ESSE

OY

A SALTY
APPRECIATION
OF TASTE
AND TEMPTATION

BLOOMSBURY
NEW YORK · LONDON · OXFORD · NEW DELHI · SYDNEY

THE

ROWAN JACOBSEN

NTIAL

PHOTOGRAPHY DAVID MALOSH STYLING ADRIENNE ANDERSON

STER

BLOOMSBURY USA
AN IMPRINT OF BLOOMSBURY PUBLISHING PLC

1385 BROADWAY   50 BEDFORD SQUARE
NEW YORK   LONDON
NY 10018 USA   WC1B 3DP UK

WWW.BLOOMSBURY.COM

BLOOMSBURY AND THE DIANA LOGO
ARE TRADEMARKS OF BLOOMSBURY PUBLISHING PLC

FIRST PUBLISHED 2016

ISBN: HB: 978-1-63286-256-3
EBOOK: 978-1-63286-257-0

LIBRARY OF CONGRESS CATALOGING-IN-PUBLICATION DATA
HAS BEEN APPLIED FOR.

2 4 6 8 10 9 7 5 3 1

DESIGNED AND TYPESET BY BENJAMIN WILKERSON TOUSLEY
PRINTED AND BOUND IN CHINA BY C&C OFFSET PRINTING CO. LTD

TO FIND OUT MORE ABOUT OUR AUTHORS AND BOOKS VISIT WWW.BLOOMSBURY.COM.
HERE YOU WILL FIND EXTRACTS, AUTHOR INTERVIEWS, DETAILS OF FORTHCOMING EVENTS
AND THE OPTION TO SIGN UP FOR OUR NEWSLETTERS.

BLOOMSBURY BOOKS MAY BE PURCHASED FOR BUSINESS OR PROMOTIONAL USE.
FOR INFORMATION ON BULK PURCHASES PLEASE CONTACT MACMILLAN CORPORATE
AND PREMIUM SALES DEPARTMENT AT SPECIALMARKETS@MACMILLAN.COM.

This be the cup, brimming fathoms of nectar
This, the well that flows from forever
This be the saltcellar, trencher of tears
and also the teardrop, stone-wept from ocean
This be the stone, lost among cairns,
and there, another, hidden in middens
This be the hull that casts off its seed
Thus grows the reef, encrusted with life—
This, ancient vessel, anchored to reef
This be the ark where life resides
and this, tiny cradle, bearer of treasure
This be the oyster, slow-rocked by tides.

—Mary Elder Jacobsen

INTRODUCTION

A good oyster smells like the sea breeze skipping over the shore. A bad oyster smells like a murder victim. I prefer the former. But I like how even the latter helps exemplify the essence of the interface: An oyster conveys its life experience directly to your senses.

Was it raised in the briny Atlantic or a brackish bayou? Warm water or cold? Rich or thin? Did it develop down in the pluff mud of the Carolina Lowcountry, or in a floating bag tossed by wind and waves in Willapa Bay? Did its ancestors hail from Japan or the James River? The whole story is there in front of you. You can read some of that story with your eyes, but to really understand, of course, you have to eat it. And when you do, even if you aren't yet familiar with the language of oysters, you can usually get the essence right away. Every oyster is a tide pool in miniature, a poem built of salt water and phytoplankton that nods to whatever motes of meaning shaped it. It is the sea made solid. The bay gone sentient.

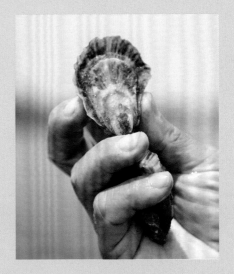

Not that solid. And not that sentient. An oyster is basically seawater with a purpose. It threatens to collapse back into sea-ness at any moment, the way an emulsion looks for an excuse to give up. This in-betweenness, neither solid nor liquid, can be the oyster's unique allure or its primary offense, depending on the audience. Assuming that you are in the first camp—and if not, gentle reader, you have made a terrible mistake—then you already know that an oyster's charm lies in straddling realms, in being animal, vegetable, and mineral all at once.

It's also wicked salty and goes great with beer. Sometimes I think it's that simple.

SACRIFICE, RENEWAL

A decade ago, I wrote a book called *A Geography of Oysters* that helped accelerate the oyster mania we now find ourselves in. There have always been oyster lovers, of course, and I'd been one of them since my teens, but it wasn't until the early aughts that I got a little clarity on why I loved them. It was because they were landscape. I'd been drinking a lot of wine and thinking a lot about terroir, the "taste of place." I loved the idea that wine nods to the natural conditions where its grapes grew, but I knew it was no more than a nod: Wine doesn't literally taste like its landscape. In terms of terroir, oysters make wine look like Hawaiian Punch. They are their terrain, and their flavors are a pure condensation of the place they grow. It's the salinity and temperature of the water, the particular mix of plankton they graze on, the wildness of the waves, and the essential mojo of the spot. I did my research and put together my book, hoping that there were a few other oyster geeks out there who might be interested. Turns out there were a lot. We all need living landscapes.

But strip away the veneer of terroir (or "merroir," the marine equivalent), and you find something much more primal going on. Like sushi, oysters are best eaten raw, when the living chi has not yet fled. They have a life force in them that leaves you feeling flushed. And you will pay what it takes to get that feeling. That's why oysters, nutritional nobodies, can cause people to part from their economic senses in a way generally reserved for drugs and sex. I consider them more mood than food. They won't fill you up. But they'll make you feel like the coolest alpha predator in the ecosystem.

The next time you're holding a particularly chi-laden oyster in your

Above: Smokey McKeen and Carter Newell sorting Pemaquid oysters dredged from Maine's Damariscotta River. Right: Thomas "Uptown T" Stewart has been the man behind the bar at Pascal's Manale in New Orleans for more than twenty years.

hand, sharpen your most prized oyster knife, go in through the oyster's bill (the rounded front), and cut the bottom muscle tight against the shell. Turn over the oyster in your hand and remove the bottom shell. Nestled against the white disk of muscle, you'll see a pale, pulsing drum. This is the heart. It flutters just like the pulse on your lover's neck.

Or on the neck of a bull about to get the axe on the altar of a Greek mystery cult, which is probably more to the point. Oyster culture is one of our last vestiges of live animal sacrifice, a Bronze Age atavism best experienced in places like New Orleans, where the oyster bar still serves as a temple. You walk in and immediately feel the heightened atmosphere. You take your seat with the other supplicants at the marble altar. The high priest greets you; ritual conversation ensues. Then he raises his knife and cuts the muscles of a dozen oysters as you follow his clean, rehearsed motions with your eyes: *Hoc est enim Corpus meum, quod pro vobis tradetur.* He sets the offering before you, you anoint it, and the deed is done. Wine is splashed, a little tithing for the priest, the gods are pleased, and the universe has been renewed for another day. Really, it's the least you can do.

SHARDS OF TIME

The tastiest oysters the world has yet produced can be found in the bays and bars of America at this very moment. Do not let the nostalgists tell you otherwise. The renaissance that began twenty years ago keeps making more diverse and delicious oysters in more new places. These are not your grandfather's oysters. They blow his away.

How did this happen? It's a beautiful feedback loop. Even ten years ago, as a new generation was falling in love with oysters, many of the objects of that affection were not that lovable. Some regions that had traditionally harvested wild populations were scraping the bottom of the barrel, dumping skinny critters onto the market. Other places were just beginning the transition to oyster farming and hadn't yet learned the best way to grow them. And many potentially interesting regions simply weren't producing oysters at all. Even when you did find good oysters, they were often mangled, drowned in cocktail sauce, or served as anonymously as a glass of the house white.

Today, what a world of difference. There's no coastline from BC to Baja, from New Iberia to New Brunswick, that isn't producing great oysters. These oysters are, for the most part, deeper cupped, stronger shelled, finer flavored, and more stylish than their predecessors. For that, thank innovative new farming techniques, but also credit the surge of interest from both producers and consumers. Everybody wants to be an oyster farmer. And everybody else wants to eat their local farmer's oysters.

To me, the watershed moment may have been the day in 2011 when I walked into the newly opened Island Creek Oyster Bar in Boston and took in the weathered gray woods, the acute light, and the caged wall of oyster shell. It was a space that could have been designed only by people who understood where oysters come from, and cared to share that story. The menu listed not just the name of each oyster and its provenance but the name of the oyster farmer. CUTTYHUNK: Cuttyhunk, MA, Seth Garfield. EAST BEACH BLONDE: Ninigret Pond, RI, Nick Papa.

That was the beginning of a beautiful trend of oyster bars run by oyster farmers, or closely affiliated with them. From Merroir on the Virginia coast to Hog Island on California's Tomales Bay, the journey from bay to plate has grown ever shorter, and the knowledge base of those on the front lines ever greater. I almost take for granted the platters of immaculate oysters being turned out by lightning-quick shuckers who will gladly debate the relative merits of tide tumbling and beach finishing as they work.

Above: A cosmopolitan collection of bivalves at Eventide Oyster Bar in Portland, Maine. Right: Fifth-generation oyster farmer Adam James stands in a field of Hama Hamas at low tide.

So we find ourselves with an unparalleled diversity of oysters to try, and places to try them. There are more than three hundred different oysters in North America, and god knows how many oyster bars, many popping up in places just beginning to come out of their Red Lobster shells.

Which brings me to this book. It is no comprehensive field guide. So many oysters, so little time (and space). Of those three-hundred-plus oysters, we've managed to give a third their moment in the strobes. Think of this as the book to accompany a new exhibition: "Ninety-nine Ways of Looking at an Oyster." It should tell us a bit about the many things an oyster can be, and even more about the ways we respond to that unique coastal landscape that has sustained and inspired us for 160,000 years.

Criteria for inclusion? Flat-out yumminess, of course. Or histori-

cal significance. Or uniqueness. Some had colorful stories to tell. Some had quirks. But above all, we wanted character. Oysters are stunning. Oyster farms are stunning. Oyster farmers are stunning, in a Swamp Thing sort of way. Oyster culture crackles with wabi-sabi authenticity. What oyster growers actually farm are poignant shards of time, miraculously transportable. They make you aware of mortality—yours, theirs, the guy wielding the knife—and profoundly thankful for the beautiful ride. That's what we've tried to capture in this book.

THE ART OF THE OYSTER

An oyster is not a ham sandwich. This little hermit focuses just enough cosmic energy inside its cave to merit a moment of your attention. The following dos and don'ts are suggestions to help make the most of that moment. But this isn't the Japanese tea ceremony, either—we're talking happy hour here—so don't get all orthodox about it. There's an art to eating and appreciating an oyster, but—as with all the social arts—part of the art is in not drawing attention to the artistry. Get it right, don't linger, move on.

DO UNDERSTAND WHAT YOU'RE EATING

An oyster is a filter feeder. All life long, it sits attached to a rock or a shell in some bay, pumping water across its gills, straining out the phytoplankton, and transforming this marine forage into protein. Oyster farms are the greenest protein producers on earth (no feed!). An oyster wants to grow up, grow strong, and reproduce as many times as possible before the Grim Reaper arrives, shucking scythe in hand. Anytime the water is warm enough for it to feed, it builds up its body and its shell. When the water gets really warm, usually in summer, it spawns, ejecting sperm or eggs into the water.

These form larval oysters, which swim around for two weeks looking for something hard (rock or shell) to attach to. As soon as they "set," they are called "spat." They never move again. Oyster hatcheries trick oysters into spawning by cranking up the water to summer temps. Then they trick the larvae into setting on tiny grains of sand instead of whole shells. Oyster farms buy this quinoa-sized "seed" and grow it in protected environments. Oysters are the animals that farm like plants.

"Spat," "spawn," "seed," "set," "flupsy"—lots of weird and colorful terms populate the oysterverse. I have used them sparingly, but sometimes there's no way around it. You don't need to know this terminology to enjoy an oyster, but it might make the experience a tad richer. Because all the terms are in the glossary, I don't define them every time they appear in the text.

DO KNOW YOUR SPECIES

The flavor, texture, and vibe of the five species of oysters grown in America are as different from one another as is that of a cow, a pig, a sheep, a goat, and a bison. The **Pacific** (*Crassostrea gigas*) species is the workhorse of the oysterverse, responsible for at least three-quarters of the oysters produced worldwide. France, Ireland, England, Australia, New Zealand, and the West Coast of North America all depend on the Pacific oyster, as does its native Japan. It grows fast and hearty, tastes good (cucumber is the go-to descriptor), and isn't picky about its waters. It can be really pretty (like that sexy little Naked Roy on page 29), with ruffled shells fanned in pastel, or strong and silent, its shell buffed gray-green by abrasion on the beach. The **Kumamoto** was an obscure and unheralded species from southern Japan before war and California brought it to fame (story on page 79); now its conspicuously fruity essence makes it the most beloved oyster in America. The button-sized **Olympia**, which once enjoyed an empire from British Columbia to Southern California, is too small to be taken seriously except by those few of us who know it to be a brassy masterpiece (as is so evident on page 51). Its hefty cousin, the **European Flat**, the native oyster of Europe, is more like a metal monster straight out of Marvel Comics: Iron Oyster. It's a mouthful of crunch and iodine. Tough to farm, it's quite rare these days, though it thrives in deep, wild basins from Maine to Scotland. Only those from Brittany's Belon River can be called Belons (page 241). The **Eastern** oyster grows wild from New Brunswick to Texas and builds reefs so large people have camped on them. Today the wild ones are few and far between, but every farmed oyster on the Gulf and Atlantic Coasts is an Eastern, prized for its robust shell (like the Gulf Coast brute on page 95) and its pure

Preceding pages: Tonging for Malpeques on Prince Edward Island. Above: A gigantic Pacific oyster in Willapa Bay. Right: In the Southeast, oysters often grow on intertidal flats.

sea-salt savor. Honorable Mention: **The New Zealand Flat** oyster, cousin to the European Flat (can't miss the family resemblance on page 251), native to New Zealand and Chile, now jetting in to the West Coast to make the occasional summer appearance.

DON'T TAKE THE EASTERN OYSTER FOR GRANTED

If you grew up on the Gulf Coast or East Coast, the Eastern oyster is about as exotic as the seagull. It's everywhere, stuffing turkeys, lining driveways, keeping the cocktail sauce honest. You'd be forgiven for thinking it's common. But you'd be like kids in Alba who think the whole world shaves truffles over its spaghetti. Familiarity breeds complacency, but it's time we woke up to the fact that we have one of the world's greatest foods clinging to our eastern shores, and nowhere else. No oyster builds reefs like the Eastern; no oyster evokes the ocean with such hyper-realism. Eagle, shmeagle; nothing says "America" like *Crassostrea virginica*.

DON'T FALL FOR CUTESY NAMES

I'm sitting at a bar with four French Hogs, two Sea Cows, a Fat Bastard, a Little Bitch, a Naked Cowboy, and a Lady Chatterley.

It sounds like a joke waiting for a punch line, or a demented version of "The Twelve Days of Christmas," but it's also the state of oyster naming today. Oysters, like European wine, were once named for the places they came from. Apalachicola, Bluepoint, Wellfleet, Malpeque, Belon. But as wild oysters disappeared and aquaculture arose, you might have thirty different farms selling Wellfleets, each using different techniques, culling to different standards, and so on. The better growers naturally wanted to differentiate themselves, so they developed their own brands: the 13 Miles and Hog Islands of the world. It made sense, and honestly, most of the oysters I look for are branded names from a single farm. But, as happened with wine, growers and distributors soon discovered that a saucy name was a great way to grab customers' attention, especially since information about the actual oysters was often hard to come by. Sometimes those oysters are good—French Hogs, Sea Cows, Fat Bastards, and Naked Cowboys are all great oysters—but a titillating name on an unfamiliar oyster should be a red flag. Real wine drinkers don't buy Mommy's Time Out.

DO TELL A WILD FROM A FARMED OYSTER

Wild oysters will be irregular in shape, owing to their irregular existences. They may be long and skinny or stumpy and gnarled. Their shells will almost always be scuffed, and will have a divot near the hinge where they were attached to a rock or shell. Farmed oysters will be perfect teardrops, paisleys, or cornucopias. (For a good side-by-side comparison, see the Wild and Cultivated Chincoteagues on page 117.)

DON'T ASSUME THE WILD IS BETTER

This ain't salmon. Oysters spend their entire lives attached to one spot. They free-range as often as broccoli. The farmed ones are usually better. (But not always: See the Wild Onsets on page 175.)

DO KNOW A TUMBLED OYSTER WHEN YOU SEE IT

And geek out for your tablemates. We are in the midst of a tumbling revolution in the oyster world. It started when Keith Reid, up in British Columbia, discovered that regular jostling would chip off the soft growing edge of his Pacific oysters—which by nature like to grow long and skinny—and force them to "cup up." The result was the Kusshi (page 27), a bonsai masterpiece that is polished, round, and firm. Soon Chelsea Gem, Shigoku, Blue Pool, and the rest got in on the game, and now half the growers in North America seem to be tumbling their oysters to some extent. You can always tell a tumbled oyster by its smooth shell, stumpy stature, and deep cup.

Above: Tumble baskets at the Nisbet Oyster Farm on Willapa Bay.

DO IGNORE THE R RULE

The old *r* rule, which goes back centuries, states that you should eat oysters only during months that have an *r* in them, September through April. In other words, avoid oysters during the summer. This had something to do with safety (bacteria counts are highest in warm summer water, and higher still if oysters bake in the air like petri dishes for days before being consumed, which happened regularly in the old, pre-refrigeration days) and something to do with reproduction: Oysters spawn during the warm summer months. As they convert their energy reserves from glycogen to gamete, they can stop tasting sweet and start tasting like something that crawled out of a bait pile. The conventional wisdom was to steer clear in summer, let them reproduce, then resume in the fall. But today's farmed oysters are spawned in hatcheries, are iced as soon as they leave the water, and they stay that way all the way to your plate. You can eat them year-round.

DON'T ENTIRELY IGNORE THE *R* RULE

On the other hand, I have yet to meet the oyster that wasn't at its peak between November and January, so I reserve most of my serious shucking for fall and winter, when oysters are reliably mind-blowing. Thanksgiving, Christmas, and New Year's were made for oysters. In that spirit:

DO THINK ABOUT SEASONALITY

Oysters vary in flavor throughout the year. Phytoplankton starts blooming in spring, when water temperatures and hours of photosynthesis rise, and that's when most oysters really start to feed and grow. At this time of year, they can have a fresh, green flavor. Oysters like to spawn in summer, when temperatures peak. As they convert their energy stores to gamete they taste gamy and soft. After they spawn—which can involve ejecting as much as a third of their body weight—they tend to look shriveled and translucent, and they taste of little more than seawater. In the fall, they begin to bulk up again in preparation for the long winter dormancy. By early winter, they have stuffed themselves with glycogen and amino acids to prevent freezing and starvation, and they can be crazy sweet. They should look fat. Through the winter, they live off their reserves, and they can be very thin by the time that first spring algae bloom hits. This cycle is especially true for more northern, cold-water oysters, and less applicable to Gulf of Mexico oysters, which never stop feeding entirely and never have to plump up quite as much in the fall. But in general, if you're disappointed by an oyster in spring or summer, try it again in late fall before you give up on it. It might be a different animal altogether.

DON'T SETTLE FOR SNOT-ON-SHELL

While it's true that the art of oyster appreciating is at an all-time high in North America, it's also true that as every dive bistro has been reborn as an oyster bar, there are more scrambled, shrunken, watery oysters being sold on the half shell than ever before. An oyster should be plump, opaque, and whole. Its meat should fill most of its shell, with just a little room for liquor (the watery juice inside the shell). It should not be translucent or gray. (A translucent oyster is basically a bag of seawater.) It should not be spawny, indicated by a creamy white belly, a mouth-coating texture, and spawning veins if you look closely enough (which you probably shouldn't do). It should not be covered in shell fragments (though sometimes a fine dusting of plaster near the hinge is unavoidable; consider it your nightly Tums) and, equally important, it should not have a broken belly, the result of an inexperienced or hurried shucker. Think of it as a poached egg: The pleasure of bursting it open, of savoring the mix of sweet muscle and salty belly, is reserved for you.

DO CHEW

You need to mix that sweet muscle and salty belly. You need to taste the thing.

DO SAVOR THE LIQUOR—TO A POINT

For years, many of us have been advocating for more liquor appreciation. "It's part of the gestalt," we told everyone, and everyone listened. But the oysters we had in mind filled 90 percent of their shells, with just a thin envelope of liquor around them. Too often, I see a shrunken oyster floating in a tablespoon of seawater. Don't feel compelled to swallow this broth. It's going to overwhelm the oyster with saltiness, so pour some out. The bigger and plumper the body of an oyster, the more "stuff" it has to balance the salinity of seawater and the more liquor you'll want.

DON'T MAKE STUPID APHRODISIAC JOKES

Mea culpa. This seemed kind of fun a dozen years ago, and we all ran with it. Now it feels stale.

DO TRY SHUCKING YOUR OWN

Think of the money saved! And the party adulation.

Above: There are
as many styles
of oyster knife as
there are styles
of oyster. Look
for a strong,
thin blade and a
grippy handle.

DO USE A GOOD KNIFE

The blade should be thin and strong, which means cheap knives won't cut it. You need to be able to wriggle the blade between the shells, and you need to use some force to pry the oyster open.

DON'T DROWN THEM IN MIGNONETTE

So you've jettisoned cocktail sauce along with your Smash Mouth CDs and other signs of your ignorant youth, and now you think you're Thomas Keller because you ladle vinegar over your oysters. Next time, bring an eyedropper with you. Three drops usually does the trick. Ditto for lemon: one wedge per dozen.

DO LOOSEN UP ABOUT DRINK PAIRINGS

Sure, sure, dry, crisp white wine with oysters. Dry, crisp beer. Both good. Now try martinis, margaritas, and manzanilla. Try flowery rosés. Try off-dry chenin blanc and sake. Vinho Verde on the rocks. Get a little louche with absinthe. Plant a Bloody Mary next to a plate of Olympias. Down sweet ice cider with salty Island Creeks. Guinness with Kelly Natives. Gin and tonics with anything. Maybe a Chupacabra's Delight (page 282). And lest we forget: lemon water.

DO ADMIRE THE SHELLS

People never know what to do with the shell after eating an oyster. They look around for a discard bowl. But the artful solution is obvious: Return the shell right back to its spot on the bed of ice, facedown. Most of an oyster's artistry lies in its bottom shell. That's where you get the gorgeous purple and green fans of color, the rune-like patterns and architectural flourishes. And as you eat through your dozen and the shells accumulate, you get to appreciate the uniqueness of each. When you're done, you've created a sort of clock of bones, a memento mori to mark this moment of your life. Then it gets whisked away.

SALISH SEA

About 100 million years ago, a 50-mile-wide, 200-mile-long wedge of land finished its 200-million-year cruise across the Pacific and parallel parked beside the continent. The incident was not without its fender benders. Vancouver Island was left crumpled and craggy. Millions of years later, when the Olympic Peninsula smacked into the continent, these two pieces of land teamed up to isolate one of North America's jewels: a temperate, rich, island-studded inner sea stretching a hundred miles up into British Columbia and another hundred down into Puget Sound. Fed by the Strait of Juan de Fuca, it became a playground for herring, salmon, orcas, and every other form of coastal denizen, including the Salish peoples, who prospered so in this paradise that they had time to do things like make totem poles and other art—the sure sign of a society that didn't have to spend every waking minute grubbing for calories. Their ancestors had been the first people to reach the New World, paddling their kayaks along the "Kelp Highway" of coastal resources that stretched from the edge of Asia up around Alaska and down the west coast of North America, and they knew exactly what to do with the calorie-laden beaches of this coastline-intensive paradise of fjords, islands, and straits. They invented clam gardens—possibly the first form of aquaculture in the world, in which beds of perfect clam habitat were built into the intertidal zone—smoked oysters ad infinitum, trapped salmon in weirs, and generally lived ridiculously well until Captain Cook and his men showed up in 1778, jonesing for otter pelts and spewing microbes in all directions.

The name Salish Sea is actually a recent one, coined in 1988 by a marine biologist hoping to stress that, although the BC portion is called the Strait of Georgia, and the U.S. segment Puget Sound, it's all one

Preceding pages: The floating Hollie Wood Oyster Farm in Baynes Sound, the heart of the BC oyster industry. Left: Aaron Friend checks vats of algae being grown for bivalve baby food at the Jones Family Farm hatchery on Lopez Island.

big lovefest of post-national ecosystems. It also happens to be one of the most oyster-intensive regions on earth. From the coasts of British Columbia, through the San Juan Islands, to the northern reaches of Puget Sound (southern Puget Sound has very different characteristics and is covered in the next chapter), these are amazingly productive waters.

The sequence of oyster development on Vancouver Island played out just as it did in San Francisco: gold rush, settlers, towns, oyster bars, exhaustion of native oysters, relaying of Eastern oysters, exhaustion, and eventual recovery using the Pacific oyster. Thanks to the superb sleuthing of Brian Kingzett and others at Vancouver Island University's Centre for Shellfish Research, we can follow the story in the local papers of the time. The first oyster bar popped up in the frontier outpost of Victoria in 1859, with the gold rush in full swing. By 1862, the *British Colonist* was editorializing in favor of white settlers stealing the oyster trade away from Native women: "Need any be idle when the very squaws are making four and five dollars a day, in bringing in oysters from Victoria Arm, Sooke or Cowichan and peddling them around town? They monopolize the whole trade; not a white nor civilized man enters the field against them. This need not be so—ought not to be so. There is money to be made at it. People do not get enough oysters to eat."

Apparently the Native women lost out not to locals but to Americans, because three years later the same paper is full of ads for oyster saloons featuring Olympia oysters, and the editor is complaining about "our total dependence on Olympia for bivalves." That problem got solved a year later with the discovery of beds of beautiful oysters in Baynes Sound, the mile-wide strip of water that divides Denman Island from Vancouver Island, which "has almost driven Olympia oysters out of this market. Our Island bivalves are larger and better flavored than any brought from the American side, and are said to rival the Shoalwater Bay oysters with which the San Francisco market is supplied." The oysters were all *Ostrea lurida*, the only native of the West Coast, and the fact that they are now all called Olympias tells you how well they survived elsewhere.

Twenty years later, the Baynes Sound beds were done, too small and slow growing to keep up with demand—and Baynes Sound would limp along on imports of Easterns until its savior arrived in the form of the Pacific oyster from Japan. Today Baynes Sound is the heart of the BC oyster industry, and the Pacific oyster is the only beast in town. BC oysters aren't terribly diverse: To mangle Tolstoy, all happy BC oysters are happy in the same way. They tend to come in the suspension-culture style BC helped pioneer: delicate, thin-shelled, beautifully colored specimens that spend their lives in trays suspended from floats in deep water. Many of the most interesting come from the Discovery Islands, the remote archipelago that separates Vancouver Island from mainland BC, where neither the few residents nor their oysters feel any pressing need to conform to the mainstream.

Nick Jones of Jones Family Farms shares some oysters with his daughter, Bear.

If all you're familiar with is Atlantic or Gulf of Mexico oystering, BC can seem like another planet: huge rafts moored in slowly undulating waters that glint like quicksilver, rimmed by snaggletooth mountains and raked by storms. Big barges, big winches, and lots of plastic trays, with not a grain of sand or a blade of marsh grass in sight. Counterintuitively, the big-water lifestyle leaves them so fluted and colorful that they sometimes look more like chanterelles than oysters.

In flavor and body, the Salish Sea oysters also tend to be more dainty than their robust Washington State cousins, less earthy, more pickled melon rind. They also tend to be fairly similar. If it's novelty you seek, look to the San Juan Islands, the last oyster frontier in the Pacific Northwest. The San Juans have everything an oyster farmer dreams about—stunning beauty, light populations, aboriginal water quality, and a location right at the business end of the Strait of Juan de Fuca that washes them in salty, nutritious Pacific upwellings—but aquaculture has barely developed, mostly because the islands are a royal pain to get to or from. That may soon change as growers look for sites farther from the megalopolises that are eating the coastline. The flavor of the San Juan Islands is just about perfect—a nice balance of salt and sweet, mineral and melon—so, in the future, keep your eyes peeled. You can even find them in the present—if you know where to look.

BAYNES SOUND

BAYNES SOUND,
VANCOUVER ISLAND

SPECIES Pacific

CULTIVATION Seed is grown in stacks of plastic trays suspended from rafts in the deep waters of Baynes Sound and occasionally tumbled. Some oysters are beach finished.

PRESENCE The full peacock. Lots of shimmery black and purple in an art deco scheme.

FLAVOR Meaty melon. In winter, sweet as heck. In high summer, a passing whiff of spawny Brie can make them tougher to swallow.

OBTAINABILITY Virtually every oyster bar on the West Coast will have a couple of BC oysters on its list. In Vancouver and other BC cities, most of the list will be local. They can commonly be found in the Northeast, too, but as with all frilly Pacific oysters their crinkled edge doesn't make a tight seal, so they tend to leak as they travel. Best sampled closer to home.

SUMMER ICE

JERVIS INLET,
BRITISH COLUMBIA

SPECIES Pacific

CULTIVATION Suspended from rafts in plastic trays sixty feet deep in the water column.

PRESENCE Can vary, depending on their origin, but they generally have that "cool mint" vibe.

FLAVOR Mild and moderately salty, with less funk and more cream.

OBTAINABILITY Only in summer. Regulars at the Grand Central Oyster Bar.

BAYNES SOUND IS A LONG CHANNEL BETWEEN the eastern edge of Vancouver Island and the western shore of Denman Island. Current cranks through these narrows, which not coincidentally hold one of the densest concentrations of oyster farms in the world. In Deep Bay, a particularly sheltered cove of cedar and fir tucked into the southern corner of the sound, you can almost hop from one side to the other on oyster rafts. This is the home of Kusshi, Stellar Bay, Chefs Creek, Paradise (on top in the photo), and, of course, Deep Bay. A mile or three away is the rest of the Baynes Sound gang, Fanny Bay and Buckley Bay and Ships Point and Komo Gway and Phantom Creek and various other names that come and go like the tides. Whatever you call them, they are almost all suspension-grown Pacifics with beautiful if delicate shells and melon-rind flavors. Some spend their last few months on the beach, toughening up; these are the pick of the litter.

In the summer, however, you might want to look for Summer Ice (bottom), grown on the opposite side of the Strait of Georgia near the mouth of Jervis Inlet, a massive (and massively deep) fjord that cuts fifty miles into the BC interior. This is big country: mile-high cliffs, half-mile-long waterfalls, fir trees, and mist. But even in these untrammeled parts, summer waters can be full of bacteria, and young oysters' minds can turn to love, so Summer Ices are dropped sixty feet into the deep dark, where it's eternal winter. They stay clean, in mind and body, and make for perfect summer companions.

BLACK PEARL

QUADRA ISLAND,
BRITISH COLUMBIA

SPECIES Pacific

CULTIVATION Broodstock is selected from the blackest shells of each generation, and the resulting seed is grown out in plastic trays suspended in deep water and gently hand-tumbled to preserve the fluting. Also gently hand-massaged (tongue-massaged?) by sea urchins.

PRESENCE Tiny, gleaming, fragile, with an inner fire. What it lacks in stature it makes up in spirit. Leads with its fat belly, like a little Buddha.

FLAVOR Light and green, with modest salinity and lots of leafy notes on the finish.

OBTAINABILITY Strong in BC, Toronto, and Montreal. In the States, you have to know someone who knows someone.

BLACK PEARLS ARE GROWN BY THE OUT LANDISH Shellfish Guild, an eight-farm cooperative making a go of it in the geographically challenged Discovery Islands. If some titanic toddler had tried to plug up the flow of water between Vancouver Island and mainland BC with a bucket of island-sized rocks, the result would resemble the Discovery Islands. The sea still manages to snake through the islands, but the archipelago is more land than water. It's light on people but heavy on marine mammals, salmon, shellfish, and stubborn iconoclasts. Tethered to "civilization" by a string of ferries and trucks, it's a tough place to produce most things, but it's ideally situated for shellfish, with impeccable water quality and myriad beaches and deepwater sites. You can find everything from the delicate, tray-raised Black Pearls to beach monsters like the six-inch Sea Angels—if you can find them. Most everything Out Landish grows gets claimed by Canada. Black Pearls are, in a sense, the anti-Kusshi. Both are small, suspended, tumbled oysters, but Kusshis undergo intensive mechanical tumbling, resulting in their postmodern golf ball feel, while Black Pearls are gently hand-tossed for a more neoclassical vibe. Part of the reason Black Pearls' intensely wavy purple-black shells are so striking is because of Out Landish's most charming innovation: Sea urchins and sea cucumbers are added to every tray to graze the algae away.

FANNY BAY

BAYNES SOUND, VANCOUVER ISLAND

SPECIES Pacific

CULTIVATION Seed from Taylor Shellfish's Hawaii and Washington State hatcheries is raised in upwellers and suspended trays until large enough to be hardened on the beach.

PRESENCE The elegant fluted edge and scruffy shells, the creamy-white belly and formal black mantle, make Fanny Bays a nice mix of city and country. These are models in muck boots.

FLAVOR Moderate salt and lots of cucumber, with a steely parsley kicker.

OBTAINABILITY Excellent. The farm was acquired by Taylor Shellfish, largest grower in North America, a few years back and is now one of the easiest BC oysters to find.

FANNY BAY HAS BEEN AT THE HEART OF BC'S shellfish industry since 1912, when its beaches were first seeded with oysters. It falls smack in the middle of Baynes Sound, the twelve-mile strait between Vancouver Island and Denman Island that is one long smorgasbord of oyster farms. It also falls smack in the middle of BC techniques: It starts off in suspension culture, then finishes on the cobbly beach. All this, along with its ubiquity, makes it the type specimen for BC oysters. Examine a Fanny Bay, slurp one, and you will grasp the BC oyster in all its velvet loveliness.

Nobody knows the origin of the Fanny Bay name, though many have speculated. It was first used on surveys around 1860 by Captain George Henry Richards of the British Navy, who peppered the BC coast with proper nouns, many of them whimsical, as he explored. Richards exhausted the names of British thoroughbreds of the day but also stuck to native names whenever possible. His portrait in London's National Portrait Gallery shows a staunch fellow in a tricked-out uniform with a strong nose, aggressive sideburns, and dark, distant eyes. A straight shooter, and yet there's something in those eyes . . . a private memory he can't shake, perhaps. Who was Fanny, and did she introduce him to the joys of native oysters on the susurrating shores of that gentle bay? Did he momentarily waver in his commitment to ship and country? Certainly it never made his journal. But every Fanny Bay oyster, if you quiet your mind and pay close attention, seems to carry with it the vibrational memory of something tender that went down in the purple-shadowed BC fjords long ago.

KUSSHI

DEEP BAY, VANCOUVER ISLAND

SPECIES Pacific

CULTIVATION Raised in stacks of plastic trays suspended from rafts in the deep waters of Baynes Sound, and mechanically tumbled within an inch of their lives.

PRESENCE Feels like a golf ball in your hand. Small, round, heavy, fun to hold. Inside, it looks like a puffball pushing out of the shell, filling every square inch and leaving no room for liquor.

FLAVOR Mild and salty, with a fruity, green-apple finish.

OBTAINABILITY This little fireplug turns up everywhere oyster lovers are willing to shell out big bucks for small oysters. Keep your eyes peeled for **Stellar Bay Gold**, the extra-large (read less tiny) size. **Chefs Creeks** are the beach-finished seconds.

IF JONY IVE, APPLE'S DEMIGOD OF DESIGN, had devised an oyster, this is what he would have come up with: a metallic white shell, rounded corners, and a disarmingly industrial sameness. It feels special yet sturdy; slightly yet nonthreateningly futuristic. It's the iOyster, and it was actually conceived by Keith Reid years before Jony Ive nailed the iPhone. And it has been nearly as revolutionary.

Reid, a tinkerer and oyster farmer in Deep Bay—the corner of Baynes Sound that is the Silicon Valley of oysters, with savvy growers stacked up and down the waterway—had the same problem as the other growers in his area. Deep Bay is, well, deep, meaning the only way to grow oysters is with suspension culture: You hang them from rafts. Reid perfected a stackable plastic tray that allowed him to hang thousands of oysters from each raft. The oysters love this environment—a little too much. High in the water column, with lots of phytoplankton drifting by and perfect protection from predators, the oysters graze 24/7. An oyster wants to grow long as quickly as possible, to outcompete its neighbors, and suspended Pacific oysters grow so quickly that they reach market size before their shells can thicken or their cups can develop. They never have to close their shells, so their adductor muscle stays weak.

The solution, Reid found, was to beat them up regularly. The growing edge of an oyster shell is as pliant as paint. It can be easily chipped off. So Reid began submitting his subjects to a monthly round of tumbling in a mechanical barrel tumbler he installed on a barge. Originally intended to scour barnacles and sort the oysters by size, the tumbler wound up stunting the oysters' growth while allowing their cups to develop normally. They produced incredibly deep cups, at least in proportion to their two-inch length. Their shells were glossy. They were little masterworks. As an added bonus, the agitation forced them to close their shells, giving their muscles regular workouts. Kusshis are as taut as Olympic gymnasts.

In the ten years Kusshis have been on the market, they have transformed the oyster world. Now everybody wants tumbled oysters. And Reid has kept pushing the mechanization of his system. Today his oysters are whipped through a high-speed Gravitron that leaves them dazed, stunted, and very, very polished. The shells are so perfect that any idiot can open one, and the flavor so gentle that any idiot can like one, too. (Something about the tumbling process lightens the flavor, perhaps because it increases the proportion of sweet muscle meat.) Kusshis have plenty of imitators, but no one else has managed to achieve that perfectly smooth, consistent, Mormon-clean look. It's a testament to Reid's ingenious innovations, which he wouldn't let us photograph. Trust me; it's the future.

NAKED ROY

SAMISH BAY,
SALISH SEA

SPECIES Pacific

CULTIVATION Hatchery seed is broadcast right on the beach and grown intertidally in the waves, where it achieves that natural ruffled look.

PRESENCE Think Muscle Beach: huge adductors, meaty bodies, and rippled shells from a life of workouts on the sand. If they could, these would wear a mankini and strut.

FLAVOR Adrienne Anderson, this book's stylist, who spent a good bit of time shepherding these babies around, nailed this one: "The flavor is all month of May: Milk-fed spring lamb up front, with the tiniest touch of game. The finish is pure chlorophyll, like rolling around on a freshly mown lawn."

OBTAINABILITY Samish Bay is a major producer of oysters, which go by various monikers, all of which taste the same, so in addition to **Naked Roy**, look for **Windy Point** or plain old **Samish**. All good. These are very common in the Pacific Northwest, and a happy but not shocking find elsewhere.

THE DEFINITIVE BEACH OYSTER. Samish Bay is known for its vast expanse of gently sloping tidelands, yielding huge growing grounds at low tide; its fairly placid conditions; and its sandy bottom. The combo makes for great frilly oysters with crinkly-potato-chip edges, on full display in this image. Its oysters' mildness comes from their large proportion of adductor muscles due to a life of labor on the beach, and their salt comes from Samish's riverless topography. In many ways, Samish is the unsung hero of Washington State oyster regions, getting less attention than Willapa Bay, Hood Canal, or Puget Sound, but producing a lighter-flavored oyster that many prefer.

It's also the preferred stomping grounds of Naked Roy, a retired sun worshipper who used to belong to a nudist colony in Teddy Bear Cove until it was run out by the Whatcom County Sheriff's Office. Roy broke off from the main colony and found refuge on a little point of land surrounded by Taylor Shellfish's oyster grounds. No one knows what Roy's last name is or if he knows about the oyster he inspired, but this is one oyster most appropriately eaten unadorned.

OLYMPIA
(Lopez Island)

SHOAL BAY,
LOPEZ ISLAND

SPECIES Olympia

CULTIVATION Seed is hatched at the Jones Family Farm hatchery at Shoal Bay, and the Olys are grown in open, walled trays in the three-acre lagoon for four to five years until they reach the size of fifty-cent pieces.

PRESENCE I think this is the most gorgeous oyster in the world. Unearthly blacks and blues seem to flicker before your eyes, changing every time you glance back, like hot sheet metal.

FLAVOR Huge. Fiery, peppery, and sharp, like a potato chip dipped in mustard oil.

OBTAINABILITY So, so sorry.

IN 2011, THE ARTIST JAMES PROSEK went to heroic lengths to capture the colors of a swordfish before it died. Hitching a ride on a fishing boat off the Cape Verde Islands, he waited out high seas and boredom until one day the boat hauled in a fifteen-foot-long, six-hundred-pound blue marlin. Snapping photos and jotting sketches, he managed to capture enough in the few minutes before the colors flickered and died to create a life-sized masterpiece of the fish alive. It's the color of the sea before it realizes the land is looking and gets shy. When they're wet and alive, the Olys of Lopez Island express those hues. They skew harder toward ultraviolet than the Olys of Puget Sound, and their flavor is a little more outré.

That flavor is an ancient taste of the Salish Sea. Olys have thrived in these tidal basins for at least ten thousand years, possibly much longer, and were certainly enjoyed by the first migrants paddling the coastal route from Asia to explore the new world. Nick Jones finds them incredibly easy to work with in his Lopez Island hatchery—the easiest of the five oyster species. They have a strong survival instinct. Put them in their home environment, with the right conditions, and they prove more formidable than their size might imply. Unfortunately, little Olympias are still hard sells, and Jones grows minuscule amounts. If you are incredibly lucky, you might catch them in Seattle. Otherwise, you'll need to talk Jones into that Lopez Island raw bar he's been contemplating.

Why eat Olys? Certainly not to fill up: With each having the heft of a Skittle, you could easily down a hundred for breakfast. Instead, think of Olys as magic timepieces. This works best if you open your own. Grab a paring knife, slip it under the top shell like a jeweler fixing a watch, pop it open, and bring it up to your nose to catch that fleeting whiff of tide pools. You'll teleport to an entirely different space—think glaciers, sealskin umiaks, furry toes padding across a long beach of tiny rainbow shells—and stay in that space for as long as it takes to dispatch your little time portals.

PENN COVE SELECT

SPECIES Pacific

CULTIVATION Beach-raised in Samish Bay, then transferred to mesh bags and hung from rafts in Penn Cove on Whidbey Island.

PRESENCE These suckers strut their stuff. Frills, flutes, and flourishes. Mardi Gras flair. Twenty years at the top of the charts. Lady Gaga, eat your heart out.

FLAVOR Cucumber and seaweed salad in ponzu sauce. The scent is straight out of a sushi bar.

OBTAINABILITY Ian Jefferds's Penn Cove Shellfish is one of the leading distributors in the country, and his flagship oyster is an anchor everywhere from the Grand Central Oyster Bar to Elliott's Oyster House. You can't miss it.

TO ME, A PENN COVE SMELLS MORE like a Pacific oyster than anything in the world—which makes sense, since it is a Pacific oyster, but somehow Penn Coves precisely capture that sharp, fruity cucurbit note that is the essence of Pacifics. They are also a showcase for all the baroque flourishes a Pacific oyster is capable of producing, which is how they have managed to lock down Seattle's Most Beautiful Oyster award more times than owner Ian Jefferds can keep track of (and he likes to keep track).

What fascinates me about Penn Coves is their dual nature. They start off as classic frilly beach oysters in Samish Bay, kissing cousins to Naked Roy. In that gentle bay, oysters' knife-thin growing edges aren't as likely to get ground off by wave and rock. But then, just when those Samish beach oysters think they know what life is all about, they get yanked from the bay and hung from rafts in deep waters, where they fatten, purge, salt up, and practice their acceptance speeches.

SHOAL BAY FLAT

SPECIES European Flat

CULTIVATION Seed is hatched at the Jones Family Farm hatchery at Shoal Bay, then grown in walled trays in a three-acre lagoon for two years until they reach the size of teacup saucers.

PRESENCE Oval, and wider than they are long, these Flats shimmer a coppery green and feel like money, especially with the creamy mother-of-pearl interiors. Each one has about a dozen fine ridges, almost like a scallop.

FLAVOR The briniest Flats I know, deeply astringent with hazelnut-skin tannins and a lingering battery-terminal zap.

OBTAINABILITY Anthony's, in Seattle, takes a thousand a week —the whole harvest.

WHEN YOU HAVE SOME DOWNTIME, take a Google Earth flight over Lopez Island, a pristine jumble of foggy, fertile, lichen-splashed mountains tossed into the Salish Sea midway between Washington State and Vancouver Island. Drill down on the perfect horseshoe of a bay on its northern tip. This is Shoal Bay. You'll quickly notice a tiny lagoon on the beach fed by a tinier inlet. This is the lagoon where Nick Jones runs his farm and hatchery, and if you're a member of the Ostrea clan—Olympias (*Ostrea lurida*) or European Flats (*Ostrea edulis*)—it's heaven on earth.

Unlike the Crassostrea oysters, Ostreas don't like intertidal life. They can't close their shells as tightly or as long—which is why Flats are always shipped with rubber bands around them—and they hate temperature extremes. All they want is a bathtub of a bay where they can stay safe and submerged, and that's what they get in the Jones lagoon. Twice a day the most pristine water in the Pacific Northwest pumps fresh food in. During summer the water gets opaque with phytoplankton.

Flats are supposed to be difficult to grow in captivity. Don't tell Nick Jones. He finds them easier than the other oysters, with only Olys being easier. Of course, when you're simultaneously running a renegade hatchery, an oyster and geoduck farm, a tender, a fish brokerage, a sausage company, and a farm with hogs, goats, sheep, and cows—plus you're raising four kids on the side, and you're starting to get into wheat and barley with the goal of making Salish Sea whiskey—your oysters are the least of your challenges.

Unlike some of their kin, these Flats don't come across like Spartans having a bad day. The fruity Salish Sea burnishes their metallic core into a soft, approachable luster. These are Spartans having a good day. Still not super easy to be around, but they know how to live.

HOOD CANAL
to PUGET SOUND

The first time I visited Seattle, in the mid-aughts, I found myself at Elliott's Oyster House on Pier 56—not unusual for anyone who is roaming the waterfront or hopping a ferry across Puget Sound, both of which I was doing.

I popped onto a bar seat and ogled the back wall. There must have been thirty metal tubs of oysters displayed, each backed by a handsome black sign listing the name, cultivation technique, and provenance of that oyster. BARRON POINT, BAG TO BEACH, SKOOKUM INLET. KUSSHI, SUSPENDED TRAY, VANCOUVER ISLAND. This was completely unlike the scrawled list of mystery names at the Grand Central Oyster Bar or the generic oyster served up at most joints in the country. I stole a glance at the supplicants to my left and right and thought, *I'm not alone.*

Sorry, San Francisco, and nyah-nyah, New York, but Seattle sculpted the oyster culture we now find ourselves in. Like grunge and specialty coffee, Seattle's nerdy knack to take itself seriously, to miss the irony, was what allowed its little block party to go viral. A white-mopped, blue-eyed eccentric named Jon Rowley was the Kurt Cobain of oysters—gifted, quixotic, difficult—and he convinced a whole generation of media and consumers that they'd been missing out.

What made Seattle the oyster mecca was happenstances both

Preceding pages: The Hama Hama barge delivers another load of Hood Canal oysters. Left: Beach picnic, Hood Canal-style.

historical and geological. The collision of continental plates 34 million years ago forced up the Olympic Mountains on one side and lit the line of volcanoes that became the Cascades on the other, leaving a jumble of jagged valleys in between. Later, glaciers oozing off the wet Olympic Range gouged a steep, deep channel to the sea: Hood Canal, the closest thing to a fjord in the Lower 48. (George Vancouver actually scrawled "Hood's Channel" on his original 1792 chart.) Rising seas then flooded Hood Canal and Puget Sound, leaving a warren of narrow, interlinked channels and inlets.

The area's near wipeout of its native Olympia opened the way for imports of the Eastern oyster from the East Coast beginning in the late 1800s. The Pacific oyster followed a few years later, and an anything-goes mentality has held ever since. Unlike the East Coast, which has carefully protected its native oysters against interlopers, the West Coast lost its native oyster industry before anyone was thinking about ecology. That freed it for experimentation with any species it liked, and that has made Puget Sound easily the most diverse oyster-growing region in the world. More different species of oysters are grown in more different ways in more diverse seascapes than anywhere else. And they all find their way into Seattle's humming raw bars, where locals know a beach oyster from a tumbled oyster and have strong opinions about it.

The locals aren't afraid to get wet, either. Recreational shellfishing is a way of life in Puget Sound, from gathering oysters to digging for geoducks, the world's strangest and most delicious clams. Even Seattleites who wouldn't know a geoduck from a firehose are happy to pay $125 to freeze their asses off at Taylor Shellfish's annual Walrus & Carpenter picnics—"'A pleasant walk, a pleasant talk, / Upon the briny beach'"—at midnight in January, when minus tides expose beds of Totten Inlets, *virginicas*, and Olympias, and pop-up oyster bars take over the flats for a few surreal hours.

Although Hood Canal and the South Sound—as the finger inlets at the terminus of Puget Sound are collectively known—come within a couple of miles of touching, they couldn't be more different in character, and each has its own champions. Hood Canal is one long, lean line. If you're driving north through Washington State on Route

Left: Caleb Davis checks a bag of Baywater Sweets in Thorndyke Bay. Above: Adam James pilots the Hama Hama barge at dawn.

101, there comes a moment when you hit Hood Canal and the vista opens up to the north. It's a unique view in America: Nowhere else do you see a thin line of salt water, flanked by mountains, stretching toward singularity. It looks like a river, which of course it was as the glaciers melted.

It takes a good two years to grow a market-sized oyster in Hood Canal, sometimes longer. That's two to three times as long as it takes in the South Sound, and the reason is obvious if you happen to wade through the two basins. In Hood Canal, you look down and you see your foot on the bottom. In the South Sound, your leg disappears into split-pea soup. There's just so much more food in the water in those skinny inlets, and the current runs fast through them, whisking it all past the oysters like an endless parade of dim sum carts, and the oysters get astoundingly fat astoundingly fast. Is that good? Depends on your allegiances. Hood Canal folks would make the whiskey argument that you never get layered complexity without slow development; they prefer the refined cucumber of Hood Canals over "skunky" South Sounds. South Sounders find the Hood Canals anorexic, not to mention ruinous for cash flow. The rest of us don't have to choose. We get to have it all, and Olys and Kumies besides, in the ridiculous oyster playground that is Western Washington.

BAYWATER SWEET

SPECIES Pacific

CULTIVATION Seed is started in crab pots, then transferred to bags staked to the beach, then finished in tumble bags attached to longlines in the intertidal zone, harvested at one year of age, and delivered directly to individual restaurants.

PRESENCE Beautifully fluted little auburn-black oysters with deep cups and a tail that curls up like a scorpion's.

FLAVOR The most refreshing of Hood Canal oysters, with an exceptional sweet-salty miso finish.

OBTAINABILITY Baywater's tiny annual production is snapped up by a handful of restaurants in Seattle, notably Elliott's Oyster House, the Walrus and the Carpenter, and The Brooklyn. Best bet: the Bainbridge Island Farmers' Market.

JOTH DAVIS IS SENIOR RESEARCHER FOR TAYLOR Shellfish, senior scientist for the Puget Sound Restoration Fund, affiliate professor at the University of Washington, and the past president of the National Shellfisheries Association. Oh, yeah, and on weekends he grows a little locket of perfection called a Baywater Sweet. The bay water in question is that of Thorndyke, near the mouth of Hood Canal, and it has a mineral quality to it that I associate with the rippled black sands of the bay. It tastes like the Perrier of the sea, and it carries through to the oysters, giving them a stony depth.

The operation is Zen simple. Undeveloped Thorndyke Bay is nothing but a half-moon of cobble backed by knobs of fir trees, and Joth and his son Caleb, who took the reins in 2014, have no buildings or equipment on the beach, so all you see is a few bags staked to the sand. At low tide it feels like a giant Japanese rock garden. Just wind, the wash of waves, wheeling gulls, and the sound of one million oysters clacking.

CHELSEA GEM

ELD INLET,
PUGET SOUND

SPECIES Pacific

CULTIVATION Oysters are grown in mesh bags attached to longlines. Floats on the bags rise and fall with the tides, shaking, tumbling, and polishing the oysters.

PRESENCE The dusky grays and lavenders of a Chelsea Gem make it look like the home of a modish Scandinavian sea elf. The shells are as smooth and polished as any oyster in the world, with unblemished alabaster interiors. The meats are never robust, and the whole thing is about the length of my pinky.

FLAVOR A big hit of shiso leaf (that classic sushi garnish), with its tingling zip of horseradish and geranium. Sweet in spring, salty in winter, cucumbery year-round.

OBTAINABILITY Chelsea Gems have developed a cult following. Although Eld Inlet remains their home base, they are now farmed throughout South Sound in significant enough quantities to make them regulars in Seattle and much of the West Coast, and increasingly visible on the East Coast as well.

LADIES AND GENTLEMEN OF THE JURY, I submit to you that oysters are art, not food, and I present for your examination Exhibit A: the Chelsea Gem shell. Petite, classy, flawless of color and curve. You could hang it from your earlobes. It gets that way through gentle and relentless tide tumbling, a system invented by John Lentz, who started Chelsea Farms in 1987. Lentz quickly learned that, in the nutrient-rich waters of South Sound, he had to chip off the growing edge of his bag-grown oysters or they would grow too quickly, getting long and leggy, with little depth and fragile shells. After years of Lentz and his wife shaking every bag by hand to force the oysters to cup up and strengthen their shells, he had a brainstorm: Let the tides do it! He attached his bags to longlines in the intertidal zone, attached floats to the other end of the bags, and watched them rise and fall with the tides, tumbling the oysters on top of each other. In addition to strengthening them, it had an unanticipated side effect: The constant jostling of shell on shell polished them into multicolored jewels. The Chelsea Gem was born, and spawned a revolution still sweeping the Pacific Northwest and now making inroads in the Southeast. Everyone loved the elegant, manageable look and the lighter flavor imparted by off-bottom life. Lentz died in 2014, but his children now run the farm, and the current 3.0 version of their tumbling system is cranking out the best Chelsea Gems yet.

HAMA HAMA

HAMMA HAMMA
DELTA, HOOD CANAL

BLUE POOL

HAMMA HAMMA
DELTA, HOOD CANAL

SPECIES Pacific

CULTIVATION Hood Canal gets the best sets of wild oysters in Washington, and many of those settle in right on the Hamma Hamma Delta. Most of those are shucked and sold by the pint. For Hama Hama singles, hatchery seed is grown out on longlines or bottom planted.

PRESENCE As sinewy and turbulent as a Rodin bronze, softened by a gray-green patina. You can feel the potential energy waiting to go kinetic.

FLAVOR Nettle soup, with lots of vibrant, herbaceous spring greens and briny sea stock.

OBTAINABILITY Excellent nationwide. In business since the 1950s, Hama Hamas have perhaps the best name recognition of any Pacific oyster, as well as the best pints of shucked oysters to be found.

SPECIES Pacific

CULTIVATION Hama Hama seed is tumbled in mesh bags attached to floats that rise and fall with the tides, flipping the oysters.

PRESENCE Always deep-cupped and smooth-shelled, with a creamy meat inside. In spring, they'll have a translucent purple growing edge.

FLAVOR The green Hama Hama flavor is still there, but in Blue Pools it's tamped down to a milder, white miso-shiitake soup. Sweetest in spring, saltiest in fall.

OBTAINABILITY Best place to obtain them: at the Hama Hama Oyster Saloon, sitting at the open-air bar with a glass of bubbly while the wind pounds the tumble farm and, if you're lucky, a whale passes just beyond, working the deep waters where Hood Canal's ledge drops into the abyss.

IF YOU SHOULD BE FORTUNATE ENOUGH TO FIND YOURSELF ON THE HAMMA HAMMA FLATS on a minus tide and you gaze back west toward shore, here's what you'll see: clouds reflected in a skein of water at your feet, the image shot through with eel grass and oyster shell. Halfway to shore it rises to a line of purple-fringed oyster reef, backed by the classical black arch of the Hamma Hamma Bridge where Route 101 crosses the river. Then wall after wall of evergreens, tiers of terrain feathered like stage scrims rising into the clouds. And then suddenly the mist lifts and the icy crags of the Brothers materialize far above. It all feels numinous, hallucinatory, compressed, and implausibly lit, like a Maxfield Parrish painting.

Of all the rivers that pour out of the Olympic rain forest, the Hamma Hamma is the most focused. (Yes, the river name uses double *M*s while the oyster company uses single; it's an old feud.) It comes barreling out of the mountains like a jade-green freight train, dropping from its six-thousand-foot headwaters to sea level in just eighteen miles of waterfalls and gloom, scouring mud off the delta and building bars of fine, firm gravel where oyster reefs rise like prickly-pear thickets. Over the years, the James gang, whose people have oystered and timbered in the Hamma Hamma watershed since the 1890s, has named the bars. There's Gold Bar, Seed Bar, H Bar, I, Helicopter (don't ask), Mexico, and Skinny Bar. Some are exceptionally fine at recruiting wild seed sets; others are ideal fattening beds. Farm manager Adam James has them all mapped out and rotates crops through the different beds. At daybreak you'll find him on the water in the Hama Hama barge, winching up crates of market-sized oysters.

At low tide, you'll find him at Hama Hama's tumble farm, checking on the new crop of Blue Pools (right side of the photo). Back in 2010 the James family began growing some of their young Hamas in bags that flip in the tides right on the tip of the delta. Another hundred yards and the channel plunges six hundred feet deep. A hundred yards in the other direction and you have regular beach-grown Hama Hamas, but the difference is extraordinary. A few months of flipping transforms Blue Pools from rough green country oysters into refined, black-tie boulevardiers.

KUMAMOTO
(Washington)

CHAPMAN COVE, PUGET SOUND

SPECIES Kumamoto

CULTIVATION Seed is hand-planted directly onto the firm gravel of Chapman Cove, then moved over the three to four years of a Kumie's life to progressively richer fattening beds, then hand-harvested at low tide.

PRESENCE Always small, always deep-cupped, never scary. What sets Chapman Cove Kumies apart from others are the celadon tinge to the meat and the rake-like ridges on the shell. Those are your marks of authenticity.

FLAVOR Sweet and fruity, with a melon nose and a rich finish like celeriac vichyssoise.

OBTAINABILITY Excellent. Taylor Shellfish produces close to four million Kumies each year. Expect to pay a bit more for them.

CHAPMAN COVE IS A NONDESCRIPT BROWN PUDDLE at the very, very, very end of Puget Sound. The water's brown. The flats are brown. The grass is pretty brown. At low tide it drains completely and turns into a few dozen acres of unimpressive, pebble-strewn bottomland. Unimpressive, that is, until you realize that all those pebbles are Kumamoto oysters. Chapman Cove is Kumamotoville. A single square foot of Chapman produces a dozen Kumamotos, plus a pound of Manila clams, every year, making it some of the most productive agricultural land on earth.

To get there from the Pacific, ocean water has to flow through the Strait of Juan de Fuca, hang a right at Port Townsend, sneak past Whidbey Island into Puget Sound, cruise south past Seattle, scooch around Vashon Island and Tacoma, cut back west at Anderson Island, snake past Henderson, Budd, and Totten Inlets, and squirm through the seven-mile crevice of Hammersley Inlet into Oakland Bay, then turn right and make its way halfway up the bay to the little cove carved out of the eastern woods. Frankly, it's a wonder any ocean water makes it in here at all, a good 215 miles from the sea. But just enough does to give it a moderate salinity, and whatever mix of planktons grows in this strange, isolated spot must be exactly to a Kumamoto's liking.

Kumamotos are contrary oysters. They can't be scattered willy-nilly over the beds, like Pacific oysters can; they must be hand-planted instead. While other oysters can be spawny and skunky in summer, that's when Kumies are in their prime. And while every other bivalve on earth grows like gangbusters in the ultra-rich waters of nearby Totten Inlet, Kumies, mysteriously, fail to thrive. They never get fat, and they have high mortality. So Taylor Shellfish reserves all of Chapman for Kumamotos.

Why go to the trouble? Because there is quite simply no other oyster like a Kumie, that most beloved of bivalves. It packs the sweetness of a Pacific oyster with none of the bitter or funky notes. Instead of cucumber, it veers toward the related yet more floral melon. It is very easy to like. Because of that, and its epic popularity, some oyster purists refuse to have anything to do with the diminutive mollusk, but this is like refusing to listen to Mozart. Beauty never bores.

OLYMPIA
(South Sound)

TOTTEN INLET,
PUGET SOUND

SPECIES Olympia

CULTIVATION Seed oysters are grown in bags staked low on the beach for about four years until they reach the size of your big toe. Occasionally they are scattered loose on the flats, a risky proposition for such flyweights.

PRESENCE The watermelon radish of the sea. Shimmery green shells opening into fragile, pink-tinged hearts.

FLAVOR Like a mermaid's Bloody Mary. (Brunch planners, take note.) Spicy celery salt and Clamato juice morphs into mushrooms and smoke after a few chews.

OBTAINABILITY Best in decades. A handful of growers in Puget Sound raise them commercially, and restoration projects are underway in California, Oregon, Washington, and British Columbia.

OSTREA LURIDA IS NAMED FOR THE IRIDESCENT gleam of its shell. It lacks the protective outer finish of other oysters, so those uncanny pearlescent shades bleed right through. A bed of Olys scintillates with an oily sheen as you walk over it. It's enough to trigger pagan impulses. It's also depressingly rare. A handful of pristine beds of Olys survive on the west coast of Vancouver Island, and nowhere else.

Still, there's hope. This pipsqueak, once abundant from California to southeast Alaska, can still be found throughout its home range, though cryptically. Roll over a rock in San Francisco Bay and you might find a few Olys clinging to the crevices. A surprisingly irrepressible population thrives in downtown Victoria, BC. The little survivor isn't going to go extinct anytime soon. Yet commercially, it went extinct long ago, because you can't make money raising Olys. Too small, too slow, and too strange. The nineteenth-century western historian Hubert Howe Bancroft deemed them "of an inferior kind, being small and having a coppery flavor." His observations echoed those of the American conchologist William Cooper, who encountered them in Washington Territory in the 1850s and astutely observed that they "possess the same peculiar coppery flavor remarked in the European mollusk eaten for the first time." *Ostrea lurida* and *Ostrea edulis* are closely related; think of *lurida* as the Baby Belon. Unlike the other commercial oysters, which broadcast sperm and eggs into the water column and are done with it, these two flat oysters both nurture their young. Fertilization occurs within the females, which release live young two weeks later. That peculiar coppery essence must somehow be related to their steely mothering instinct.

SEA COW

SPECIES Pacific

CULTIVATION Seed is tumbled in mesh bags attached to floats that rise and fall with the tides for roughly one year, and is harvested at a petite size.

PRESENCE Sea Cows have the classic small size and deep cup of a tumbled oyster, but they don't quite develop the perfect purple-striped sheen of a Blue Pool, their twin in everything except terrain, staying more gray-green.

FLAVOR With oysters, as with wine, there's always a question as to how far one can push the descriptors before inspiration tips toward farce. Partly it's just a matter of having the balls to go for it, and in that category it's hard to top Island Creek Oyster Bar's description of the taste of Sea Cows: "Like birthday cake. They are sweet, sweet, sweet, with a nice cake frosting thing going on with a dollop of melon sorbet right on top and the slightest hint of cucumber and minerality. Quite frankly, these oysters blew our mind." Bravo.

OBTAINABILITY Better than its namesake, but still unusual enough to make a naturalist perk up.

STELLER'S SEA COW WAS A MANATEE-ON-STEROIDS that plied (well, bobbed) Pacific seas until the eighteenth century, when we ushered it into oblivion. It was one of the most remarkable creatures we ever shared the planet with, topping out at thirty-three feet long and twenty-four-thousand pounds. Put twenty manatees together and you'd have one Steller's sea cow. Like its cousins, it didn't like to do much. It just cruised along the coasts of the Pacific with its trawling motor on, eating kelp all day long. It was first described by the naturalist Georg Wilhelm Steller in 1742 while he was marooned with other survivors of a shipwreck on an island in the Bering Sea, living off sea cows. Steller's description makes it clear why the species had been hunted to near extinction by native peoples, and was finished off just twenty-six years after discovery by Europeans. Not only was the slow, trusting sea cow incredibly easy to catch, but a single specimen served up a year's supply of meat that Steller compared favorably to beef, while the calves had flesh "just like veal." Better still was the fat, "so sweet and fine flavored that we lost all desire for butter. In flavor it approximates nearly the oil of sweet almonds."

What does this have to do with oysters? Well, like the original, Sea Cows are an unlikely wonder of the Pacific Northwest ecosystem. They are curvy and fat, a product of the 24/7 all-you-can-eat plankton buffet that is the South Sound, but the tumbling process tamps down the distinctive South Sound musk so the sweet green melon notes shine through. The name also serves to remind people that oysters are the livestock of the tidelands, grazing on its green micro-meadows and turning it all into sweet protein.

To qualify for membership in the Order of the Tumbled Tasters, you need to sample Sea Cows, Blue Pools, and Chelsea Gems side by side. Sea Cows and Blue Pools are the same seed, equipment, and parent (Hama Hama Oyster Company), but grow in very different waters; Sea Cows and Chelsea Gems are grown cheek by jowl by different people (Hama Hama and Chelsea Farms) using slightly different techniques. Method versus merroir. Because you need to know.

STEAMBOAT

HAMMERSLEY, TOTTEN,
AND ELD INLETS,
PUGET SOUND

SPECIES Pacific

CULTIVATION Seed oysters are staked bag-to-beach at various intertidal zones throughout South Sound, then scattered on the beach to harden their shells and strengthen their muscles. In less than a year they are robust half-shell specimens. Shortly thereafter, they are destined for the grill.

PRESENCE Strong, ruffled shells scuffed a khaki-lichen color from life on the beach. Inside, the ivory meat is almost obscenely ample.

FLAVOR Sweet and earthy, with lots of funky bacon fat and matsutake on the finish.

OBTAINABILITY You'll find these everywhere, under a variety of aliases, including **Totten**, **Skookum**, and **Hammersley**.

STEAMBOAT ISLAND GUARDS THE SPOT WHERE the finger inlets of the South Sound come together. As the geographic center of South Sound oyster culture, it's the name Taylor Shellfish assigns to its Pacific oysters coming from the various finger inlets, which all share the unmistakable South Sound character: full, sweet meats and a mouth-filling, musky character. All are impressive, but keep your eyes peeled for the Totten, which is especially plush. This Venus reclining in her shell is downright Rubenesque, all frilly frame, pulchritudinous pudge, and eau de civet. Baroque but beguiling.

TOTTEN INLET VIRGINICA

TOTTEN INLET,
PUGET SOUND

SPECIES Eastern

CULTIVATION Seed is grown out in mesh bags and then bottom planted on the firm intertidal flats of Totten Inlet.

PRESENCE The khaki TIV shell is clean and firm and could easily hail from Maine or the Cape, but inside it is buttery and opaque in a way you don't see back east.

FLAVOR Starts off like a briny East Coast oyster, then it brings on da funk, with a mushroomy finish reminiscent of raw-milk Camembert. An extraordinarily rich, lingering umami.

OBTAINABILITY Virginicas don't spawn well in Pacific waters, and several vintages of TIVs died in succession, making the oyster harder to get ahold of than a case of Heady Topper. But after a recent run of success, TIVs are again arriving en masse.

HOW SPECIAL IS TOTTEN INLET? JUST ASK TAYLOR Shellfish's Marco Pinchot: "Totten Inlet is the greatest oyster-producing bay that we have. Nothing even comes close. Some areas can grow an oyster very quickly, but generally it will have a thin meat and a brittle shell. And other areas can grow really fat meats and hard shells, but generally they're very slow-growing areas with few nutrients. Totten Inlet is an anomaly. You can grow an oyster that's very fat and very firm very fast. It's the only place that can do all of that. Pacifics grow great there. Virginicas grow great there. Olympias grow great there. And Virginicas and Olympias don't grow great many places."

No one has yet figured out what mysterious forces are at work in Totten Inlet, but when you crack open a Virginica or even a regular Pacific while at Totten, you get the sense that it has been mainlining chi for months, and you want to fall to your knees and scratch at the dirt in pagan obeisance to whatever inhabits this little haven of fecundity. The flawless meat almost spills over the shell. Life has been very, very good to this oyster. And now it's being good to you.

The original TIVs actually date to the 1890s, when the founder of Taylor Shellfish began importing Eastern oysters by train and planting them in what he called "the Eastern Bed" of Totten Inlet. That practice died with the rise of the economically superior Pacific oyster, but the family always remembered the extraordinary qualities of that oyster, which combined its species' firm brine with Totten's ripe complexity. In the mid-2000s, Taylor Shellfish revived the tradition. It hasn't been all sauvignon blanc and roses—spawning and raising virginica seed in Pacific nurseries remains puzzling—but when it works, there's simply no other oyster like it.

NORTH PACIFIC

Oyster mania took hold on the West
Coast in 1849, when San Francisco's
forty-niners found that they could not live
on gold dust alone and began slurping
San Francisco Bay's oysters like bar nuts.

Those oysters, being Olympias, were barely larger than bar nuts, and they were few and far between. San Francisco Bay is ringed by prehistoric shell mounds, but those mounds are dominated by clam and mussel shell. Oyster shell seems to have disappeared from them at least two thousand years ago. Small and slow-growing, Olympias were made for overharvesting. The oyster entrepreneur John Stillwell Morgan spent 1850 searching the bay for serviceable oysters and found few. This situation would later instigate Hubert Howe Bancroft, chronicler of California history, to claim that "there is actually no such thing as a California oyster . . . The only California product of the kind that bears any resemblance to an oyster is a little soft-shelled parasite, more like a barnacle than anything else, a handful of which can be squeezed up into a pulp with slight pressure. They are not fit for consumption." Harsh words for the divine Oly! Clearly he never tasted the good ones.

Back then, the good ones were merrily wriggling their mantles in Washington Territory's Willapa Bay (then called Shoalwater), six hundred miles from the nearest population center. Shaped like a jai alai basket ready to catch the nutrient-rich upwellings flung from the

Preceding pages: Oyster pens from the Nisbet Oyster Company in Willapa Bay. Left: Founder John Finger and friend check bags of Hog Island Sweetwaters in California's Tomales Bay.

Pacific, protected by a long thumb of barrier beach, and so shallow that half its volume turned into mudflats every low tide, Willapa grew millions of the plumpest Olympias anyone had ever seen. And San Francisco devoured them. The "Shoalwater Bay Trade" delivered a fresh boatload of Willapa oysters to San Francisco every few days for decades.

Adding insult to injury was the completion of the transcontinental railroad in 1869. Most consumers still found Olys to be small and weird, definitely last-resort oysters, so one of the first things the railroad brought west were iced barrels of Eastern oysters to be planted in Willapa Bay and San Francisco Bay for fattening and sale. Once Easterns were available, the price on Olys collapsed. By 1894, San Francisco was famous for the quality of its Eastern oysters (Jack London worked as both an oyster grower and an oyster pirate), and Willapa Bay was equally divided between Easterns and Olys.

None of it would last. By 1910, Olympias had been overharvested into oblivion everywhere except in southern Puget Sound, near Olympia—which is when they acquired their name—and the water quality in San Francisco Bay was becoming too poor to farm anything but salt. (You still see the remnant Technicolor salt ponds when you fly in to SFO.) Water quality in Willapa remained—and remains—sky-high, but in 1919, Willapa Bay's Eastern oysters suffered a massive die-off and the action switched to Japan's more forgiving Pacific oyster.

The Japanese had been farming oysters in Matsushima Bay for centuries, and the Americans soon learned that they could ship spat-covered shells from Matsushima Bay (hand-packed in old wooden sake cases, covered in straw mats, and watered twice a day during the voyage with fresh seawater) considerably cheaper and with better survival rates than with Eastern oysters by train. Seed would be shoveled off a barge into the bay, where it would grow to market size in a year. Each year, one hundred thousand cases of seed would arrive in Washington State. World War II managed to sabotage that arrangement for only a few years, but it was just long enough for the industry to start thinking about breaking its dependence on Japanese seed suppliers. In the 1970s, West Coast hatcheries began producing their own oyster seed, ending the Japanese trade.

Today, you can divide the North Pacific oyster scene into two styles. Willapa Bay, Gray's Harbor, and Oregon are the home of old-school, large-scale oystering. Big barges, industrial shucking houses, and very salty oystermen. The Bay Formerly Known as Shoalwater still singlehandedly produces about 10 percent of the nation's oysters. Considering their fine flavor, surprisingly few of them are sold in-shell as singles for half-shell service, but at least a tub of shucked Willapa Bay oysters is still one of life's affordable treats.

California, meanwhile, is the pioneer of half-shell hip. Back in the 1980s, when oysters were about as trendy as quahogs, a handful of restaurateurs and aquaculturalists helped awaken the Bay Area to the beauty of a local oyster perfectly presented—and helped acclimate the public to paying for the pleasure. When the last shucking operation in California, Drakes Bay Oyster Farm, closed in 2015, it left only high-end half-shell operations from the Kumamoto fields of Humboldt Bay to the picnic paradise of Tomales Bay, where on a weekend you can barely navigate U.S. 1 for the cars spilling out of the oyster farms, and the smell of grilled jumbos fills the air. Unlike the full-figured oysters of Oregon and Washington, California sports a lean, clean, salt-and-graphite style of oyster. It's all high cheekbones and ice, and it's very hard to resist.

And don't forget those little soft-shelled parasites. Reports of their death have been greatly exaggerated. True, you won't find any beds of Olympias in the region, but all along the coast you can still find them anywhere rock meets the low-water line, even in San Francisco Bay. They tend to be "cryptic," the zoological term of art for "concealed." Look for them under rocks or anywhere else they can avoid sun, cold, and predators. My favorite place to go on Olympia safari is Shell Beach on Tomales Bay. Go at an extreme low tide, when the cliffy, Pacific Plate side of the bay is exposed, and you'll find them hugging the shoreline, melding into the rock like insurgents, awaiting a less mucky future when they can retake the coast from Monterey Bay to Shoalwater. It could take millennia, but they will. For us, we simply get to enjoy the geological eye blink that is Tomales Bay, the evanescent flavor of the San Andreas Fault.

DISCOVERY BAY

DISCOVERY BAY,
WASHINGTON

SPECIES Pacific

CULTIVATION Most Disco Bay oysters are raised in suspended trays in the deep waters of the bay. Some are beach finished.

PRESENCE A frilly shell with gunmetal-blue highlights mark this as a suspended-culture oyster (the only option in deep, stormy Disco Bay).

FLAVOR The earthy mushroom of Willapa meets the crispy pickle of the San Juan Islands. A nice balance of Washington State flavor zones.

OBTAINABILITY Strong in Seattle, spotty elsewhere on the west coast, and nearly nonexistent back east. Look for **Snow Creek**, a suspension-cultured oyster from the bay, and also **Otter Cove**, a thick-shelled wild oyster harvested from Hood Canal beaches and salted up in a rack-and-bag system in Discovery Bay.

DISCOVERY BAY IS ONE OF THOSE jaw-droppingly gorgeous spots that Western Washington seems to tuck all over the place behind a scrim of Douglas fir. When I was first exploring the world of West Coast oysters, I used to spend a fair amount of time in nearby Port Townsend, and I still remember the first time I went for an aimless drive and quickly wound up gazing in awe over the cliffs of Discovery Bay and out to the wild Strait of Juan de Fuca beyond. I wasn't the first to have a mystical moment at the bay. The explorer George Vancouver was so impressed when he sailed into it in 1792, its two wide arms rising high to embrace him, that he named it for his own ship. With instant access to the Pacific, and miles of virgin fir stretching in all directions, it was an ideal logging port, an identity it still clings to as that world winds down. Today, the best things about Discovery Bay are its rugged beauty and its shellfish.

Discovery Bay often gets lost among Washington State's Big Four: Willapa Bay, Hood Canal, Puget Sound, and Samish Bay. Only a handful of farms operate here, and its production is minuscule, but it grows excellent oysters. It's perfectly positioned to catch the nutrient-rich upwellings that rise from the deep Pacific and pour down the Strait of Juan de Fuca and funnel straight into the bay, and its deep, cliff-lined waters stay icy year-round. The high-food, low-temp ocean combo keeps its oysters sweet and savory, and I always try one when I see them.

DRAKES BAY

DRAKES ESTERO,
POINT REYES NATIONAL
SEASHORE

SPECIES Pacific

CULTIVATION Spat from Drakes Bay's mature oysters was captured using "remote setting": Clean shell was placed in a saltwater tank and oysters were added and encouraged to spawn. The spat set on the shell, which was hung in clusters from wires attached to wooden rafts in the estero.

PRESENCE Drakes Bays were known for their groovy colors and dramatic flourishes—a side product of their bag-free lifestyle. They acquired their green hue from the envy dripped into the estero over the years by Park Service bigwigs eyeing the oyster farm from the shallows.

FLAVOR Bitter tears of sorrow.

OBTAINABILITY RIP. But look for **Drake's Little Bajas** (or, as I call them, Drake's Diasporas), fine oysters that the Lunny family is now growing in Baja, California—one of the few places that can match Drakes Estero for brine.

DRAKES ESTERO IS A PEACEFUL OASIS of alternating fog and steely light tucked into the tawny grasslands of the Point Reyes Peninsula, just north of San Francisco. It's where Sir Francis Drake touched down in his circumnavigation of the globe in 1579, and besides the Golden Hind, it specializes in catching upwellings from the deep Pacific as they plow into the coast. This gives it some of the most pristine water quality of any bay in North America— easily the best in California—and it always made the oysters grown in it a special treat. The oyster farm in Drakes Bay was established in 1935 and thrived until 2014, when the National Park Service closed it down. Of all the oysters profiled in this book, this is the only one that you absolutely, positively can't find. What you see is the last photo that will ever be taken of a Drakes Bay oyster. This is an elegy.

Here's what happened. When the Park Service took over Drakes Estero in 1972, as part of its vision for Point Reyes National Seashore, it gave the oyster farm a forty-year lease, with the option of renewal if things were going swell. Everybody thought they were. After Kevin Lunny bought the farm in 2005, he turned it into one of the most beloved brands in California. But in 2012, when the lease was up, the Park Service told Lunny he had to go. When he asked for justification, the Park Service claimed the farm was harming calving harbor seals in the estero. It turned out that motion cameras had been quietly installed in 2007, and these had the proof. But then further digging by an independent researcher found that a Park Service employee had cherry-picked the evidence and misrepresented colleagues' work, and what the cameras actually documented were seriously unfazed seals. Lunny sued. "Save Our Drakes Bay Oyster" signs popped up all over Marin County. An independent seal expert was tapped to evaluate the photos. His report made it very clear that the seals were unharmed by the farm, yet somehow, when the Department of the Interior issued its final ruling, it claimed just the opposite. By the time a reporter at *Newsweek* uncovered the report in 2015 and scandal erupted, the Supreme Court had already ruled against Lunny. The last few million oysters were hauled out of the estero and composted.

So we are left with only our memories of driving through the misty, windy hills, dropping down to the shell-strewn shore of the estero, and marveling at one of our most shining examples of humans and nature working in harmony. I can see why, in the Park Service's view, allowing the oyster farm to continue operating in a wilderness zone might have muddied the waters, but I do wonder how a more nimble entity might have celebrated such a gem.

ELKHORN

WILLAPA BAY,
WASHINGTON

SPECIES Pacific

CULTIVATION: Cultch (old shell) seeded with baby oysters is attached to longlines raised a foot off the bottom in the intertidal zone.

PRESENCE Fractal. Feels like the truest expression of whatever algorithm defines the curve of a Pacific oyster's shell. Some can be huge.

FLAVOR Meaty, mineral, muskmelon.

OBTAINABILITY The Shotwells grow a lot of Elkhorns on their leases—it's a beautiful sight, the clean lines stretching far across the bay—and the oysters turn up at bars throughout the Pacific Northwest and frequently in New York as well.

ELKHORNS ARE CLASSIC, old-school oysters farmed for twenty years on thirty acres in the heart of Willapa Bay by Steve and Andi Shotwell, with the assistance of their twin boys, Ray and Tom. They employ the two traditional methods that have been used in Willapa Bay for decades: longlines and bottom culture. In the past, for both, cultch would be spread on the bottom of the bay in spring, when the oysters in the bay were ready to spawn. The spat would settle on the shell, which could either be kept in place (for bottom culture) or drilled with holes and strung on longlines, which would then be elevated on poles driven into the mud. Raised off the bottom, the longlined oysters would have better access to food and be protected from some bottom-dwelling predators. Both styles tend to produce clustered oysters with irregular shapes, which can be a challenge to shuck, so producers of half-shell oysters have mostly gravitated toward mesh bags and other, more intensive gear, but sometimes it's nice to hold a spectacularly curvy and pointy Elkhorn in your hands and appreciate the beauty of keeping your operation as simple as possible. There's something sublimely mathematical about the Pacific oyster: Why not let Elkhorns be Elkhorns?

GOLDEN NUGGET

TOMALES BAY,
CALIFORNIA

SPECIES Pacific

CULTIVATION Seed is raised in the shallow, upper end of Tomales Bay (very close to TBOC's retail store and picnic spot) in bags attached to floats that rise and fall with the tides, tumbling the oysters and giving them perfectly smooth shells and fat meats.

PRESENCE Remarkably blubbery, these are the gavage-fattened geese of the oyster world. The black, shiny shells recall graphite—so handy, since the flavor does, too.

FLAVOR Graphite and cream. Artichokes in butter. Foie gras. Fatty is what I'm saying.

OBTAINABILITY I've never found these anywhere except at TBOC's retail store and picnic grounds on the edge of the bay.

WHEN THE SAN FRANCISCO BAY oyster industry tanked in the early 1900s amidst a storm of mining sediment, pollution, and typhoid flares, most of the main players decamped to Tomales Bay, thirty miles up the coast, a sun-speckled slot of pure ocean water connected to San Francisco by the North Pacific Coast Railroad. John Stillwell Morgan's Morgan Oyster Company was one of them, and in 1913 it became the Tomales Bay Oyster Company, which has been raising oysters in the same spot ever since. Back then, Eastern oysters, brought as seed from the East Coast, were the critter du jour; but in 1928, TBOC, as it's affectionately known, partnered with the California Department of Fish and Game to try a wild experiment: importing Pacific oyster seed from Japan. Needless to say, things went well. The Pacific oyster has ruled the roost in California ever since, and TBOC has been a big part of it.

TBOC's next evolution happened when it began letting customers picnic on the grounds. Big hit. Now the place is a madhouse every weekend. How mad? Eighty thousand oysters will disappear by Monday.

Most of those oysters are TBOC's fine Preston Points, grown beside Hog Island Sweetwaters out where Walker Creek pumps nutrients into the open end of the bay. But a few years ago TBOC owner Tod Friend tried his hand at a tumbled oyster, and the results were remarkable. Tumbled in the closed southern end of the bay, which can get both plankton-rich and hypersaline in summer, as rain becomes nonexistent and the California sun bakes the water out of the San Andreas trench, the oyster can get obscenely rich and briny—the kind of thing to make a prospector run down the street shouting "Eureka!" while holding it aloft. But to do that you'll need to pay a visit to Tomales Bay. Golden Nuggets don't travel.

GOOSE POINT

WILLAPA BAY,
WASHINGTON

SPECIES Pacific

CULTIVATION Seed from Hawaii is grown in Willapa Bay in cylindrical tumble-cages attached to longlines for six months, then bottom planted for an additional six months to develop a round, frilled edge.

PRESENCE Goose Points combine smooth, sizable cups with a nearly round, thin growing edge.

FLAVOR Like a cucumber sandwich rolled in salt and parsley, with a stony, astringent finish.

OBTAINABILITY The Nisbet Oyster Company has long-standing connections to Portland, Oregon, and that's still Goose Point Central. They ship both shucked and live oysters online.

MOODY WILLAPA BAY FEELS A WORLD APART from the cramped confines of Puget Sound. Fog and drizzle swirl in from the 50-degree ocean. The whole place feels soggy, green, vibrant, oxygen-rich, and slightly blurred, as if you're inside a terrarium. The Pacific is literally just around the bend. This is the land of lonely beaches and oyster boneyards. The Nisbets' shell pile is the size of a Walmart, and it's not even one of Willapa's big ones. But after thirty-five years of focusing on shucked oysters, Kathleen Nisbet-Moncy, daughter of the founders, has spent the past three developing a top-end single oyster. Goose Points are named for the nearby head of land where Kathleen grew up, and they capture the essence of the spot: salty, crackling with untamed energy, and robust. The Nisbets raise their own seed in Hawaii, then grow it out in black mesh cylinders attached to longlines. This produces a young, semi-tumbled oyster, but then the oysters get scattered on the muddy floor of the bay, where they are given lots of breathing room. From minerals in the mud, they develop a full-bodied flavor. From the space, they grow into a wide oval, almost like an open hand, giving them a unique look: deep cup surrounded by dainty frill. Serve these and you get points for both presentation and canny sourcing.

HOG ISLAND ATLANTIC

TOMALES BAY,
CALIFORNIA

SPECIES Eastern

CULTIVATION Seed is raised in off-bottom racks and bags in the intertidal zone of northern Tomales Bay.

PRESENCE Like a tubercular John Keats, this transplant seems to be struggling to thrive in a foreign environment and pining for home, even as its isolation has imbued it with a tragic beauty and a fiercely lyrical love of life.

FLAVOR Insanely savory and fruity, with a bitter green-tea finish, this is one of the world's great oysters.

OBTAINABILITY *Crassostrea virginica* is notoriously finicky to grow in the Pacific, and seed supply is tight. Only a trickle of these make it to market, and they trickle only as far as Hog Island's three oyster bars (Marshall, Napa, San Francisco Ferry Building).

"IT WOULD TAKE THE PEN OF A POET guided by the imagination of an epicure to do any sort of justice to the oysters of San Francisco," a partisan paper opined in 1909. "The oyster of San Francisco is famous. Its celebrity has gone forth to the ends of the earth, carried by the eloquent tongues of the gourmand, native or visitor, who has tasted, smacked his lips, tasted again, and instantly has become the willing slave to the appetite for the delicious bivalve that thrives upon the oyster beds of San Francisco Bay."

That oyster, weirdly, was the Eastern oyster, planted upon the beds of the bay from 1869 until the early twentieth century. And though none has been so foolish to plant oysters in that bay for nearly a century—and even back then those Eastern oysters struggled to flourish in the cold Pacific—suspicion has lingered among oyster nerds that something was lost when the Eastern oyster stopped coming west.

The closest you can get to those famed oysters of yore might be the Hog Island Atlantic, raised in small quantities by Hog Island Oyster Company in Tomales Bay. Hog Island's John Finger was the first in our era to play around with Eastern oysters on the West Coast. He sent seed up to Taylor Shellfish, which used it to perfect its Totten Inlet Virginica. Both companies have struggled to get their *virginicas* to market ever since, but when it works, it's magical. Something happens to Atlantic oysters when they touch the Pacific. They lose their salty edge and turn a little bit fruity. A tenderness softens their Calvinist core. They become Romantics.

HOG ISLAND SWEET-WATER

TOMALES BAY, CALIFORNIA

SPECIES Pacific

CULTIVATION Seed is grown in tumble bags on the northern end of Tomales Bay, near the mouth, then transferred to bags attached to off-bottom racks in the intertidal zone and harvested after one year.

PRESENCE Deep-cupped from its early months in the flip bags, but sporting a stylish frilly edge from its rack-and-bag finish. Slate black, deep purple, California cool.

FLAVOR An intense mix of brine and honeydew nectar unlike anything else on the market. Sweetwater indeed.

OBTAINABILITY The most famous and successful oyster in California history. Hog Island grows several million Sweetwaters per year. The only problem is that their own oyster bars—particularly the one at the Ferry Building, which singlehandedly unloads two million of them each year—absorb most of the production. For the ur-experience, head out to the self-serve picnic tables at their headquarters on Tomales Bay.

THE OYSTER THAT WOULD TRANSFORM California was born in 1983, when the marine biologist and surfer John Finger, a rangy young guy with a pearl earring and sun-bleached hair, scored a five-acre aquaculture lease in Tomales Bay, north of San Francisco, directly atop the San Andreas Fault, where the Pacific Plate and the North American Plate continue to grind in opposition an inch or two per year. Oysters had been grown in Tomales Bay in the past, but no one in California had ever grown singles for half-shell service, and Finger suspected that was where the market was headed, with California increasingly hungry for anything fresh and local. Young seafood distributor Billy Marinelli agreed, and sold the first oysters Finger produced to Chez Panisse and Zuni Café—the two flag bearers of California Local. Grown using French-style racks and bags where the salty, nutrient-dense Pacific upwelled from the depths and funneled into skinny Tomales Bay and met the fresh waters of Walker Creek (referred to as "sweetwater" by the old-timers), this oyster was a revelation of flavor and form. To set it apart from the old guard of oysters, he gave the oyster—and the operation—an intentionally quirky identity, naming it for a nearby isle where settlers used to corral their swine. (This inadvertently sowed much confusion, since other Hog Island oysters, undoubtedly named for the same reason, turn up in Maine's Damariscotta River, Virginia's Eastern Shore, and Rhode Island's Narragansett Bay.)

Soon, Finger brought aboard fellow marine biologist Terry Sawyer, and soon after that the two opened a retail spot near their farm. Customers were eating their oysters on the premises as soon as they bought them, so Hog Island added some picnic tables and began lending out shucking knives. Some people wanted to grill their bivalves, so they added some Webers. Beer and wine followed, and suddenly Hog Island was the sizzling weekend destination spot in the Bay Area and had inadvertently created the vertically integrated "bay-to-plate" model many savvy oyster farms now follow: Island Creek, Rappahannock, Little Creek, Hama Hama, and even Taylor Shellfish have all gone to Hogwarts.

Today, Hog Island farms 160 acres in Tomales Bay and is charging hard into Humboldt Bay. Hog Island also grows superb Kumamotos (in the southern, less dynamic part of the bay, confirming Kumies' contrary nature) and even some flats ("French Hogs"). For those, you'll need to make the piggy pilgrimage.

KUMAMOTO
(California)

HUMBOLDT BAY, CALIFORNIA

SPECIES Kumamoto

CULTIVATION Seed sets on shell that is strung on longlines raised a foot off the bay bottom and harvested at two to three years of age. Look for the telltale "scar" near the hinge where the oyster was attached to the mother shell.

PRESENCE Chic shells and a fragile, mannered elegance sets these apart from the thick, rustic Kumies of Washington. It's Catherine and Heathcliff.

FLAVOR Tastes scintillating, like the flashes of light sparking off the dark bay.

OBTAINABILITY All over the frickin' place. Look for extra-gorgeous **Redwood Curtain Kumamotos**, which are grown in swaying SEAPA baskets.

THE WINSOME LITTLE "KUMIE" is native only to the Yatsushiro Sea, in Kumamoto Prefecture on the island of Kyushu at the far southern tip of Japan, where it has been harvested on the flats since the mid-1800s, though it was never popular because of its shrimpy size. The Japanese preferred the larger Pacific oyster that lived in Matsushima Bay on Japan's northern Pacific coast instead, and that was what they always sent to American growers as seed until World War II shattered that arrangement. Yet, just two months after the bombing of Hiroshima and Nagasaki, America asked Japan to send eighty thousand boxes of Pacific seed again. The Japanese said, *Sorry, things have been a little crazy around here lately, there's nothing happening in Matsushima Bay,* and instead scrounged up thirty boxes of Kumamoto seed. American farmers were thoroughly unimpressed with the slow-growing Kumamotos and eagerly reverted to Pacifics when the seed became available two years later, but by then the Kumie had established a beachhead on the West Coast, in part because growers hoped it could replace spawny Pacifics in summer. (Coming from warm southern Japan, the Kumie never spawned in the cold waters of the West Coast.) Soon after that, a Japanese chemical plant began pumping clouds of mercury into the Yatsushiro Sea, driving the native Kumamoto into extinction and poisoning thousands of people in the process. Humboldt Bay became the Kumamotos' last hideout, and even there, back in that era of oyster-meats-by-the-gallon, nobody wanted it. The floor of Humboldt Bay was littered with millions of unsellable Kumies.

Enter a fast-talking twenty-something bundle of entrepreneurial verve named Billy Marinelli. In the early 1980s, Marinelli had developed a fledgling business distributing oysters to San Francisco oyster bars, and he began buying Humboldt Bay's unwanted Kumamotos for two dollars a dozen. The established oyster bars, still selling beefy East Coast Bluepoints in those days, wanted nothing to do with the little Kumies. But a new wave of restaurants celebrating local cuisine was rising, so Marinelli took his little oysters to them. Alice Waters fell hard for Kumies. Chez Panisse was one of his first takers, and Zuni Café was right behind. Soon Marinelli had turned an entire generation into Kumamoto lovers.

Today, Humboldt Bay remains one of the few places on earth that can grow happy Kumies. And grow them it does: The bay is filled with millions attached to longlines. They are very different in appearance and flavor from the Chapman Cove Kumamotos of Puget Sound, and debates rage over which is the best and truest exemplification of what many feel is the most delicious oyster of all.

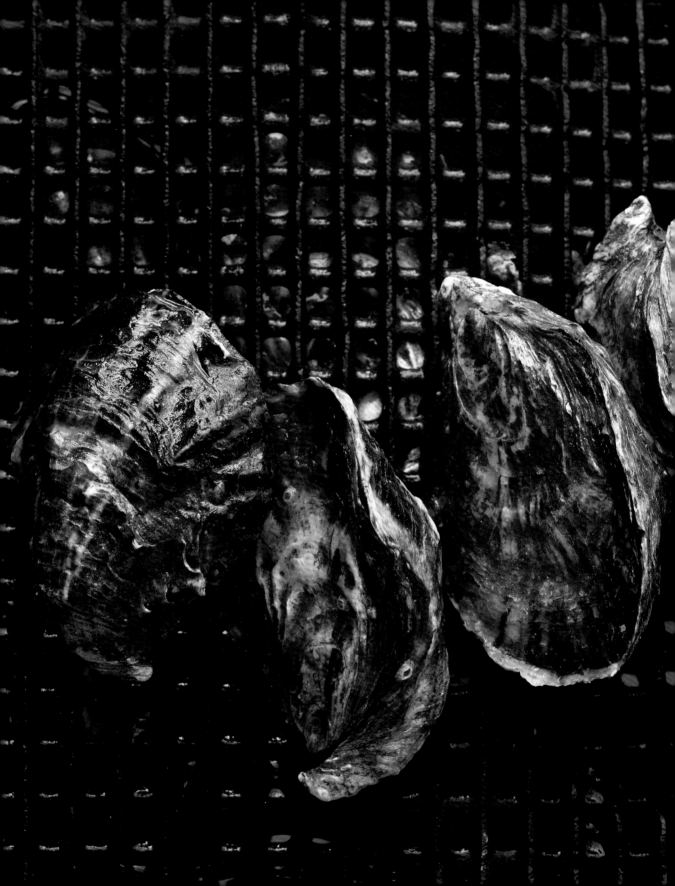

SHIGOKU

WILLAPA BAY,
WASHINGTON

SPECIES Pacific

CULTIVATION Seed from Hawaii is grown out in plastic mesh bags attached to longlines that tumble up and down with the tides, reaching market size in six to eight months.

PRESENCE Small, scooped, and slick, with Ridley Scott color palettes, these feel like they got beamed out of some Pacific Rim fusion future.

FLAVOR Strong, clean cuke and salt, finishing with water chestnut and Jerusalem artichoke.

OBTAINABILITY Shigokus are legion. Taylor Shellfish has installed 1,400 longlines in Willapa Bay, each holding 39 bags producing 150 mature oysters every six months. You do the math.

THERE ARE TUMBLED OYSTERS, and then there's the Shigoku, tumbled with a vengeance by the angry Pacific as it pours into and out of Willapa Bay every twelve hours. In addition to the tides, Shigokus are shaped by the wind. Grown on the "Oyster Gardens," a flat expanse of fattening beds in northern Willapa Bay named by oystermen for its tonic effect on oysters, Shigokus are two miles due east of the bay's mouth, where wind and wave can work them like sandpaper. The choppy surface shakes the floats and the attached oyster bags up and down like a machine. It's a much higher-energy environment than, say, South Puget Sound, and the oysters become that much more manicured.

Taylor began playing around with the Shigoku in 2007, after noting the success of the Kumamoto and especially the Kusshi. They named it for a Japanese term meaning "ultimate," reinforcing the rule that small, cute oysters must be named like manga characters (a rule dutifully obeyed by Shibumi, Chunu, and others, yet flouted by Sea Cow). A storm-of-the-century obliterated that first experiment, but Taylor rebooted, and now they are cranking out picture-perfect Shigokus on a massive scale. I almost always use Shigokus when I lead tastings because they are such reliably charming companions, because they don't require much commitment, and because the tumbling process gives them a top shell that is pop-top easy to open. The ultimate zipless shuck.

Occasionally an oyster nerd will reject a Shigoku like an undersized bluegill. Fortunately for such nerds, Taylor Shellfish has now released the **Fat Bastard**, a double-stuffed Shigoku (about three inches) and the **Grand Cru**, a *triple* stuffed. Most Grand Crus wind up in Hong Kong, center of the bigger-is-better oyster cult.

GULF
of MEXICO

Go now. Go, while you can still crawl through New Orleans summoning plates of oysters by pooling your pocket change.

Preceding pages: Dead soldiers at Pascal's Manale in New Orleans. Left: Wild Gulf oysters dredged in Pass Christian, Mississippi.

Stand at the counter at Casamento's or Pascal's Manale and let the shucker clutter the bar with the biggest damn oysters you've ever seen in your life, puddled in strangely thick shells. Tabasco, oyster, beer. Wash, rinse, repeat. Another dozen? Don't think twice. Go, because someday you'll want to regale future generations of oyster lovers with stories of Louisiana oysters in their prime. Big as your hand, you'll tell them. Three bucks a dozen.

They won't believe you.

Abundance is profound in itself. The difference between parceling out tiny portions of a precious resource and going hog wild on one almost too cheap to meter is a difference of kind, not degree. Wild Gulf Coast oysters aren't always the tastiest or prettiest oysters in the world, but they are huge and untamed. If today's domestic oysters are dainty fatted calves, kept in their little pens, these are the bison. It always feels like a battle taking one down. That and their unlimited supply can make any Joe staggering down Bourbon Street feel as fortunate as Meriwether Lewis gazing in wonder at the herds of the plains.

The early European explorers actually had trouble wrapping their heads around the abundance of oyster reefs they encountered on the Gulf Coast, or getting their compatriots back home to believe them. In 1720, Pierre François Xavier de Charlevoix, the Jesuit Priest who had been exploring the northern wilds of New France (and commenting favorably on its oyster culture; see page 217), traveled down the entire length of the Mississippi River in an aborted effort to reach the Pacific Ocean and wound up exploring the western coast of Florida as a consolation prize. "This coast is the Kingdom of Oysters," he reported, "as the great Bank of Newfoundland, and the Gulf and the River St. Lawrence are that of the cod-fish. All these low lands, which we coasted as near as possible, are bordered with trees, to which are fastened a prodigious quantity of little oysters of an exquisite taste. Others, much larger and less dainty, are found in the sea in such numbers that they form banks in it, which we take at first for rocks on a level with the surface of the water."

Oysters in the trees? This caused a stir in Europe, where they had never seen a mangrove.

The heart of Gulf Coast oystering has always been Southern Louisiana, where thousands of oystermen got to live as hunter-gatherers, some of the last in the nation, and all of us benefited. Until 2010, if you bought oysters in a supermarket east of the Rockies, you bought Gulf oysters. Yet, the generation before mine tells me that we'd already missed the golden era. That what seemed to us like paradise on earth was already a pale shadow of the real thing. Until the mid-1900s, Louisiana oysters were abundant, briny, and distinctive: Every bayou or lake had its own flavor—some grassy, some more like driftwood, some sweet, and some salty—and everyone asked for their favorites by name. Grand Bayou. Bay Batiste. Bayou Cook. Basin Bois. Lake Washington. Caminada Bay. Every day, barrels of oysters, their provenance clearly marked, were boated up to New Orleans. Then the national distribution Goliaths took over the business. They bypassed New Orleans entirely, loaded their tractor-trailers right at the docks, and didn't care where their oysters were coming from. Everything sold for the same price, whether it was a bland river oyster or a Lake Washington classic. Soon Gulf oysters became synonymous with "cheap and plentiful."

That all changed with the BP oil spill in April 2010. As oil crept toward the coast, the state of Louisiana opened the floodgates on the levees in the Mississippi River, hoping the surge of freshwater through the bayous would push the oil away. What it did was turn many of the oyster grounds fresh for the next few months. And oysters can't live in freshwater. When the experts surveyed the grounds in July, they found killing fields. Many reefs suffered 90 percent mortality. Some were gone entirely. Meanwhile, ironically, in Mississippi, Alabama, and Florida, increasing salinity killed production as predators rushed into the saltier water.

Jason Hulse shows off his Louisiana pride while shucking at Pêche.

Now, years later, Gulf Coast production is still less than half of what it used to be, and prices more than double. That dark cloud still hangs over the entire Gulf Coast. And I won't sugarcoat it: It's pretty dark. But when the light is just right and I squint real hard, I swear I can see a silvery edge starting to glow around that cloud. If the prevailing winds hold, it might even become a ray of hope.

April 15, 2015: I'm leaning against the marble oyster bar of Pêche on Magazine Street when the steamy cumulonimbi part and a bolt of sunshine cuts through the window and gilds us all. It lights up a chalkboard in the corner. And on that chalkboard is written: **OYSTERS**. **Louisiana**: Area 3, Caminada Bay, Beauregard Island; **Alabama**: Murder Point, Isle Dauphin; **Massachusetts**: Island Creek.

Honestly, I'm stunned. Having read about the desperation of the Gulf Coast industry for a couple of years, I came into town like the Grinch, waiting to hear all the Whos in Whoville crying boo-hoo. And instead they are all singing. Christmas came just the same.

New Orleans in the twenty-teens is the best oyster town it has ever been. Sure, Gulf Coast production is down, but all that has meant is that supermarkets in Dubuque are no longer getting their cut-rate oysters. Casinos in Illinois are suffering. New Orleans ain't suffering. If anything, it has stopped taking its abundant reefs for granted. The entire city seems to be turning to friends and strangers alike and saying, "Look what we've got!"

The French Quarter alone inhales fifty thousand oysters *a day*. And now it seems like the rest of the city is gunning to surpass it. There have never been so many oyster bars in New Orleans, and, more important, never so many serious ones. From Pêche to the Curious Oyster Company in the new Dryades Public Market, you will find prime oysters proudly identified by provenance for the first time in half a century. And it isn't just New Orleans. Gems such as Saltine in Jackson, Mississippi, and Kimball House in Decatur, Georgia, are reinventing what a southern oyster bar should be, serving carefully curated oysters of impeccable quality. Some are wild Louisianans identified by harvest area (1 to 28); others are coming from the first wave of Gulf Coast farms.

Yes, farms. Oyster farming, which could never get a foothold in the region when the wild reefs were so productive, is at last coming on strong. The clear leader is Alabama, where some of the saltiest coastlines on the Gulf are producing world-class oysters that can hold their own anywhere. The patron saint for all this is Dr. Bill Walton, who once grew oysters on Cape Cod, but in 2009 took a position with Auburn University with the goal of revolutionizing oyster farming on the Gulf Coast. And he has done so.

Other states are now following Alabama's lead. And I can't wait. I'm already relishing that moment a few years from now when I begin my oyster crawl in Apalachicola and head west, following I-10 past Mobile Bay and Portersville Bay and Pass Christian, stopping at seaside bars every few miles to sample the local bivalves, past Lake Borgne and Terrebonne Bay and Vermilion Bay and on to Galveston Bay and Lavaca Bay and Padre Island. It'll be epic. Unprecedented. And pricey. And that's just fine.

One side effect of the decline of the wild reefs is that Gulf Coast oysters are no longer quite so cheap. (For now, prices are holding in New Orleans, where every hole-in-the-wall seems to be offering fifty-cent oysters as loss leaders during happy hour—and when is it not happy hour in New Orleans?) That means the days may be numbered when you can knock back two dozen sloppy, sketchy oysters after work every day while standing at the counter and jawing with the shucker—which is truly a shame—but it also means that the days of Gulf Coast oysters being derided may be numbered, too. Because when people pay more for oysters, farmers can afford to grow them right. And when you give a Gulf oyster space, salty water, and an occasional shake to keep it from growing too fast, you get an oyster that's the envy of the world.

Right: Casamento's oyster loaf may be more famous, but I'll take the charbroiled oysters any day.

APALACHICOLA

APALACHICOLA BAY,
FLORIDA

SPECIES Eastern

CULTIVATION Wild oysters are tonged by hand from small skiffs.

PRESENCE Thick, encrusted shells from life at the bottom, and ivory meats from eating high on the hog. The interior of the shells is often tinged old-pearl yellow.

FLAVOR Depends which way the wind's blowing. If it's blowing river water over the oyster beds, expect a nearly saltless experience; if the river water's going the other way, they can be gloriously briny, buttery, and shrimp-sweet. The best oyster I ever tasted was pulled straight out of Apalachicola Bay with tongs by a guy named Kendall. It was slick with mud and as sweet and briny as saltwater taffy.

OBTAINABILITY Few and far between these days. Wild harvests are at an all-time low. For that Apalachicola savor, look for Tommy Ward's **13 Mile** oysters (pictured here), which grow on his private leases thirteen miles west of town in the saltiest and most remote part of the bay.

APALACHICOLA BAY, THE BULGE IN the Florida Panhandle, is about eighty miles from anywhere. It has been formed over eons by the Apalachicola River, the thick, brown, sluggish, gentle giant that drains southern Georgia and much of the Florida highlands. Picture a mini-Mississippi before the petro-industrial complex moved in. The river is lined with cypress and tupelo swamps—and is the source of the world's finest tupelo honey—and it discharges a steady flow of rich, sediment-filled water into a warm bay that is just a few feet deep. Add to the mix the barrier islands that rim Apalachicola Bay, which keep the bay relatively calm (a boon for oysters and oystermen both), and relatively brackish (which keeps at bay most oyster predators, which can only thrive in salt water), and you've got an oyster metropolis.

Or had. Once the rock star of the Gulf Coast, shipping fifty thousand cans of oysters a day by railroad in the late 1800s, Apalachicola Bay needs to spend some time in rehab. Some of the blame goes to the state of Georgia, which began diverting the river water for Atlanta's insatiable needs in 1989, but even more goes to the double whammy of drought and overharvesting. A trickle of its former self, the river no longer dilutes the salt water in the bay sufficiently, and salt-water-loving predators and diseases have moved in. Reefs are down to a tenth of the size they were just ten years ago, meaning that even when things go well, there aren't enough oysters in the bay to quickly repopulate. The fishery was declared a federal fisheries disaster in 2013. Many of the six hundred oystermen who used to work the bay full-time in small boats—dropping fifteen-foot tongs into the soup to spoon up a handful of oysters at a time, then culling them on wide running boards—have given up trying to catch a living out there. The eighty or so who still do are now limited to five bags a day, down from twenty. In all likelihood, oystering will be shut down in the bay for some time. In early 2016, heavy rains in the region gave Apalachicolans some hope. Stay tuned.

CAMINADA BAY

CAMINADA BAY,
LOUISIANA

SPECIES Eastern

CULTIVATION Seed from the neighboring LSU hatchery on Grand Isle is grown out in off-bottom cages in a few feet of water until the oysters are very large.

PRESENCE Cyclopean. These saucer-eyed giants feel almost mythic in their power. A wanderer of the Louisiana coast could easily be waylaid by them and not come home for years. The crusty purple shells feel ancient.

FLAVOR Mild, fresh, and yeasty, like salted dough dipped in the bayou. The essence of Lafourche Parish.

OBTAINABILITY The first full-size Caminada Bays hit the market in 2015 and quickly made a cannonball-size splash in New Orleans. Look for them and their kissin' cousins—**Beauregard Islands**, grown in the same manner a mile east—at Pêche and other new-wave oyster bars.

FOR FOUR GENERATIONS, Jules Melancon's family has harvested oysters from the waters of Caminada Bay and Beauregard Island, near Grand Isle, Louisiana. Jules spent his teen summers tonging and carrying hundred-pound sacks of oysters from his grandfather's four hundred acres of leases, but the land subsidence and saltwater intrusion that has doomed so much of Southern Louisiana turned those leases too salty, and the reefs succumbed to saltwater predators. So in 2011 Jules teamed up with his friend Jim Gossen, a legendary seafood distributor on the Gulf Coast with a particular love of oysters and a desire to see the tradition continue, and became the first oyster farmer in Louisiana. With cages to protect his flock from marauding oyster drills, he has been able to produce the platonic ideal of a Louisiana oyster: a huge, plump dumpling of an oyster with the biggest adductor I've ever seen on a farmed specimen. The sweet adductor balances the salty belly and gives a lot of chew to the oyster—just like Louisianans like it. It can be more than a mouthful, but just do what I've seen the Cajuns do: Take the edge in your lips and start working it in like chubby linguini. It fries wonderfully, too.

GULF

GULF OF MEXICO

SPECIES Eastern

CULTIVATION Wild

PRESENCE Massive, mean, and muddy. Spackled, gritty shells and fat, sloppy meats, with one giant "eye" gazing back at you. The kind of thing that makes a Manhattanite run in fear.

FLAVOR "Chewy blancmange" in the words of Adrienne Anderson, this book's stylist. Sometimes watery, with a subtle scent of Ol' Muddy, and sometimes tasty, with a lightly briny, earthy, Jerusalem artichoke flavor.

OBTAINABILITY Funny thing. For half a century, Gulf oysters have been the dominant oyster in America. Any generic oyster you saw in a restaurant, casino, or supermarket was bound to be a Gulf oyster. That all changed in 2010, when they got scarce and prices per sack climbed. Still, where people think oysters should cost ten dollars a dozen, you'll find them.

A GULF OYSTER CAN BE ANY wild oyster from Florida to Texas, but most of them come from Louisiana's ample reefs. Being wild, they are completely unmanicured, and being dredged by the sack and sold by the truckload, they are always a crapshoot. They can be a little mild, a little languid—as M. F. K. Fisher put it—or they can be great, especially for those who like their aphrodisiacs meaty. You just never know.

Here's the insider's tip for you: Look for specific areas. Louisiana's wild reefs are divided into twenty-eight different harvest areas. Restaurants and retailers are required to keep the tag indicating where oysters were harvested from, and to produce it for any customer who asks. Don't be shy about this: It will tell them you're serious about your oysters, which they should welcome. In fact, more and more oyster bars are listing the area right on their menus and chalkboards. Many aficionados favor Area 3, a large zone east of Lake Borgne that tends to produce many of Louisiana's best half-shell oysters, thanks to its location farther into the Gulf of Mexico, where the saltier, rougher conditions give the oysters more sea essence. I've also had good experiences with Area 15, in Terrebonne Parish.

In theory, Gulf oysters are the same species as East Coast oysters, but if so, these are the mastiffs to the East Coast collies. If oysters could drool, these would be the ones. Gulf oysters are big-boned and big-eyed, with layered, poured-concrete shells. Perhaps the year-round feeding and mating molds them—it's a lifestyle thing—but they must have some genetic uniqueness, too. For that alone, it's my hope that more people outside the region will come to appreciate these gentle giants. As a jiggly conveyor of horseradish, they most definitely have their place.

MURDER
POINT

PORTERSVILLE BAY, ALABAMA

SPECIES Eastern

CULTIVATION Seed oysters from Auburn University are grown in mesh baskets attached to longlines in about five feet of water, constantly rocked by the waves and winds. The oysters are run through a sorting tumbler very frequently to deepen the cups.

PRESENCE Movie-star handsome. Murder Points are shaken, stirred, and culled to a state of creamy-white pulchritude.

FLAVOR Cream-of-potato soup with brioche on the side. Or, as Lane Zirlott prefers to describe it, "butterlove."

OBTAINABILITY The Zirlott family released their first crop of Murder Points in 2015. They are on track to produce two million a year, so by the time you read this, expect to find them in all the top Southeast oyster bars.

BACK IN THE ALABAMA COAST'S surprisingly lawless days, a notorious band of thugs called the Copeland Gang ran roughshod over the territory. They lived in some scruffy cabins on Copeland Bayou, where the marshes of the Fowl River open onto Portersville Bay, and they did whatever was doable: burned houses, looted stores, stole horses and slaves, and pilfered oysters, always fading back into the bayou. One day, an eighty-three-year-old oysterman named Steven Lawson, who lived in a house made of oyster shell, accused the Copelands of stealing oysters from his beds. Undoubtedly he was correct, but it was still a bad call. In response, the Copeland Gang arrived at Lawson's shell house, where he was sitting on his porch, and beat him to death with a bat. For further measure, they propped him back up in his chair and shot him with a shotgun. After that, the point near Lawson's home came to be known as Murder Point (it had been "Myrtle" before that), and the shell house was always rumored to be haunted. (It was leveled in 2014.)

Brent Zirlott grew up on the waters of Portersville Bay, within spitting distance of Copeland Bayou. He always gave the bayou and the shell house a wide berth, but when Auburn University started an oyster-farming program right on the bay and turned over a couple of acres to Zirlott and his wife, he knew exactly what to call his oysters. "Oysters worth killing for" is their motto.

They are, too. Murder Points have perfect teardrop shapes, smooth pastel shells, and button-tufted meats that push against every available millimeter of shell space. They achieve this the hard way—through constant handling. Brent's son Lane, who manages the farm, is a big, strong guy, and before he installed their Australian longline system, he used to shake every bag of oysters by hand. "Anyone can grow an oyster," he says, "but you gotta raise an oyster. You gotta talk to it a little."

To me, the Zirlotts and their Murder Points are a heartening glimpse of the future of Gulf Coast oystering. Five generations of Zirlotts have made their living on these waters. Brent was a shrimper, and he still owns two ninety-seven-foot trawlers, one of which Lane used to captain. But shrimping at that level involves spending as much as a month at sea at a time, and relies on a lot of unknowns. Lane has a young family, so when the opportunity to move from hunter-gatherer to farmer came up, he jumped at it, and quickly fell in love. He says you can taste that in the oysters, too. "A little butter, a little love."

PELICAN REEF

CEDAR KEY, FLORIDA

SPECIES Eastern

CULTIVATION Seed is raised in off-bottom trays in the shallow waters of Florida's Gulf Coast.

PRESENCE All the colors of a Florida Gulf Coast beach: sand and stone, streaked with gray and green. The shells are deep cupped but delicate.

FLAVOR Beautifully balanced sweetness and salt, with a creamy corn chowder finish.

OBTAINABILITY Excellent in Cedar Key. Spotty elsewhere.

THE FIRST TIME I ATE A PELICAN REEF, I went back and checked the tag, so sure was I that a mix-up had occurred. Surely this was a Barnstable or a Duxbury oyster. That clean sea flavor with the sweet-corn finish. The scooped cup and natty racing stripes. No way was this a Florida cracker. In earlier wanderings I'd encountered exactly two Florida oysters—the scraggy little intertidal "coon oysters" of my Mosquito Lagoon childhood, and the wild, thickset heavyweights of Apalachicola—and this was neither of those. But the tag panned out. Here, on one of the most pristine and unknown curves of Florida coastline, a world-class oyster had appeared out of nowhere.

I wouldn't have been so surprised, however, if I'd carefully checked my copy of *The Oyster Industry*, the bivalve bible from 1881. Its author, Ernest Ingersoll, was a man who paid much more attention to the numbers of boats and the prices of bushels than he did to flavor, but something about Cedar Key turned him into Brillat-Savarin. "The Cedar Key oysters have a different taste from anything I have experienced elsewhere," he wrote, "and one which will commend itself to those who like a saltish oyster; but there is a flavor about them, in addition to their saltness, which distinguishes them at once from anything else. On the whole, they must be pronounced good."

Cedar Key, a dreamy cluster of islets flanked by the swaying greenery of Big Bend Seagrasses Aquatic Preserve, is known for its sport fishing and clam farming. By the time you've left the mainland and crossed four bridges to join Cedar Key's seven hundred other castaways, you have entered a whole different Florida. Cedar Key was once a kind of kid sister to Apalachicola, producing similar oysters in much smaller quantities, but the wild oysters tanked in 2012 when the extended drought drove salinity levels too high. It has been a clam-farm powerhouse since 1995, when the state enacted a net ban and retrained fishermen to grow clams. In 2012, some of those clam farmers decided to give the tenderer bivalve a try. Bingo. In those salty (25 parts per thousand) subtropical waters, the oysters turned into classics. They still face an uphill battle—Florida oysters carry as much baggage as Florida politicians—but resistance is falling, one slurp at a time.

POINT
AUX PINS

GRAND BAY, ALABAMA

SPECIES Eastern

CULTIVATION Seed is raised in cylindrical Australian SEAPA-brand "oyster baskets" that hang from longlines and are designed to maximize "rumbling," as the Aussies call it. Harvested at eighteen months of age.

PRESENCE Spiffy black-and-white shells, deep cups, and creamy-white meats. A class act.

FLAVOR Like a can of creamed corn simmered in seawater. Sweet, savory, delicious.

OBTAINABILITY Strong along the Gulf Coast from Alabama to Houston.

THE MOMENT WHEN I REALIZED everything I thought I knew about Gulf oysters was wrong came in 2012 when I slid my first Point aux Pins into my mouth. Up to that point, most Gulf Coasts I'd experienced had been wild, mild, and lax. Like most people, I'd assumed that was just how they grew down there. But here was a crisp, salty oyster in a polished semiformal shell that could have come out of Maine or the Cape. Its umami was matched by its sweetness, and it finished clean. I was shocked, then very excited when I began to anticipate the future masterworks coming out of Grand Bay.

Today a dozen oyster farms are up and rolling on the Gulf Coast, with many more on the way, but in 2009, Steve Crockett was "the first penguin in the water," as he puts it. He's still the lead penguin, thanks in part to his extraordinary growing site. Crockett lives on Point aux Pins, a sandy spit of longleaf pines that forms the eastern edge of Grand Bay, a national wildlife refuge and one of the best pine savanna habitats remaining on earth. Grand Bay has neither development nor freshwater, meaning Crockett's oysters are some of the saltiest in the Gulf—about 25 ppt on average. Crockett lives in a beach house a couple of hundred yards from his oysters, and miles of sand road from the nearest town. By day, the waters are filled with pompano and pelicans; by night, heat lightning crackles within the clouds. If I was going to kill one oyster grower and take over his life, it would probably be Steve.

RESIGNATION REEF

GALVESTON BAY, TEXAS

SPECIES Eastern

CULTIVATION Wild

PRESENCE Burly and baroque, with a rusty tinge to both the meat and shell. The bill gets supremely crinkly, as if fried in molten salt, and the lining can be posh purple.

FLAVOR Check the drought. In normal times, so much freshwater pours into Galveston Bay that it stays at a mildly briny 10 to 20 ppt. But when a few years of drought baked Texas like a ginger crisp, the Galvestons turned into virtual Katama Bays.

OBTAINABILITY A handful of restaurants in Houston and New Orleans are leading the charge on this one.

ONE OF MY ALL-TIME-FAVORITE OYSTER names, and just one of the dozens of single-reef oyster appellations coming out of Galveston Bay. Others to look for include Ladies Pass, Elm Grove, Possum Pass, Lost Reef, Found Reef, and, best of all, Todd's Dump. It's a concept spearheaded by Tracy Woody, the leading oystermen in the region, and it's laudatory. I don't know of anywhere else in the country taking terroir down to the microlevel of individual reefs. But according to the great Texas food writer Robb Walsh, the differences are there: Oysters from the northernmost reefs, such as Lost Reef, are fatter and sweeter, while oysters from the southernmost reefs, closest to the Gulf outlet, including Ladies Pass and Elm Grove, are considerably brinier.

When most people in the country think "Galveston," they think "oil," and they get particularly agitated about a happy hour featuring raw animals harvested from beside the tanker shipping channels. But the water quality in Galveston Bay is quite good, and the oysters can be some of the best on the Gulf Coast. Unfortunately, in recent years, overharvesting, drought, water diversions, and hurricanes all took their toll. Then in 2015, massive floods threatened to kill many existing reefs by turning the water too fresh, but had the positive side effect of filling the bay with fresh nutrients and eliminating many salt-loving predators. "God pushed the reset button" is how Tracy Woody put it. Look for a bumper crop from Galveston in 2017 or 2018.

SOUTH ATLANTIC

For a few years, I've been referring to the Southeast as the sleeping giant of the oyster world. But now I can't, because the giant isn't sleeping anymore.

When I wrote my first oyster book ten years ago, I didn't even bother including a chapter on the Southeast. Why? Because I'd conceived the book to be an aid to people attempting to navigate the extensive oyster lists in places like the Grand Central Oyster Bar, Shaw's Crab House, and Elliott's Oyster House, and back then you couldn't find a southern oyster in a northern oyster bar. Chefs literally said to me, "I'd never serve an oyster from south of the Mason-Dixon Line." The perception was that southern oysters were muddy, bland, and dangerous. The reality, as usual, was more nuanced. The only southern oyster most people in the north had encountered was the wild-harvested Gulf of Mexico oyster, which at the wrong time of year can indeed be insipid (thank you, Mississippi River) and risky to those with weak immune systems (thank you, *Vibrio vulnificus*). Other oysters from the South were guilty by association.

Back then, it's true, the northern oysters were almost always more savory and polished. But that's because the southern oysters were wild. Wild oysters tend to be gnarlier than their cage-grown

kin, and they proliferate in brackish water (where salt-loving oyster predators can't survive). They're also much cheaper, sold by the sack instead of the individual piece, meaning less time to cull and clean them before shipping. As the only regions that managed to preserve their native oyster reefs, the Gulf Coast and the Southeast were never forced to start farming them, and their reputation suffered. Somehow many oyster bar chefs and patrons got it in their heads that cold-water oysters were automatically saltier, comelier, and safer.

Then Virginia began farming oysters that gave the northeastern stars a run for their money. The trick was to use the sea, as the northern farmers had been doing. Marinating in the Atlantic brine of the Eastern Shore instead of the brackish bays, the oysters grew intensely salty and savory, and they did it in half the time of their northern peers. True, in November, as it prepares for a six-month hibernation, a slow-grown Maine oyster is going to have an unmatched sweetness and density; but conversely, in April, it's going to be bony beside that zaftig Virginian.

After Virginia, the oyster industry cast its eye down the southeast coast and saw paradise: more than six thousand miles of shoreline unmarred by a single metropolis. The giant may have twitched first in Virginia, but now its eyes are open in the Carolinas. Growers are quickly mastering the art of raising half-shell oysters in marine environments, which in the Southeast means regular tumbling to promote shell strength and cup depth. With a longer season and faster growth, they can undercut northern producers on price, and they are poised to become a staple at oyster bars across North America.

But that should not preclude you from visiting the region itself to partake in a culture that can't be shipped in FedEx boxes. Those wild oyster reefs still survive in the Carolinas, and each has its own discerning clientele. Some swear by the Bulls Bays from north of Charleston, others by North Carolina's Stump Sounds or Crab Sloughs. It's the kind of local micro-knowledge that used to exist everywhere.

What never existed elsewhere is the excellent Lowcountry habit of the oyster roast: shovel clusters of wild oysters onto a metal sheet over a beach fire, cover with wet burlap sacks, steam until the oysters "smile," transfer to a picnic table, eat, swig beer. It's a great way to

Preceding pages: A brilliant morning in the ACE Basin; a Charleston oyster roast; and a Lowcountry shucking pedestal. Below: South Carolina oysters that have set on bamboo poles. Right: Lowcountry boot drier.

remind yourself that we used to have a relationship with oysters that had nothing to do with chalkboards or Muscadet.

Not that there aren't plenty of chalkboards and Muscadet to be found in the region. In fact, if you think the Northeast has a sizzling oyster culture, just check out what's happening in the new urban South. Exhibit A: Travis and Ryan Croxton. In 2011, when the founders of Rappahannock Oyster Company bought the storm-smashed marina next to their farm and turned it into a tasting room called Merroir, they had no idea they'd found the golden goose. Great Virginia oysters, great Virginia wine, great Virginia view. It's been packed ever since. That goose has since given birth to a gaggle of goslings, including Rappahannock (Richmond), Rappahannock Oyster Bar (DC), Eat the Rich (DC), and Rocksalt (Charlotte and Charlottesville). The proliferation shows the insatiable enthusiasm for oysters in the South, even far inland, and it marks the reemergence of a distinct oyster culture. Not only are the oysters you find in a southern oyster bar wholly different from what you find up north, but this is also the only region in the country where they'll bring your bucket of steamed "clusters" to the table, hand out oyster knives, and trust you not to raise their insurance premiums.

The success of Southeast oyster farms has also helped to revive the wild oyster fishery—something many people thought we'd never see in our lifetimes. Not only do the aquaculture operations take the pressure off the wild stock, they also help to replenish it by seeding the bay with billions of larvae every time the farmed oysters spawn. And the filtering capacity of hundreds of millions of caged oysters has improved water quality and reinvigorated seagrasses. From a nadir of 23,000 bushels in 2001, Virginia's annual harvest has climbed to more than 500,000 bushels—the best in thirty years.

ATLANTIC EMERALDS

NORTH RIVER, NORTH CAROLINA

FROM LONG ISLAND TO GEORGIA, certain wild oysters found in very salty waters have the discomfiting habit of developing green gills in winter. The rest of the oyster will be unchanged, while the gills have turned a color we don't like to see in our meat. They are considered unsalable, but while your domestic compatriots quiver in fear, you, Oyster Nerd, will be feeling a frisson of superiority, because in Marennes-Oléron, France's oyster Mecca, you have fed on beaucoup Fines de Claire Verte, bearers of blue-green gills and exorbitant price tags. You may even know (but of course you do) that the pigment, known as marennine, is produced by a blue diatom called *Haslea ostrearia*, is a heroic antioxidant, and is always associated with excellent flavor. The French adore it so, they actually isolate the diatom and add it to their finishing ponds. In America, not so much.

Green Gills have been a problem in the Southeast since forever. Ernest Ingersoll noted them in his 1881 bible *The Oyster Industry*, pointing out that "the existence of it does not impair the quality of the oysters, but it does materially affect the sale, because people generally are ignorantly afraid of it." An illustrative account appeared in the November 20, 1879, issue of *Forest and Stream* magazine, in which a company of sportsmen dined in an oyster saloon in Richmond, Virginia, and were served a plate of Green Gills. Downplaying rumors that the oysters derived their color by dining on "copperous banks" created by the festering remains of Civil War soldiers, the waiter assured the sportsmen that "dey's de best oyster comes here. Dey gets green from eatin' seaweed." To no avail: The sportsmen rejected the oysters, and Virginia failed to become America's Marennes-Oléron.

But now the Outer Banks just might. Down in Smyrna, North Carolina, near the Shackleford Banks, there's a wild harvester of some notoriety known as Clammerhead. Looks like a biker, talks like a philosopher. After years of frustration trying to convince buyers that the Green Gills he pulled from his leases were not just safe but special, or *spéciale*, Clammerhead has decided that the best defense is a good offense. He's trademarked the name Atlantic Emeralds and will be giving distributors and restaurants the full-court press. Who knows? Perhaps it won't be too long before foodie pilgrims make their way to the Outer Banks to worship the wild exemplar of what in France they can only find tamed.

SPECIES Eastern

CULTIVATION Wild harvested in the North River, near Beaufort, in the winter months.

PRESENCE Quartz flesh, jade gills.

FLAVOR Very sweet and salty, with a layered, nutty green-olive depth.

OBTAINABILITY Holy Grail. Be in the vicinity of the Outer Banks between late October and late February and look for a guy named Clammerhead.

BODIE ISLAND

ROANOKE SOUND,
NORTH CAROLINA

SPECIES Eastern

CULTIVATION Seed is raised in off-bottom cages on the bay side of Cape Hatteras National Seashore and tumbled periodically throughout its two-year life-cycle to deepen the cup and strengthen the shell.

PRESENCE Auburn shells with deep cups and a pockmarked surface, these embody the rugged southern Atlantic look.

FLAVOR Nicely balanced between sweet and salty, with a bright Atlantic zing.

OBTAINABILITY Much celebrated on North Carolina's Outer Banks (try the Coastal Provisions Oyster Bar in Southern Shores) and distributed around the country by Wanchese Fish Company.

JOEY DANIELS IS A BURLY, red-bearded, fourth-generation member of the family behind North Carolina's Wanchese Fish Company, a major player in East Coast seafood since the 1930s. For years, Daniels worked from the company's Virginia office, but he wanted to come home to Wanchese, a rough-and-tumble seaside community on the southern end of Roanoke Island. He was also sick of seeing more and more local fishermen go under, swamped by imports. So when he learned about oyster farming, it sounded like the perfect way to get himself home and to keep a few local guys employed year-round.

It was. Daniels scored a sweet ten-acre lease on the inside of Cape Hatteras, within sight of the Bodie Island Lighthouse (pronounced "body"). There the Atlantic pours through the Oregon Inlet break in the Outer Banks, infusing the sound with fresh seawater and keeping his lease around a near-perfect 24 ppt salinity. Unlike most newbie oyster farmers, he had all the infrastructure and distribution he could ever need through Wanchese Fish. He constantly experiments with different growing techniques, keeping his eyes on a pretty big prize: Daniels's goal is to turn the Outer Banks into an oyster powerhouse, churning out millions of big, salty Bodie Islands for delectation from Maine to Miami. Don't be surprised if he succeeds.

CAPERS BLADES

SPECIES Eastern

CULTIVATION Wild oyster clusters from Capers Inlet are chiseled apart into singles and purged in racks near the surface.

PRESENCE Pure of purpose, these are the greyhounds of the oyster world. Long, lean, fine-boned, and sharp. Deep as a dugout. Like a shark, they have to keep moving forward or they die.

FLAVOR A cherry-sweet salt lick of an oyster, sending certain quadrants of your tongue into jackpot mode. Photographer David Malosh swears by the stone-fruit finish.

OBTAINABILITY A good portion of the Capers Blades supply gets gobbled in Charleston restaurants like The Ordinary and Husk, where they are staples.

THE SALT MARSH CREEKS of the South Carolina Lowcountry tend to produce clusters of long, thin, knife-edge oysters that race to outgrow each other in that warm, intertidal environment. Traditionally served as part of a Lowcountry oyster roast, their meats tend to be, let's face it, scrawny, and they tend to come with a bit of Lowcountry terroir still clinging to them, which hardly matters if you're picking through them in the dark, drunk as a skunk, Tabasco and saltines flying in all directions, but on the half shell they can be a bit substandard.

This problem was solved in 2007 by Clammer Dave, the artist formerly known as Dave Belanger, who began chiseling apart his clusters into single blades (common) and finishing those blades in racks in the richest part of the water column (unheard-of). Like rough hogs fattened on acorns for a few sweet weeks before slaughter, the oysters get plump and sweet while retaining the rich, supersaline, pluff-mud nature of the bottom of Capers Inlet. The result has blown people away, from Charleston chefs to ostrea-savvy visitors from afar. It's an oyster seemingly made for shooting, perhaps even shotgunning, by the dozens. They just keep sliding down. Now others in the region have begun using Clammer Dave's techniques, and more and more oyster nerds are heading for King Street to run with the big dogs.

CHINCOTEAGUE
(cultivated)

CHINCOTEAGUE BAY, VIRGINIA

SPECIES Eastern

CULTIVATION Hatchery seed is grown out in off-bottom trays.

PRESENCE Farmed Chincoteagues (left in photo) look like they've been under attack: pockmarked, strafed with boring-sponge holes, scuffed white. Their beauty is on the inside.

FLAVOR A concentrated, unapologetic salvo of salt. Plain and simple. Have emergency pilsner on hand.

OBTAINABILITY Common. Also known as **Chincoteague Salts**.

CHINCOTEAGUE
(wild)

CHINCOTEAGUE BAY, VIRGINIA

SPECIES Eastern

CULTIVATION Wild

PRESENCE A randomized jumble of rusty green substrate, these clearly have been successfully impersonating rocks for years. If the cultured Chincoteagues look like they are under attack, these look like they've been through the wars—and survived. What doesn't kill you makes you stronger, and more beautiful.

FLAVOR Strong and slightly bitter sea salt bursts with fennel and black pepper. It's all Greek to me.

OBTAINABILITY Uncommon up and down the East Coast.

AFTER THE CIVIL WAR, a number of men straggled out of the smoking wreck of Virginia and threw themselves at the coast. "Many who had been reduced from wealth to poverty were glad to avail themselves of the chance to make a support by oystering," wrote a government expert in 1881. The luckiest of them all found their way to Chincoteague Bay, straddling the Mason-Dixon Line. Oysters thrived in the huge, sheltered lagoon, and, unlike in the brackish Chesapeake, at Chincoteague they soaked up profoundly salty Atlantic Ocean water. Better still, four years of war had left the oyster beds untouched and untended. A handful of entrepreneurs were soon selling plump and briny Chincoteagues to Philadelphia and New York, and they did so well that they named their bayside enclave Greenback. Chincoteague Salts became famous not just in the mid-Atlantic states but even in Europe, selling for thrice the price of Chesapeake oysters. Naturally, the wild beds were overharvested, but the Greenback planters didn't miss a beat, buying tens of thousands of bushels of baby James River oysters and planting them in Chincoteague Bay for two or three years before sending them on to New York. That practice ended only when the cheap wild spat from the James River ran out, but now, with the advent of hatcheries and cultivation gear, Chincoteague Bay is again filled with some of the planet's saltiest oysters. Better still, the farmed trade has taken the pressure off the wild survivors, who are mounting a modest comeback. These knotty beauties (right in photo), with their thick and worn four-inch shells, are somehow comforting to hold, like worry stones: You feel their heaviness in your hand and give thanks that there are still some solid things in the world. I imagine some shattered Virginia soldier, circa 1866, probably staggered into the shallows of Chincoteague Bay, picked up one of these beauties, ran his fingers over it while gazing at the waves, the gulls, the undefined horizon, and had the very same thought.

CHUNU
MISTY POINT

SMITH ISLAND BAY,
VIRGINIA

SPECIES Eastern

CULTIVATION Raised in off-bottom cages and tumbled frequently.

PRESENCE Chunus are petite and discreet, with white, deep-cupped bottom shells and mother-of-pearl interiors. Misty Points are the same, minus the petite.

FLAVOR Firm and very salty, with the sweet iron tang of a razor clam and a mochi finish.

OBTAINABILITY Quickly becoming a standard along the Eastern Seaboard.

A FEW YEARS AGO, the men of Ballard Fish and Oyster Company in Virginia toured the oyster scene in the Pacific Northwest and saw the writing on the chalkboard. While the Southeast was still tied to the remnants of the old world of wild harvesters and shucking houses, who paid by the pound and favored oysters the size of your hand, the Pacific Northwest was brimming with snappy oyster bars where millennials in raingear threw money at tiny tumbled oysters with Japanese names. Kumamoto had begat Kusshi, which begat Shigoku, which inspired Shibumi. The Ballard boys got it immediately: Make it beautiful, make it intense, make it nonthreatening. They were already working on a flagship oyster called Misty Point (the big guys in the photo), which they were tumbling to address the brittle-shell issues that plague southeastern oysters; instead of waiting for it to reach 3.5 inches, they could tumble the heck out of it, to deepen that cup, and release it at 2.75 inches.

Chunu is the closest thing the East Coast has to a Kumamoto, and I predict it will eventually find a similar embrace. The name translates to "virgin," as in pure and pristine (there's a Chunu Waterfall in Taiwan), and this is virgin territory you'd do well to explore before all the settlers rush in. But even if Chunu does become the "It" oyster, and you feel the need to put a little distance between yourself and the madding crowd, you could simply upgrade to Misty Point: less virginity but more virginica.

CRAB SLOUGH

OUTER BANKS,
NORTH CAROLINA

SPECIES Eastern

CULTIVATION Wild

PRESENCE Heavy green-brown shells with naturally manicured paisley shapes and full, ivory meats inside.

FLAVOR Sweet and buttery, with some clammy tannins and astringent asparagus on the finish.

OBTAINABILITY A local delicacy, October through March. Try the Coastal Provisions Oyster Bar in Southern Shores.

WHEN YOU OPEN A CRAB SLOUGH, if all is right with the world, you will lift up the mantle of the oyster with your knife and a listless little ball of legs and eyes will peek out at you (a pose our smoldering model is nailing in the photo here). This is *Zaops ostreus*, the oyster crab, which lives inside oysters throughout the mid-Atlantic and the Southeast, picking food off their gills. Transparent of shell, it reveals its red inner working parts like one of those wind-up robots from Radio Shack. I've never seen a creature look more forlorn and existentially confused than your typical oyster crab, which, when you meet it, is invariably having a lousy day. If you have a heart, you will do one of two things: (1) Pop it in your mouth, chew fast and hard, and swallow. For your efforts you will get a quick hit of crabby sweetness and the satisfaction of knowing that you put a doomed soul out of its misery. (2) Throw a griddle on the stove and fry the sucker (and possibly the bivalve it emerged from) in butter. Then go back to (1). If you are lucky enough to hit a bushel of oysters all packing oyster crabs, you can think grander: The *New York Times* published a recipe for Oyster Crab Salad in 1893. Frankly, it lacked dimension or inspiration. (Steam the crabs for 15 minutes, toss in mayo, serve in a pile in a lettuce cup.) If you innovate, please send me the recipe.

Even if you don't find a crab in your Crab Sloughs, you may get a surprise when you pop open that shell. Crab Sloughs are one of the oysters that sometimes go green in the gills during the winter. (Full scoop on page 111.) Lucky you.

The eponymous slough, by the way, is down near the southern tip of Roanoke Island, exposed to the Atlantic surges pouring through the Outer Banks at Oregon Inlet. Because Crab Sloughs grow in a rough-and-tumble marine environment, they develop thick, strong, almost naturally tumbled shells and salty meats, and they are usually found as singles rather than the scrawny clusters found in calmer intertidal zones.

JAMES RIVER

JAMES RIVER, VIRGINIA

SPECIES Eastern

CULTIVATION Wild

PRESENCE This is one of the heavyweights of the oyster world, with oversized muscles and a pale potbelly, like an aging professional wrestler. The thick umber shell comes creviced with Virginia mud.

FLAVOR Very dilute yet clean, with a touch of sweet astringency on the finish, like watery white tea.

OBTAINABILITY Still treasured as a "value oyster" in the Southeast, you'll see James River oysters at many raw bars looking to keep things affordable. If ever there was a time for horseradish, this is it.

WATCH HOUSE POINT

CHESAPEAKE BAY, VIRGINIA

SPECIES Eastern

CULTIVATION Rack-and-bag

PRESENCE This tough is all about urban-camo shells and khaki meats. It may as well wear combat boots. Let's just say Arlington is not far across the bay.

FLAVOR Like an inside-out Maryland oyster stuffing: bivalve, broth, bread, and Old Bay. Touch of celery.

OBTAINABILITY Good in the mid-Atlantic and Southeast.

IN 1880, THE *NEW YORK TIMES* embedded a reporter on a Virginia oyster schooner. The resulting article begins: "The bottom of the James River is one enormous oyster-bed." How enormous? From the mouth of the river for twenty miles upstream, said the *Times*. "Go anywhere in it you may and push to the bottom a pair of oyster-tongs, bring them together, and lift them out of the water, and you will catch oysters." Virtually the same observation had been made by Captain John Smith 273 years earlier when he sailed upriver and noted that oysters lay "thick as stones" on the bottom. Smith and the early colonists complained about the twenty miles of oyster reefs that broke the surface of the water and threatened to gut their boats, though they actually lived on one of the oyster banks during a particularly lean period and survived on a diet of bivalves, bivalves, and more bivalves.

The abundance of the Chesapeake Bay's oysters is legendary, but the James River was always the powerhouse. Low salinity and circular eddies that brought new spat back to live with its parents turned it into the New York City of oysters. The 1880 *Times* article describes more than one hundred boats working a single reef for months on end without denting the population. The James River was the mother of the entire mid-Atlantic industry.

Yet, nobody ever loved it. James Rivers (top in photo) are about as close to tasteless as an oyster can be. They aren't bad—they taste like clean Virginia mountain water, which is no small thing—they just need help. Traditionally, that help was provided by moving oysters from the James to saltier grounds. In the late 1800s, James River oysters stocked most of Chincoteague, and even most of New York. A Bluepoint was a James River oyster marinated in Long Island Sound for a year or three.

But you didn't even need to go that far. For instance, raise oysters a mere thirty-five miles northeast, on the eastern side of Chesapeake Bay, away from all the rivers, and they transform. There you have Watch House Points (bottom). Bobbing in the bay right at the point where the sweet mountain waters of Virginia mingle with the Atlantic salt, they epitomize the balance that defines a great Chesapeake oyster.

LADY'S ISLAND
PHAT LADY

ACE BASIN, SOUTH CAROLINA

SPECIES Eastern

CULTIVATION Hatchery seed is grown out in off-bottom cages in the ACE (Ashepoo, Combahee, and Edisto) Basin to three inches in about fourteen months. Phat Ladies start the same, but at two inches these girls go wild, scattered free on the flats and allowed to reach market size there.

PRESENCE Mahogany shells with the classic paisley curves and deep cups holding cream-white meat. The Phat Ladies take on a green tinge, ridged shells, and a pleasant paunch from life on the bottom.

FLAVOR Holy guacamole, these are salty! With no fresh inputs, just ocean washing in and out and evaporating, at times the ACE Basin can soar to 37 ppt salt—higher than the ocean's 34. But Lady's Islands have a sweet finish that keeps them nicely balanced, while Phat Ladies finish astonishingly round and jammy.

OBTAINABILITY Admirably, Frank Roberts sells his oysters only September through April, giving the warm-water months a pass. Lady's Islands headline at dozens of Charleston venues, as well as oyster bars throughout South Carolina. The Phat Ladies croon only at The Ordinary.

THE ACE BASIN (the coastal watershed drained by the Ashepoo, Combahee, and Edisto Rivers) is the heart of Carolina Lowcountry: 350,000 acres of low-lying salt marsh, tidal creeks, oak hammocks, and precious few residents. Think *The Prince of Tides* and you'll have the scenery locked in. Its water quality is unsurpassed, and it grows a decent wild oyster—the "clusters" the Lowcountry is known for—but Frank Roberts experienced nice, cupped single oysters growing up on the Chesapeake, and he always thought he could grow an even tastier half-shell oyster in the ACE Basin. For a while, the equipment and technology to do it wasn't available in South Carolina, but about a decade ago, when it was, he became the first in the state to jump at it. Soon he was producing the best oysters the state had ever seen, unexpectedly winning over diehards as well as newbies. He grows some of his oysters in cages, to protect against the onslaught of blue crabs and stone crabs, in a few feet of water. Others are a unique hybrid between wild and farmed: He plants thousands of bamboo poles in the mudflats and lets wild oyster larvae set all over them. When the oysters reach market size, he breaks them apart and sells them as "Single Ladies."

Phat Ladies (on the right in the photo) are a partnership between Roberts and Mike Lata, the chef of The Ordinary, Charleston's best oyster bar. Lata was always searching for a local oyster with a stronger shell and deeper cup. Then Roberts discovered thirty thousand oysters that he'd broadcast as seed on the bottom of the estuary three years earlier and forgotten about. Growing loose on the pluff mud—what the Charlestonian Buff Ross calls "the mothersauce of all things Lowcountry"—they'd become exceptionally full-bodied, in every sense. Richer, bigger, greener, knucklier. The Ordinary coined the name, bought them all, and committed to buying all the others like them that he could grow. A great arrangement, though harvesting the bottom dwellers is complicated by the presence of a fourteen-foot great white shark named Mary Lee who patrols the edge of the lease, occasionally doing a sweep across the oyster grounds.

RAPPAHANNOCK RIVER

RAPPAHANNOCK RIVER, VIRGINIA

SPECIES Eastern
CULTIVATION Virginia hatchery seed is raised in off-bottom cages. Harvested at a year and a half.
PRESENCE A good example of the scuffed and dinged shells so characteristic of the Chesapeake. Good cups with smart paisley curls. Some cloak themselves in Rappahannock jade, like these sharp dressers here. Rapp meats can be particularly full.
FLAVOR At 15 ppt, one of the lowest salt profiles out there. Gentle and deep, like a low-sodium veggie stock. Screams out for caviar.
OBTAINABILITY Excellent along the Eastern Seaboard, especially DC, Virginia, and North Carolina.
(Upper left in photo)

STINGRAY

WARE NECK, CHESAPEAKE BAY

SPECIES Eastern
CULTIVATION Virginia hatchery seed is raised in off-bottom cages. Harvested at a year and a half.
PRESENCE White and brown shells flecked with black filings call to mind geological strata. Feels like you're eating time.
FLAVOR At 20 ppt, a beautiful balance of salt and sweet.
OBTAINABILITY Excellent along the Eastern Seaboard, especially DC, Virginia, and North Carolina.
(Lower left in photo)

BARCAT

CHESAPEAKE BAY, VIRGINIA

SPECIES Eastern
CULTIVATION Raised in off-bottom cages by small, independent growers throughout the Chesapeake Bay region.
PRESENCE Varies, but generally sporting a tanned top and white bottom, like so many Bay natives.
FLAVOR Varies, but generally a medium-sweet, slightly briny oyster with a touch of that classic Chesapeake root-soup essence.
OBTAINABILITY The lower-priced Barcat has become a mainstay at happy hours throughout the region. It's also sold shucked by the pint, quart, or gallon, and has been the house shucked oyster at the Grand Central Oyster Bar for years.
(Upper right in photo)

OLDE SALT

CHINCOTEAGUE BAY, VIRGINIA

SPECIES Eastern
CULTIVATION Virginia hatchery seed is raised in off-bottom cages. Harvested at a year and a half.
PRESENCE Tanned and toned, and a touch leggier than the rest of the Rappahannock line.
FLAVOR At 32 ppt, these are little lozenges of ocean screaming for lemon.
OBTAINABILITY Excellent along the Eastern Seaboard, especially DC, Virginia, and North Carolina.
(Lower right in photo)

BACK IN THE MID-2000S, when I was first digging into the fine points of oyster flavor, it could feel pretty hopeless. I'd assumed other foods would work like wine, where the top producers had been thinking for decades about how subtle changes in the environment or their cultivation practices might affect the final product. But it turned out wine was an exception. Flavor was the last thing most farmers worried about. Just getting their product to market in decent condition without going broke was plenty to occupy their days. When I asked growers what was responsible for the flavor of their oysters, I mostly received blank stares. That seems surprising today, when the saltiest oysterman can go on about merroir with a straight face; but back then, if you murmured terroir in the ear of a typical oyster farmer, you were likely to get punched.

In Virginia, where the wild oyster fishery still ruled and aquaculture was in its infancy, that was doubly true. Things didn't look good for the Chesapeake chapter of *A Geography of Oysters*. And then I discovered Travis and Ryan Croxton. The two cousins were in their early thirties, with tousled blond hair and boyish faces that looked like they'd spent more time in conference rooms than on the water—which was true. Ryan had been a graphic designer and Travis worked for the Federal Reserve. Now they were growing oysters, and not only did the website for their new company, Rappahannock River Oysters, list locations and salinities for each of their three oysters, it was map based. They had gone to wine school, and they saw what was coming as clearly as I did.

If you want to find a microcosm of the rise, fall, and redemption of Virginia oystering, you can't do better than the Croxtons' story. It all started in 1899, when their great-grandfather James Croxton decided to buy a few acres of oyster leases. Back then, aquaculture was simply a matter of buying or harvesting wild spat from the public grounds and replanting it on your leases. For the next sixty years he was a part-time oyster farmer, but his son William went into the business full-time, buying hundreds of acres of leases from other owners. But by the time he passed away in 1991, that style of oyster farming was doomed. The wild reefs had collapsed to a hundredth of their historic levels, and there just wasn't enough seed to be had. Worse, so much muck was washing into Chesapeake Bay from upstream agriculture and development that it was impossible to grow oysters on the bottom. William Croxton convinced his sons to stay out of the biz, but they kept paying to renew their leases, more out of nostalgia than anything else.

In 2001, the family received notice that their leases were about to expire. They almost let them. The Virginia harvest was down from 20 million bushels a year in the 1880s to 23,000 bushels, and the state very nearly committed the colossal blunder of allowing the bay to be seeded with a foul-tasting but fast-growing Chinese oyster. However, Travis and Ryan thought there was hope for *Crassostrea virginica*. They re-upped on the leases and began Googling "How to grow oysters." The answer, of course, was true aquaculture. Hatcheries could supply seed, and off-bottom cages could raise the oysters out of the muck and protect them from the stingrays that were chomping half the oysters in the bay. In 2004, they became the first of the new wave of oyster growers in Virginia, cold-calling Le Bernardin and nailing a standing order for two hundred oysters per week, despite the awkwardness of needing the chef de cuisine to show them how to shuck their own oysters.

Today, the Croxtons continue to farm their oysters in three spots with wildly different characteristics: several miles up the Rappahannock estuary, where the influence of Blue Ridge mountain water is the strongest; in the mid-Chesapeake, where the profile is that of a classic bay oyster; and outside the bay in Chincoteague, where the ocean dominates. They also sell a fourth oyster called a Barcat (named for a style of small, nimble oyster skiff used by independent types around Tangier Island who wanted to easily sail from oyster bar to oyster bar) that they buy from small, independent types throughout the Chesapeake region, many of whom were trained by the Croxtons. The goal was to jump-start oyster farming throughout the bay, give these baby growers a built-in market for their product, and maintain the tradition of the affordable oyster accessible to all. And it worked.

SEWANSECOTT

HOG ISLAND BAY,
VIRGINIA

SPECIES Eastern

CULTIVATION Hatched in the H.M. Terry hatchery at Willis Wharf, then grown out in bags and off-bottom trays in the shallow waters of Hog Island Bay. Harvested at around fifteen months of age.

PRESENCE Meaty, beaty, big, and bouncy. (There is also a Sewansecott Petite that is just beaty and bouncy.) The gray shells often have streaks of black on their pearlescent interiors, and they can be honeycombed with boring-sponge holes—both very characteristic of high-salinity mid-Atlantic oysters.

FLAVOR Savory and rich, like a buttered steak.

OBTAINABILITY In the past few years, these oysters have won over many top chefs up and down the East Coast. They even make it out to Hog Island Oyster Bar in San Francisco.

SEWANSECOTT WAS THE JACKIE ROBINSON of oysters, the one that broke the Mason-Dixon barrier. At the Grand Central Oyster Bar, Chef Sandy Ingber tasted it and instantly put Virginia oysters back on the menu. It has become one of his favorites. What did it for Sandy? Brine. With no nearby freshwater creeks, Sewansecotts capture the robust Atlantic waters that file through the bay every tide. They balance that drying salt with lots of sweet and savory amino acids, giving them a full-bodied, almost beefy succulence. They are not hard to like, and they have educated half the country to the greatness of Eastern Shore oysters.

Of course, the Terry family has known that since 1903, when Henry Miller Terry first settled in Willis Wharf to be an oysterman. Three generations of Terrys worked the waters of Hog Island Bay until 1988, when disease invaded the region and wiped out the oysters. The family took a twenty-year hiatus before reviving their Sewansecott brand in 2007, this time farming the oysters. Today, Heather Lusk has taken the reins from her dad, Pete Terry, and her uncle Wec Terry.

Willis Wharf is one of those places you never want to leave. The Terrys never did. As you stand at the graying H.M. Terry docks and gaze across the salt marsh, you see a single brick house snuggled into the oak hammock. It's where three generations of Terrys have grown up. Beyond the house is an endless expanse of mudflats, tidal creeks, and pine islands. You hear wind and waterfowl. It's part of an eighty-mile stretch, reaching north through Hog Island Bay toward Chincoteague, that has been designated a United Nations Biosphere Reserve. Water quality is impeccable. Oyster quality, too. Cell phone reception? Sucks.

LONG ISLAND SOUND *to* BLOCK ISLAND SOUND

There's really no place on earth where the local oysters and wine go together as well as the North Fork of Long Island. A bottle of chenin blanc. A dozen Peconic Bay oysters. Bliss.

Sure, you could make a case for Tomales Bay, California, and Sonoma County sauvignon blanc. Or French oysters and muscadet. But there, you're still talking many miles between sea and vine. On the North Fork, with a little effort, you could capture them both in the same snapshot.

Or you could just swing by Little Creek Oysters, on the water in Greenport, and capture a menagerie of local oysters and local tipples in a single shot. The little shack that was once the wheelhouse of a whaling ship, then a haven for fishermen, and finally a bait and tackle shop has been reborn as a funky oyster saloon, which says to me that Long Island oyster culture has matured. The proprietors, Ian Wile and Rosalie Rung, who also farm Little Creek oysters in Peconic Bay, will sell you whatever oysters you pick out, hand you a knife, and trust you to do the deed on the picnic tables out front while the working waterfront goes by.

Oysters aren't just a risqué novelty during midnight happy hour anymore; they're part of the fabric of every burg touched by New York waters. Whether it's happy hour on Bedford Ave, the pre-train wait in the Roman caverns beneath Grand Central Terminal, or the unceremonial "shuck yourself" style at Little Creek, oysters own this place. That twentieth-century blip when they nearly disappeared from daily life is looking more and more like an interregnum, kind of like the Yankees in the 1980s.

From the three big boys in the western part of the sound—Norm Bloom & Son, Tallmadge Brothers, and Frank M. Flower & Sons—to the myriad midgets on the East End, the common factor is perfect salinity. Sure, everybody's different, and you can find people who prefer everything from an oyster that tastes Hudson fresh to one that's Baja salty, but most of us like our brine in the mid-high range—strong enough to make your mouth water, but not enough to burn. And that's exactly what Long Island Sound delivers, like a gifted mixologist, spiking a base of North Atlantic brine with the bright minerality of New England rivers and the fresh upwellings of its famed bays.

That, of course, is what made it the oyster powerhouse of the Northeast for so long. Long Island Sound has always been packed with oysters right up to where the East River laps against the flank of Manhattan. Quality was traditionally extraordinary, which caused its own problems, as is captured so well in the saga of Saddle Rock, a twenty-foot-high bump emerging just off the eastern shore of Little Neck Bay, not far from the Throgs Neck Bridge. In 1827, with oyster mania well under way in Manhattan, a northwest wind commenced to howl for several days, blowing a lot of water out of the bay and connecting Saddle Rock to the shore. A local man named Dr. O. R. Willis reported that "this extraordinary low tide revealed a bed of oysters just below the rock. The oysters were very large, and possessed the most

delicate flavor; we collected cart-loads of them, and placed them in our mill-pond." Word got out, of course, Manhattan went gaga for Saddle Rocks, and the oyster reef around the rock was immediately exhausted. But the name lived on, and indeed still does.

So it goes. Long Island continues to crank out a tremendous number of oysters under an array of creative names, and New York eats them

all. Water quality is a lot better than you might expect for a sound sur-rounded by the heart of the Northeast Corridor, and new people are leaping into the business as fast as the towns will grant leases, from the Great South Bay to the Peconic Bay and all along the Connecticut shore.

And then, of course, there is Gotham itself. To say that no other city in the world comes close to New York's oyster scene does not do it jus-tice. Cities like Paris, Boston, and Seattle have intense oyster cultures, and New Orleans probably consumes more oysters per capita than any city in the world, but all those towns glorify their local bivalves. Gotham thinks globally. It can down a dozen Bluepoints and still have room for the best that Virginia, New Jersey, New England, Prince Ed-ward Island, BC, Washington, California, Baja, and New Zealand can offer. Any species, any style, any price point, any time of night, you can find it. The city has taken the best ideas from San Francisco, Seattle, and Paris and made them its own. One school of thought holds that the vitality of a city's oyster scene is a direct proxy for its cultural vigor. If so, then, as usual, New York wins.

BLUEPOINT

LONG ISLAND SOUND

SPECIES Eastern

CULTIVATION Wild spat is collected on cultch in the Sound. The following year the spat is moved to shallow, warmer beds in the Norwalk Islands and grown out for another two years. Harvested by dredge.

PRESENCE Dark-shelled, gnarled, and a little bit dirty, this is the real deal, the same un-manicured, sturdy oyster New Yorkers have been savoring for a century.

FLAVOR Unsubtle. Moderate brine backs lots of earthy Connecticut funk.

OBTAINABILITY You can't miss 'em. **Copps Islands** and **Naked Cowboys** are two excellent variations on the theme.

THE MOST FAMOUS OYSTER IN AMERICA, Bluepoints have been a part of New York's fabric for centuries; yet, like so many of the city's other denizens, they're actually from Connecticut. Technically, a Bluepoint is any oyster from Long Island Sound, but the bulk of them have been harvested for generations by Tallmadge Brothers and the Bloom family of Norwalk, two branches of the same family tree, who own thousands of acres of leases a few miles off Norwalk in the vicinity of Copps Island and the other Norwalk Islands. Their white-hulled oyster boats are one of the classic sights on the sound, and their cultivation technique is just as much of a throwback: Every summer, they clear underwater plots of debris, starfish, and anything else that might hamper a young oyster's development; then they spread a clean layer of cultch over the plot. When the sound's still-abundant wild oyster population spawns, the spat settle thickly on the fresh cultch, their medium of choice. The following spring, these half-inch oysters are dredged up by the bushel and moved to shallow, plankton-rich beds around Copps Island, where they grow much faster. Oysters that are threatening to grow too large may be shuttled back to beds in deeper, colder water to slow down until needed. Oysters are harvested fresh to order each day using mechanical dredges.

At least, that's how Bluepoints *should* work. The problem is that the name has always been abused. In fact, the original Bluepoints didn't even come from Long Island Sound. They were huge, meaty oysters discovered in the early 1800s off the town of Blue Point on Long Island's Atlantic-facing Great South Bay. Those briny steaks triggered Bluepoint Mania in New York City, which hasn't really abated since. Alas, the true Blue Point oyster reef abated just a few years after it was noticed, which was when city purveyors began calling the more abundant Long Island Sound oysters Bluepoints. These are now the accepted, genuine Bluepoints, but the name has been up for grabs since, and you'll find oysters from Delaware Bay, the Chesapeake, and even the Gulf of Mexico passed off as Bluepoints. It isn't illegal, just creepy.

Most "Bluepoints" you find are indeed from Long Island Sound, but with so many people using the name, quality is all over the place. The Bloom family now call their oyster Copps Island, though many restaurants still label it the more recognizable "Bluepoint." Also look for Naked Cowboy, a wild-harvested Long Island Sound oyster sold by Chris Quartuccio of Blue Island Shellfish. Quartuccio had the idea to differentiate his oyster from the masses by striking an endorsement deal with the real-life Naked Cowboy, a guitar-strumming, briefs-baring Times Square fixture. Naked Cowboys may sound gimmicky, but they tend to be true Blue.

FISHERS ISLAND

FISHERS ISLAND SOUND,
NEW YORK

SPECIES Eastern

CULTIVATION Seed is spawned in the Malinowski family's hatchery, right next to their house, in January; and raised in pearl nets in protected, brackish Island Pond for their first year; then transferred to lantern nets in West Harbor for their final one to two years of growth. Pulled by hand from the water each morning and shipped for overnight delivery.

PRESENCE Fisher Islands are like Zen house guests: They wear neutral tones and don't impose, yet their mere presence raises the tenor of the evening and keeps things real. Only after they're gone do you realize what it all meant.

FLAVOR Evanescent. The purest expression of sea you'll find, with the cleanest aftertaste. Most oysters have a land component, but Fishers Islands aren't earthbound.

OBTAINABILITY Delivered to restos throughout New York City and farther afield the day they come out of the water. Look for them at elite spots. Or order them online.

FISHERS ISLAND OCCUPIES A SWIRLING no-man's-land where the currents of Long Island Sound, Block Island Sound, and Fishers Island Sound churn together in waves of interference. Is it part of New York? Connecticut? Atlantis? It remains aloof. I've often thought it had some sort of cloaking device installed on it, so few people seem to be aware of the existence of this sizable island looming just off the Connecticut coast. Perhaps that's what preserves its Brigadoon-like purity.

Fishers Island has had a hallowed place in oyster lore since the 1960s, when Carey Matthiessen, younger brother of the writer Peter Matthiessen, began an oyster hatchery there. Steve Malinowski cut his teeth working for Carey, fell in love with the island, and started his own oyster farm in the 1980s, buying seed from Carey. In the late 1990s, when Carey retired, Steve took over the hatchery, too. His killer app is a unique pond on the ocean side of the island, which has the feel of a Japanese garden, a condensed topography of maple forest, spring, and beach. Surrounded on three sides by hardwoods, the spring-fed pond is separated from the sea by a barrier beach, but each month on the highest moon tide the sea pours over the sand into the pond. This natural lagoon stays brackish enough to support baby oysters, but it's also one of the only spots in the Northeast that's free of all oyster diseases, making it an almost miraculous oyster nursery. The Malinowskis nurture 40 million oysters a year, selling most to other oyster farms. Widow's Holes, Montauk Pearls, Cuttyhunks, Lucky13s, and many others begin life in the Fishers Island pond—as do the oysters in the Billion Oyster Project, where Sarah and Steve's son Pete is project director, working to reestablish reefs in New York Harbor using seed donated by the family hatchery.

The oysters that Fishers Island does keep are grown out in lantern nets that hang from longlines like five-tiered Japanese lanterns in the deep waters of West Harbor, which gets a daily injection of supremely cold, supremely salty water from the oceanic expanses of Block Island Sound. "It's guaranteed to be pristine," says Steve Malinowski. "We don't have to worry about water quality." Only one other farm on the East Coast (Cuttyhunk) uses lantern nets, which produce a delicate oyster with a particularly elevated flavor and appearance. They can have thin shells, but a third winter at sea toughens up Fishers Islands. I sometimes picture them out there in their silent contemplation, submerged through the long gray winter, swaying in the lonely tides.

MONTAUK PEARL

MONTAUK,
LONG ISLAND

SPECIES Eastern

CULTIVATION Seed from Fishers Island is raised in floating surface bags that are turned weekly to shake the oysters and kill biofouling, then finished for three months in cages in twenty feet of water in Block Island Sound.

PRESENCE Impeccably clean, uniform shells with deep cups and ample if not bountiful meats.

FLAVOR Tastes like the breakers in Montauk, plain and simple.

OBTAINABILITY These have become extremely popular in both eastern Long Island and New York City.

MONTAUK IS THE FARTHEST TIP of Long Island, with the best beaches, biggest waves, and briniest bivalves. Montauk Pearls, the first to be grown in the area, almost instantly became the "It" oyster after they hit the market in 2012. The perfect shells are achieved by shaking the daylights out of the oysters every week. Because they grow in just a few feet of water right in the marina in Montauk, this is doable. Owners Mike Martinson and Mike Doall then sink the oysters in the open Atlantic waters of Block Island Sound for their last three months, to acquire that "ocean finish," as they call it. The oysters are delivered by van into NYC the day they are harvested; the ocean finish transfers.

PECONIC GOLD

PECONIC BAY, LONG ISLAND

SPECIES Eastern

CULTIVATION Seed is raised in off-bottom mesh cages deep in the heart of Peconic Bay and tumbled every two weeks. Harvested at just under three inches in size.

PRESENCE Unusually symmetrical and deep cupped, with lovely sepia shells.

FLAVOR Salty and brisk, with a smoky iron tang.

OBTAINABILITY Great on the North Fork of Long Island, which was the first to catch on to these intensively cultivated oysters. Cull and Pistol Oyster Bar, in the city, was also an early adopter.

LUCKY 13

GREAT SOUTH BAY, LONG ISLAND

SPECIES Eastern

CULTIVATION Seed from Fishers Island is raised near the Fire Island Inlet in floating bags and cages that are submerged at bay bottom for the winter, then refloated in the spring.

PRESENCE Bone china. As white and fine as sun-bleached sand dollars in your hand. It's actually the saltwater power washer at work.

FLAVOR Tannic and tangy, with lots of bright Atlantic brine and an evergreen finish.

OBTAINABILITY Still quite rare. If you spot some, consider yourself lucky.

OF ALL THE PECONIC BAY OYSTERS, Peconic Golds (the bronzed cuties in our photo) are my favorite. Most Peconic oysters have good flavor but brittle shells, thanks to boring sponges that like to drill micro-holes throughout the shells to steal the calcium, compromising their integrity. Not Peconic Golds, thanks to Matt Ketcham, the hardest-working man in the seafood business. Ketcham hand-tumbles his oysters relentlessly to keep the sponges under control and force the oysters to toughen up those shells. The result is the strongest and deepest cup in Peconic Bay. They also have the richest flavor, which may or may not be coincidental; Ketcham also raises his oysters in an area rich in iron and magnesium, which I often associate with good flavor. (In tea, for example, you get much better body using water high in magnesium.) Ketcham, who runs sportfishing trips in Peconic Bay virtually every moment he's not oystering, got the aquaculture bug from his high school wrestling buddy Perry Raso, of Matunuck Oyster fame, and he fits the Raso wrestler mold: strong, stocky workaholic who doesn't like to lose. You could do worse than put your money on Peconic Golds to break out.

Like Matt Ketcham, fellow bay rat Matt Welling grew up on the water. (Both are dead ringers for their oysters, one small and tan, the other long and fair.) A transatlantic sailor with several America's Cup campaigns on his résumé, Welling applied for one of the thirteen initial aquaculture leases the Town of Islip issued a few years ago. The first twelve applications chosen in the lottery were not his. He crossed his fingers, and when the thirteenth lease was chosen, he had the name for his oyster. These are some of the first oysters in decades to come out of the Great South Bay, once the hallowed home of Bluepoints and the heart of the New York industry. GSB has always been rumored to hold the tastiest and briniest oysters in the Northeast, and if things keep going in this direction, we'll soon have some data points to examine. Who knows but that we might even someday return to the Great South Bay of 1881, as described by oyster expert Ernest Ingersoll: "With few exceptions, to be born and bred here means to be a bayman, and a curious result follows socially. The women of the village know a vast deal more than the men." The two Matts are clearly an exception to the rule.

PECONIC PEARL

PECONIC RIVER, LONG ISLAND

SPECIES Eastern

CULTIVATION Seed is raised in barrels in Southold's Shellfisher Preserve hatchery until one-inch long, then transferred to cages and grown out in the Peconic River between Southold and Shelter Island.

PRESENCE Medium-sized, nicely cupped, dappled with grays, browns, and blacks. Classic Peconic look.

FLAVOR Strongly salty and savory with a hint of edamame.

OBTAINABILITY A favorite at New York City restaurants and festivals, in part because a portion of the proceeds supports the Peconic Land Trust.

MYSTIC

MYSTIC RIVER, CONNECTICUT

SPECIES Eastern

CULTIVATION Seed from Southold's Shellfisher Preserve is raised in mesh bags, then shipped across Long Island Sound and planted on subtidal sandbars near the mouth of the Mystic River for about two years, then harvested by dredge.

PRESENCE Like a spruce-lined snowscape, the green and white ridges of Mystics scream winter in New England to me. This is a proper Yankee oyster: thick shell, prominent goosefoot ridges on the underside, and a scalloped shape.

FLAVOR Brine, turnip, and metal, with a sweetness that lingers. My wife says they taste like Old Lyme Shores.

OBTAINABILITY Widely distributed throughout the Northeast.

A BIG PART OF LONG ISLAND'S oyster revival can be credited to Karen Rivara and her husband, Greg, who spearheads Cornell's SPAT (Southold Project in Aquaculture Training) program. They have given a whole new generation of Long Island aquaculturalists the skills, stuff, and spirit needed to succeed, and we are all now enjoying the yields of that investment. The core of the East End oyster machine is the Shellfisher Preserve, an old hatchery in Southold that feels like an underground bunker. With strange fluorescent lights and cement tanks of water burbling everywhere, it's the kind of place a James Bond supervillain might hide out. Instead, you'll find Karen Rivara there, coaxing her oysters, clams, and scallops into ardor with a special mix of science, art, and voodoo. (DON'T look at the oysters when they are ready to spawn. DO rub the belly on the plastic mermaid over the tank to get them started.) The hatchery was donated to the Peconic Land Trust by the family that owned the famed (and long-gone) Shelter Island Oyster Company, with the stipulation that it continue to produce shellfish. Karen does just that, spreading her seed far and wide to members of the Noank Aquaculture Cooperative across the Peconic Estuary and Long Island Sound. She reserves just enough seed to grow a few oysters to market size in the waters just offshore from her nursery. These she calls Peconic Pearls; they are primarily used as fund-raisers for estuary projects.

The franchise player in the Noank Aquaculture Cooperative is the Mystic oyster (right in photo), grown directly across Long Island Sound on the Connecticut coast. Mystics are as pretty an East Coast oyster as you'll ever see. They are amazingly robust, with a balanced brine and a beautifully clean finish, and they are absolute joys to shuck. Grower Steve Plant's secret? "Location . . . location . . . location." He nestles them onto clean, hard sandbars at choke points in the estuary, so the tidal flow screams through, beating up the oysters and grinding down their growth edge. Instead of getting leggy, they get deep and scalloped, and the meat completely fills the shells inside. With plenty of elbow room, the oysters get almost round, cup up nicely, and produce strong shells. Slower growth means, yes, it takes longer to grow them to market size, so expect to pay a bit extra, but the quality is so much better. These stunners are serious, graduate-level oysters, and they make you wish every oyster had the chance to reach its full potential.

PINE ISLAND

OYSTER BAY,
LONG ISLAND

SPECIES Eastern

CULTIVATION Seed is produced in the Flower hatchery and broadcast on the bottom of Oyster Bay when it is an inch in size, then harvested by dredge one to two years later.

PRESENCE The opposite of boutique. Strong, irregular shells, more broad than deep, mottled in black and brown, indicating a rough-and-tumble life on the muddy floor of Oyster Bay. Inside, they are a Kandinsky schmear of charcoal, amethyst, agate, and sepia.

FLAVOR The essence of Long Island Sound, as earthy and salty as a potato chip, and equally good with beer. The finish is a rich and fruity golden raisin.

OBTAINABILITY For a concern that cranks out 10 million oysters a year, they are surprisingly hard to find in their own state. Best bet: the massive festival Flower throws in Oyster Bay every year, to which it donates forty thousand oysters.

EVER SINCE THE NOT-COINCIDENTAL RISE of the farm-to-plate movement and the oyster renaissance a decade ago, the borough of Brooklyn has been obsessed with Pine Island oysters. From Bushwick to Bed-Stuy, barely a bistro can be found that isn't sporting a pile of the local umber-tinged beauties—

No, wait. Sorry, my mistake: Actually, nobody in Brooklyn seems to have a clue about Pine Islands. Sometimes I forget that, because it seems so odd that the same crowd that will light up Instagram with luscious shots of their Mast Brothers chocolate is content to let the world-class oysters in its own backyard get shipped to Sheboygan. But that's how it has been for some time, because Frank M. Flower & Sons, the company that produces Pine Islands, is old-school. Like, no-functioning-website old-school. Like, they-harvest-with-a-retrofitted-1935-ferry-and-not-because-it's-cool old-school. Frankly, Flower & Sons has been doing industrial chic from forever.

Eighteen eighty-seven, to be exact. That's how long the family has been harvesting in Oyster Bay, which was named by Dutch settlers in the 1600s for the obvious reason. But by 1962 the wild population had collapsed due to pollution and overharvesting, so H. Butler Flower did something considered a bit nutty at the time: He built one of the first hatcheries in the country and began seeding his grounds with baby oysters. It was a wild success, and today Flower & Sons is one of the country's largest oyster producers, with one of the largest hatcheries. Every year it spreads 50 million one-inch oysters on its 1,800 acres of bottomland leases and harvests 10 million or so that have survived the year or two it takes them to reach market size. (This is a different strategy from most farms, which use protective equipment to reduce their mortality percentage, but when you've got a hatchery that can crank out as many oysters as you need, it pays to play more of a numbers game.)

Flower & Sons uses all the seed its hatchery produces, and selects broodstock from the bay's best. They are genetically unique to the bay, which has an ideal salinity of 25 to 27 ppt. The issue is finding them. Flower sells everything to national wholesalers; there's no local distribution. That needs to change, because when you're in a New York state of mind, you should be eating Pine Islands, which are literally harvested from Billy Joel's (submerged) front yard. If I were twenty-two years old with some time and a reefer truck, I'd load it with sacks of Pine Islands every day and make the one-hour run into New York City.

WIDOW'S HOLE

GREENPORT
HARBOR,
PECONIC BAY

SPECIES Eastern

CULTIVATION Two-millimeter seed is raised in upwellers in Widow's Hole, a small saltwater pool behind the Osinskis' house, until large enough to be transferred to off-bottom cages on the four-acre grounds just off the edge of their yard. Cages are winched to the surface by small boat.

PRESENCE Flaunts the classic Peconic burnt-orange algal shading over a black-and-white shell. Cups can be deep; shells can be a bit brittle. Generally very juicy inside. Slipper shells often ride along.

FLAVOR Intensely salty and undergirded by iron. Around Christmas, they are sweet as bonbons.

OBTAINABILITY Ubiquitous in Manhattan. The Widowmobile runs about five thousand oysters a week straight to NYC restaurants.

MIKE OSINSKI WAS RETIRED AT FORTY-FOUR. He'd made his millions in finance and had put himself out to pasture in Greenport, New York, savoring sunsets from the porch of his 1830s whaler's mansion overlooking Greenport Harbor. The Shelter Island Ferry pretty much cuts through his backyard. Then Osinski learned that Greenport was once the oyster powerhouse of Long Island. Huge shucking houses, huge shell piles. Then, as fate would have it, he learned that along with the deed to his house came four acres of prime bottomland. (New York is one of the only states where an individual can own, instead of lease, submerged real estate. But unless people paid the taxes on their bottomland, the state took it over; at Osinski's mansion, somebody had paid.) Around 2000 he began playing around with oysters, and starting in 2003 he went all in, driving his Widow's Holes into Manhattan once a week.

Osinski was ahead of the curve. Back when oysters were distributed like canned tuna, the revelation of a briny Widow's Hole that hadn't been kicking around a distributor's walk-in for two weeks was a game changer for many chefs. All the usual players signed on: Esca, Aquagrill, Le Bernardin . . . (Why does Chef Eric Ripert seem to be the first to discover every new oyster? He also gets credit for Island Creeks and Rappahannock Rivers.) A goofy *New Yorker* profile followed, and suddenly Osinski was the poster child for boutique oyster farming.

What impresses me is that, many years later, Osinski has stuck to his guns. He's still out on the water every day, his wife and teenage kids beside him. His oysters are still bright and lively, with a bracing freshness. And he's still a nonconformist. Everything you want in an oyster farmer.

The little critters in the photo clamping onto the Widow's Holes like limpet mines are slipper shells, aka quarterdecks, aka *Crepidula fornicata* (don't ask). Invert these little sea snails and you'll see they have a kind of shelf over half their shell, hence the common names. Slipper shells abound on the northeastern coast, and they like nothing better than to ride along on the shell of an oyster (or, of course, a slipper shell of the opposite sex). Mike Osinski was the first person to tell me I could eat them live, which I did immediately. (We were shucking together at some long-forgotten event.) They are often better than the oyster. I'm still not convinced he wasn't pulling my leg, but I've relished their mind-blowing sweetness ever since, so I suppose it doesn't matter. Thanks, Mike.

NINIGRET POND *to* NANTUCKET SOUND

When people picture the New England coast, they tend to envision the craggy coves of Maine or the sand dunes of the Lower Cape.

But when I really want to feel the essence of the shore, I head for the salt ponds of southern Rhode Island and Massachusetts. Paddling their shallow, glassy surfaces, the Atlantic audible beyond the barrier beaches, backed by red maple swamps that could teach my home state of Vermont a thing or two about fall color, I can almost smell the ghost fires of the Wampanoag smoking ten thousand years' of oysters and eels.

The groundwork for this landscape was laid twenty thousand years ago by glaciers, which scraped up bedrock into a wall of riprap as they advanced like bulldozers. When the world warmed, they retreated, leaving a jumbled ridge that formed Long Island, Fishers Island, Block Island, Martha's Vineyard, and Nantucket. The dissolving glaciers left behind braided rivers of meltwater flowing down to a sea that was hundreds of feet lower than today's. Those shifting glacial rivers, thick with sediment, acted like conveyor belts, building a rolling outwash plain of fingerlike headlands and shallow valleys. When the seas rose, the valleys turned into bays separated by the headlands. Another thousand years of wave action spread sand perpendicularly along the coast, forming barrier beaches that linked together, isolating the salt ponds from the sea except

for the occasional breachway or storm surge. They exist only here, and only now. From New Jersey southward, the coast remained glacier-free and now is just one long line of sand. Up north, in Maine, the glaciers extended another hundred miles out to sea, leaving an outwash plain that drowned long ago—as will this one, when the seas have risen another ten feet. Enjoy it while it's here.

Oyster farmers certainly do. Virtually every salt pond from SoRho to Martha's Vineyard has Eastern oysters in it. What could be better than a placid lagoon, just a few feet deep, that fills twice a day with fresh ocean water? Salinity is spectacular, plankton abundant, and the view doesn't suck.

The topography drives the cultivation methods, which are fairly uniform across the region. Tides are tiny, so intertidal cultivation is not an option. Most people grow their oysters in floating mesh bags, to take advantage of the warmer surface waters before transferring their oysters to off-bottom cages. The big divide is whether or not you finish your oysters free on the bottom. Everyone agrees that a year in the mud produces primo shells—thick, deep, and barnacle-free—but the jury is still out on whether bottom-dwelling boosts flavor. In the short term, probably not; with less access to food, the oysters take longer to fatten up. But if you have the time to let your oysters slowly reach half-shell size on the bottom, you wind up with a firmer, rounder, earthier, more layered critter. Many people chalk it up to the clay and minerals at the bottoms of the salt ponds, but no one really knows. All I know is that time is good: A two-year-old oyster beats a one-year-old of the same size, a three-year-old beats a two-year-old, and a four-year-old is dope.

The flooded salt ponds of southern New England produce some of the most intensely flavored Eastern oysters in the world. Start with the salt. New England's major rivers bend either east (to Boston) or west (to Connecticut), leaving this pockmarked coast incredibly briny. That brine combines with the clay and finishes with a mild daikon note, a potting-soil essence that distinguishes the region from Cape Cod Bay and the Gulf of Maine. I think of it as "glacial silt," and I give silent thanks to the Pleistocene every time I taste it. It's good to know that, however civilized the New England coast may sometimes appear, deep down it's the same jagged jumble of survivors and old salts it always was.

Preceding pages: Bags of young oysters floating on the surface of Cotuit Bay; Ninigret Pond oyster cages propped up for defouling with bamboo poles from an old Metropolitan Museum of Art installation; Perry Raso inspects a bag of Matunucks. Right: The motley crew at Matunuck Oyster Farm.

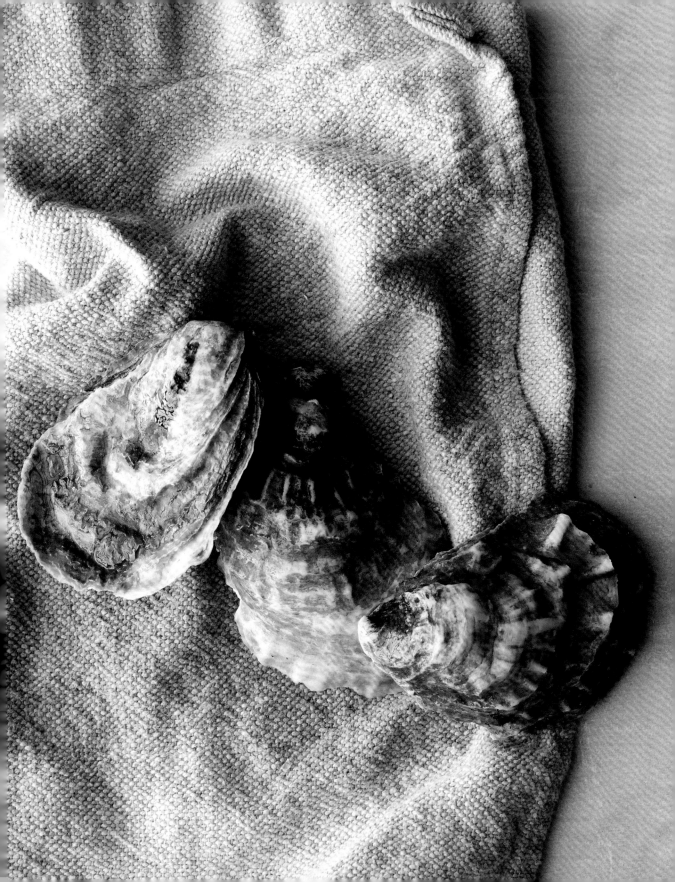

CHATHAM

OYSTER POND, CAPE COD

SPECIES Eastern

CULTIVATION Seed is started in upwellers in Oyster Pond, with the six-foot tidal flow naturally driving current through them, then transferred to floating mesh bags and finished in an all-of-the-above strategy: some in surface trays, some bottom-planted, some in OysterGro cages.

PRESENCE The shells are large, grainy, and sepia, like an old photograph. Everything about them says classic, timeless New England coast.

FLAVOR Elegant and fine, with a bracing, breezy brine and no aftertaste at all. There's a remarkable clarity and focus to the flavor. When synesthetes taste this oyster, they see diamond.

OBTAINABILITY Spotty. Although these have been around for years, and are much loved, they are very hard to find outside of Boston and the Cape.

THERE WAS A BRIEF TIME in my childhood when my family owned a house in Chatham. It was dreamy; a straight-up Cape, it looked out over Oyster Pond and the Chatham Bars Inn to the barrier islands and the Atlantic beyond. You could *smell* the oysters. And in Chatham you still can. In fact, you can even gather them. Years ago, friends of mine returned from a Chatham vacation with a cooler of the most perfectly shaped oysters I'd ever seen. They had pulled them out of the water while canoeing. I knew they were way too perfect to be wild oysters—they weren't attached to anything on the bottom, just rolling around like sunken treasure—and I was stumped until I learned that every year the town raises about one hundred thousand oysters and tucks them into its many watery crevices. Amazingly, it even tumbles them. A few bucks gets you a recreational license. Commercial cultivation of oysters in Oyster Pond started in 1976, and there have been some quiet stretches, but recently those oysters have been a revelation. Always large and ocean scented, perfect of shell and savor, they never fail to blink me back to my first encounters with Cape Cod. That landscape, those scents, are still, to me, the essence of ocean.

Chatham is the elbow of the Cape, that unique spot where it bends from Nantucket Sound to open Atlantic. Oyster Pond, the aptly named home of Chatham oysters, draws on both, as well as a richness from the land, which is, I believe, where it gets its pitch-perfect balance of flavor. The town, one could argue, has the same perfect balance: You can follow Oyster Pond out into Nantucket Sound, tucked safely behind Monomoy Island, or you can head a few yards in the other direction and wander out to Cape Cod National Seashore. Either way you go, it's the perfect spot for the stripped-down oyster experience: beach, beer, bivalve.

COTUIT

COTUIT BAY, CAPE COD

SPECIES Eastern

CULTIVATION Seed is started in a flupsy in spring, then transferred in June to floating mesh bags in Cotuit Bay. In early fall, when the seed has reached 1.5 inches in size and the Cotuit conchs and crabs have moved on, the seed is bottom planted in the bay, where it winters over. Harvest is by dredge after an additional one to two years.

PRESENCE The beige-shelled bivalves feel surprisingly heavy in your hand—the sign of a bottom-planted oyster. The teardrop shape has more roundness than most—another sign of bottom life. The bottom shell is nicely fluted in the "coon's foot" pattern.

FLAVOR Slurping once, slurping twice, slurping chicken soup with rice.

OBTAINABILITY Chris Gargiulo grows several million Cotuits per year, and they are regulars in New England and New York. He is also one of the few growers who will ship directly to individuals.

THE FINELY SHELTERED HARBORS OF COTUIT and its neighboring village of Osterville (originally Oysterville) were an oystering hot spot for the Wampanoag until 1648, when the tribe sold the twenty square miles of prime coast to Myles Standish and the Plymouth Colony for the price of "one great brass kettle seven spans in wideness round about, and one broad hoe." Bad call, Wampanoag, no matter how broad that hoe was. (The local watering hole, Kettle Ho, celebrates this swindle.) Cotuit Bay kept cranking out the "ersters" for the English and Americans for hundreds of years. In the 1800s, they were hauled by wagon to the railroad in Barnstable and shipped to Boston. In 1912, the Cotuit Oyster Company was founded, though the exact leases and building sites used today had already been in use for half a century. Life was good until World War II, when the Army chose Cotuit as its site for Camp Can-Do-It. Amphibious commando units from the 594th Engineer Boat and Shore Regiment trained for their assault on the beaches of the South Pacific by storming the oyster beds, which never recovered.

Aquaculture came to the rescue. Cotuit still had perfect water for oysters: just enough fresh input to keep the salinity at a mouthwatering 30 ppt, and lots of unspoiled coastline. Current owner Chris Gargiulo, who grew up outside Boston in a family that loved to vacation on the Cape, took a gamble on the farm, ditching his career in law enforcement and jumping full-tilt into oystering in 2004. After experimenting with various methods and discovering that Cotuit Bay had a robust population of boring sponges that happily turned his oysters into pincushions, he settled on his current system, which makes him one of the only people on the Cape to bottom plant his oysters in the mud, safely away from the sponges, where they develop exceptionally thick shells, "because they're fighting off everything that's crawling over the top of them." Our gain.

EAST BEACH BLONDE
NINIGRET CUP
NINIGRET NECTAR
WALRUS & CARPENTER

NINIGRET POND,
RHODE ISLAND

SPECIES Eastern

CULTIVATION Two-millimeter seed is
raised in the solar-powered flupsy, then
transferred to floating bags as it grows.
At one inch it is moved to stackable trays
hanging from the raft, and at two inches
it is transferred to off-bottom cages or
cast loose on the bottom of the pond and
hand-harvested in the shallow water.

PRESENCE The shells can be green or
white, but the cups are always just right.
These are all tumbled enough to keep
the meats compact and tight. The Nectars
are the smallest and densest by far.

FLAVOR Brine and ozone;
a boardwalk in the rain.

OBTAINABILITY Strong from New
York to Boston.

NINIGRET POND IS THE DEFINITIVE SALT POND IN RHODE ISLAND, 1,700 unspoiled acres bounded by barrier beaches and never more than a few feet deep. It's also the definitive model for cooperative aquaculture. Jim Arnoux and Nick Papa (who grow separately but both sell under the name East Beach Blondes, occupying the Northwest corner of our Pondapalooza photo here) and Rob Krause (Ninigret Cups, Midwest) all share a solar-powered, floating nursery raft where they raise their baby oysters before transferring the adults to cages and racks on their individual three-acre sites. Each grower uses subtly different techniques, but the oysters share what I think of as the Ninigret profile: small, deeply cupped, and very salty (Ninigret Pond gets no more than a smidgen of freshwater). The owners cover for each other and generally make life as an oyster farmer a little more fun. Ninigret Nectars (southwest in photo), the new kid on the block, isn't part of the co-op but isn't far away; owner Matt Behan tumbles his oysters the most frequently to keep them small and special, which is how he likes them. "Oysters are a delicacy like Champagne or caviar," he says. "You don't see Champagne in a mug, and caviar is not sold in grinder form." Okay, Matt, point taken, but when they start handing out the caviar grinders and mugs of Champagne, I will be first in line.

Our tour of Ninigret Pond ends with Walrus & Carpenter (southeast in photo), the art school counterpart to the salty dogs. W&Cs have lovely green shells, an artichoke finish, and a different vibe. There are a couple of things I like about Jules Opton-Himmel's operation. One is his seasonal CSA model. Instead of hawking skinny oysters year-round to make ends meet, Opton-Himmel sells most of his oysters by pre-order during the holidays, when they are at their best, with pickups in Brooklyn and Manhattan. The other thing I like is his infrastructure. In 2010, the Metropolitan Museum of Art featured an exhibition called Big Bambú that was composed of thousands of bamboo poles lashed together. It looked like a roc had built its nest on the roof of the Met. After de-installation six months later, Opton-Himmel scored the bamboo, which seemed a lot friendlier than the poly gear used for most aquaculture. Those poles still hold his oyster trays. You can see them on page 154, or if you attend the on-farm dinner series he hosts each summer.

FIRST
LIGHT

POPPONESSET BAY,
CAPE COD

SPECIES Eastern

CULTIVATION Seed is grown in
trays staked to the intertidal flats
of Popponesset Bay.

PRESENCE A perfect calcified
Madeleine: One taste will whisk you
away from the vicissitudes of life to a
coastal scene outside of time and
culture where you may hear the echo
of great spaces traversed.

FLAVOR Salty, savory, and
bright as the dawn.

OBTAINABILITY Distributed
throughout Boston and Cape Cod.

HOW LONG HAS THE WAMPANOAG TRIBE been living
off the tidelands of Cape Cod? Twelve thousand years, they'll tell
you. Give or take. They call themselves "People of the First Light,"
a fitting name for the native societies who were the first in America
to catch the dawn rising out of the Atlantic each morning. Of
course, this also made them the first in the Northeast to encounter
Europeans, which didn't go so well. After contact, a plague swept
through the Wampanoag and killed almost all of them. By the time
the Pilgrims arrived a few years later, the Wampanoag were down
to a skeleton crew. Still, they made a big impact on the Pilgrims and
helped them squeak through that first brutal winter in Plymouth.
As one Pilgrim wrote to friends in Europe, "Oysters we have none
near, but we can have them brought by the Indians when we will."

Eventually some of the Wampanoag descendants settled in
Mashpee—on the underside of Cape Cod on Nantucket Sound—
where part of their traditional tribal lands lay around the lovely,
leafy Popponesset Bay. In 2009, they decided to reclaim one of
their traditions by cultivating oysters on five acres of the intertidal
zone. First Lights capture the bright essence of saline Nantucket
Sound and mix in a fresh Mashpee sweetness—a combo little
changed from the oysters those hungry Pilgrims greedily received.
Like other New England oysters, First Lights peak in flavor around
Thanksgiving. Just saying.

KATAMA BAY

SPECIES Eastern

CULTIVATION Seed is raised in upwellers, then transferred to off-bottom cages and tumbled periodically (several growers use wind power) to remove fouling organisms and encourage cup depth. Harvested after two-plus years.

PRESENCE The shells are big and deep and range from bleached white to classy brown. Inside, the white shells are often splotched with yellowed-ivory patches. The meats can be thin, as you often find with oysters growing in a full-salt environment.

FLAVOR The full salt lick. (But this may change; see text.) Scatter Katama Bays on the beach at Martha's Vineyard and watch the brine addicts gather. At the end comes a subtle pop of papaya.

OBTAINABILITY Strong in the Northeast. In summer, they rarely make it off Martha's Vineyard alive. Twelve growers farm in Katama Bay, producing several million oysters per year that are mostly marketed under their own brands. The star is Jack Blake's **Sweet Neck**.

IS KATAMA BAY A BAY OR A CHANNEL? It depends on when you check. In the north, Katama Bay narrows to a channel that separates Chappaquiddick Island from the rest of Martha's Vineyard, and until 2007 that was its only connection to the sea. Water would flow in, warm up, and spend some time in the bay before finding its way out again. The oysters were salty, but they balanced that salt with a fat sweetness from the rich plankton soup that slow-cooked in the cul-de-sac of the bay. Then, in 2007, the Patriots' Day Storm blasted a hole in the barrier beach to the south, opening another channel, and Katama Bay became a thoroughfare for the sea. The currents quintupled, making life hard on the oystermen, and the oysters turned into throat-searing salt bombs with shells that were sandblasted white by churning beach sand. They were still good oysters, as long as you had lots of beer on hand.

In 2015, the barrier beach finally healed itself. It's a natural cycle: Storms punch breaches through the barrier islands, and the currents immediately begin to fill the breaches with sand. No one knows how long Katama Bay will stay a cul-de-sac this time—the next major storm could come in a year or twenty—but, for now, the oyster growers are looking forward to the sweet life.

MATUNUCK

SPECIES Eastern

CULTIVATION Seed from Maine is grown out in mesh bags attached to metal racks in the clear waist-deep waters of Potter Pond.

PRESENCE Matunucks are all about delicacy and grace. Small, white teardop shells painted in burnt siena encase dainty, tender meats. They want you to like them.

FLAVOR A light broth ending with sweet white miso. Salty but utterly manageable, Matunucks never impose.

OBTAINABILITY Solid. Perry Raso produces one million Matunucks a year. Most are sold in New England. An icy bed of them can always be found on the pewter bar at Matunuck Oyster Bar. Even better are the **Potter Ponds**, which are bottom planted for a season in the name of cup depth and shell strength.

THE UNSTOPPABLE FORCE KNOWN as Perry Raso grew up digging clams on the Rhode Island coast. He got hooked on the idea of raking money out of the mud, and hasn't really looked back. The money has just gotten much bigger. By junior high he was scuba diving for steamers and littlenecks and was a champion wrestler, and later he got into grad school in marine biology on the strength of his drive and his scuba. He learned about aquaculture and gave it a go in Potter Pond, his favorite clamming spot among Rhode Island's coastal salt ponds. The gorgeous pond turned out to be ideal for oyster farming, with rapids sluicing through from nearby Point Judith Pond and firm, shallow bottomland that made for incredibly easy access. Raso developed a system of off-bottom rack-and-bag culture now known as "Raso Racks" and began growing some of New England's tastiest oysters, named for the local beach.

Potter Pond included a broke-down hovel of a bar constantly flickering in and out of existence. Raso bought it for the dock access, planning to try out a "clamshack" with the pond's oysters, beer, and not much more. On July 1, 2009, opening day, he tended the oyster farm in the morning, as usual, then came in to see if Matunuck Oyster Bar had any customers, and found "pandemonium." It has been pandemonium ever since, with a steady crush of people jockeying for a seat at the ever-expanding restaurant, which is now a showcase for one of the shortest farm-to-table journeys in America, as well as other Rhode Island oysters. Raso has added a barge for pre-lunch tours of the oyster farm, and a six-acre organic vegetable farm around the corner that supplies the restaurant. The farm is on the conserved estate of Captain John Potter, and Raso now lives in the captain's 1740 gray-shingled Cape, overlooking the farm and the pond where young Perry first learned that there was money in mud.

MOONSTONE

POINT JUDITH POND, RHODE ISLAND

SPECIES Eastern

CULTIVATION Seed is started in an upweller, then moved to mesh bags and grown in compartments beneath a floating raft until large enough to be bottom planted in the clay of Point Judith Pond. Harvested by small dredge.

PRESENCE The sign of a Moonstone is how heavy it feels. It's like hefting a rock. The shell is bombproof, the muscle corded, the meat—well, meaty. Tends to be a bit scalloped from its final life stage on the bottom.

FLAVOR Strong and beefy, rich as bone broth.

OBTAINABILITY One of the best known of all Eastern oysters, Moonstones have a huge following.

QUONSET POINT

NARRAGANSETT BAY, RHODE ISLAND

SPECIES Eastern

CULTIVATION Seed is raised in plastic trays sunk fifty feet deep in Narragansett Bay's East Passage.

PRESENCE Like artisan pottery, the shells are finely cut, deeply scooped, and covered in a ginger glaze.

FLAVOR Extraordinarily salty with a concentrated daikon chaser. Good with sake.

OBTAINABILITY As the flagship oyster of one of the country's leading shellfish distributors, these aren't hard to find. And even if you can't, **Beavertails** and **Umamis** will brine you just the same.

THERE'S TWO WAYS TO PRODUCE A BRILLIANT oyster in New England. One is to luck into one of those magical spots with incredible flavor, and plant your oysters on the bottom so they slowly milk every drop of merroir from the landscape. There you have Moonstones (right, in photo). The other is to produce a lot of oysters and cull mercilessly, only releasing the cream of the crop under your flagship name. That's what American Mussel Harvesters does with Quonset Points (left). Any oyster that doesn't have the Quonset shape and cup depth becomes a Beavertail (a reference to the elongated shape, which, conveniently, reflects the tip of Conanicut Island, home of Beavertail State Park). There's also a cocktail-sized version (2.75 inches versus 3.5) called an Umami. All have that Quonset Point brine, a product of Narragansett Bay's glacially scoured East Passage, which cuts between Conanicut Island and Newport's Aquidneck Island at depths exceeding one hundred feet, and which funnels cold Atlantic water in and out of the bay. Quonset Points are grown BC style, with stacks of six plastic trays, each holding one hundred to two hundred oysters, suspended from longlines up to fifty feet deep in the channel. The East Passage is one of the only places on the East Coast you can do that, and it shows in the unique oyster. Salty water is denser than freshwater, so the farther down you go, the saltier you get. Quonset Points are very, very salty. They also have delicate shells, typical for a suspended oyster, and they always have a handsome wash of ginger on the shells contributed by some algae that is their companion (and likely food supply) down in the deep.

Like Quonset Points, Moonstones have been around for decades. These are the deans of Rhode Island shellfish, the most recognizable names, but they are stylistic opposites. Quonsets are pure water column, Moonstones are pure benthos. Grown by John and Cindy West, with the help of their twin daughters, Moonstones get the full boutique treatment. In the early days, they are shaken regularly so they don't turn into "potato chips." In the fall, they go down to the soft bottom of Point Judith Pond, which Moonstone founder and marine biologist Robert "Skid" Rheault singled out as having the finest flavor of all Rhode Island's salt ponds in a study years ago. There, they get deep and tough; they stay protected from barnacles and other colonists, so their bottom shells are a smooth, silky white; and they take on that familiar Moonstone beefiness. Interestingly, the water that fills Point Judith Pond goes on to stock Potter Pond, where Matunucks grow, but Matunucks are as light as Moonstones are heavy; apparently, method and mud trump agua.

PLEASANT BAY

LITTLE PLEASANT BAY,
CAPE COD

SPECIES Eastern

CULTIVATION Seed is grown in floating mesh bags and then transferred to wire cages sitting on the bottom of Little Pleasant Bay in just a few feet of water, semi-exposed on minus tides. In the winter they are dumped on netting on the bay bottom, then returned to the cages in spring and harvested at two years of age.

PRESENCE Like other top Cape oysters, Pleasant Bays have large, deep-cupped white shells, but they soften this with a mysterious, mossy wash.

FLAVOR Conch chowder with turnips, heavy on the salt. Might that briny burn finish with a hint of Kraft macaroni and cheese? Tasting is believing.

OBTAINABILITY About half a million Pleasant Bays reach market size each year. Rare, but not that rare.

PETE ORCUTT WAS AHEAD OF THE OYSTER CURVE in 1983 when he decided to quit fishing and start oystering. "They caught all the fish," he says. "Now I'm growing them." He endured the years of aquaculture resistance and poor seed availability, and now is enjoying the fruits of his labors, working the bay every day with his children Jeff (fifteen years on the farm) and Danielle (seven), although, after thirty years in the business, Pete admits that his primary focus is to "grow the effing things and get them out the effing door"—a sentiment every true farmer can appreciate.

As one of the only operations on the Atlantic side of Cape Cod, Orcutt scored a prized spot: Little Pleasant Bay, tucked deep behind the barrier beaches of Orleans, one of the wildest spots on the Cape. Extreme salinity, low tides, lots of marsh, deer on the beaches, great white sharks patrolling the inlets. That sort of thing.

Although the tides in Little Pleasant Bay are modest—a few feet max—the oysters are grown in a corner of the bay that catches a long fetch of wind blowing off the Atlantic. Even in their earthbound cages, the oysters rock in the waves. That, along with the practice of dumping them on netting on the bay bottom each winter, results in dinged *wabi-sabi* masterpieces of beauty and struggle.

WILD ONSET

SPECIES Eastern

CULTIVATION Wild

PRESENCE The shells are magic, green and luminous, as if lit from within. Gnarled and pock-marked from life in the wild, they yield a watery gray meat that would be a bad sign in a cultivated oyster, but here goes along with full flavor.

FLAVOR Earthy and deep, like a pot of black bean soup, right down to the hint of cumin. It's the purest expression of the region's signature potting-soil note. Some have notes of green pepper and tobacco leaf.

OBTAINABILITY Erratic, as you'd expect from wild game. First, the oysters have to have a good set, then a few years later, somebody needs to wade around the Onset shallows with a hammer and gather the things, and then they need to get bought by a distributor and, well, distributed. But Ben Lloyd of Pangea Shellfish is a huge fan of Wild Onsets, and he does his best to spread the gospel.

WE ALL HAVE A CERTAIN REVERENCE for wild foods. If it slithered out of a bayou, clung to the side of a reef, or popped up between the roots of a pin oak, it must be divine. And it's true, certain wild foods possess an ineffable otherness that makes their domesticated cousins taste tediously tame, but for every chanterelle or chinook, there's a stringy wild turkey riddled with birdshot. Many wild foods disappoint.

So it is with oysters. Most people assume a farmed oyster must be inferior to a wild one, because when they hear the word "aquaculture," they think of salmon. Farmed salmon have pale flesh and soft meat compared to their wild kin, because they get neither the diet nor the workout of the free-rangers. But, being immobile filter feeders, farmed oysters get the exact same diet (water) and exercise regimen (nada) of wild ones. And since farmed oysters are perfectly spaced, while wild ones set at random on top of each other and have to grow long quickly, curving around obstacles and reaching for open access to passing food, farmed oysters almost always have deeper cups, better form, and plumper meat. Wild oysters are usually long, skinny, and warped. "Bananas" is the term of art.

Yet, every now and then you get a wild oyster that really does feel like Neptune reached out of the waves and slapped you upside the head. Wild Onsets can be leggy, but their shells have a stunning green patina from the same algae they feed on, and their flavor packs a rich, gamy leather note you rarely find in cultivated oysters. They are picked off the rocks around Onset (tucked into the corner of Buzzards Bay) by local fishermen, so they're more of a hobby than a business, but it's the kind of hobby you'd do well to take up, or at least to cultivate friends who take it up. Wild Onsets are just plain special. And, actually, this is old news. Already by the late 1800s, Bostonians considered oysters from the upper corner of Buzzards Bay to be tops, with those from other New England locales, even Wellfleet, several rungs down. Taste them for yourself, and spread the info to your very good oyster friends—but to no one else.

CAPE COD BAY

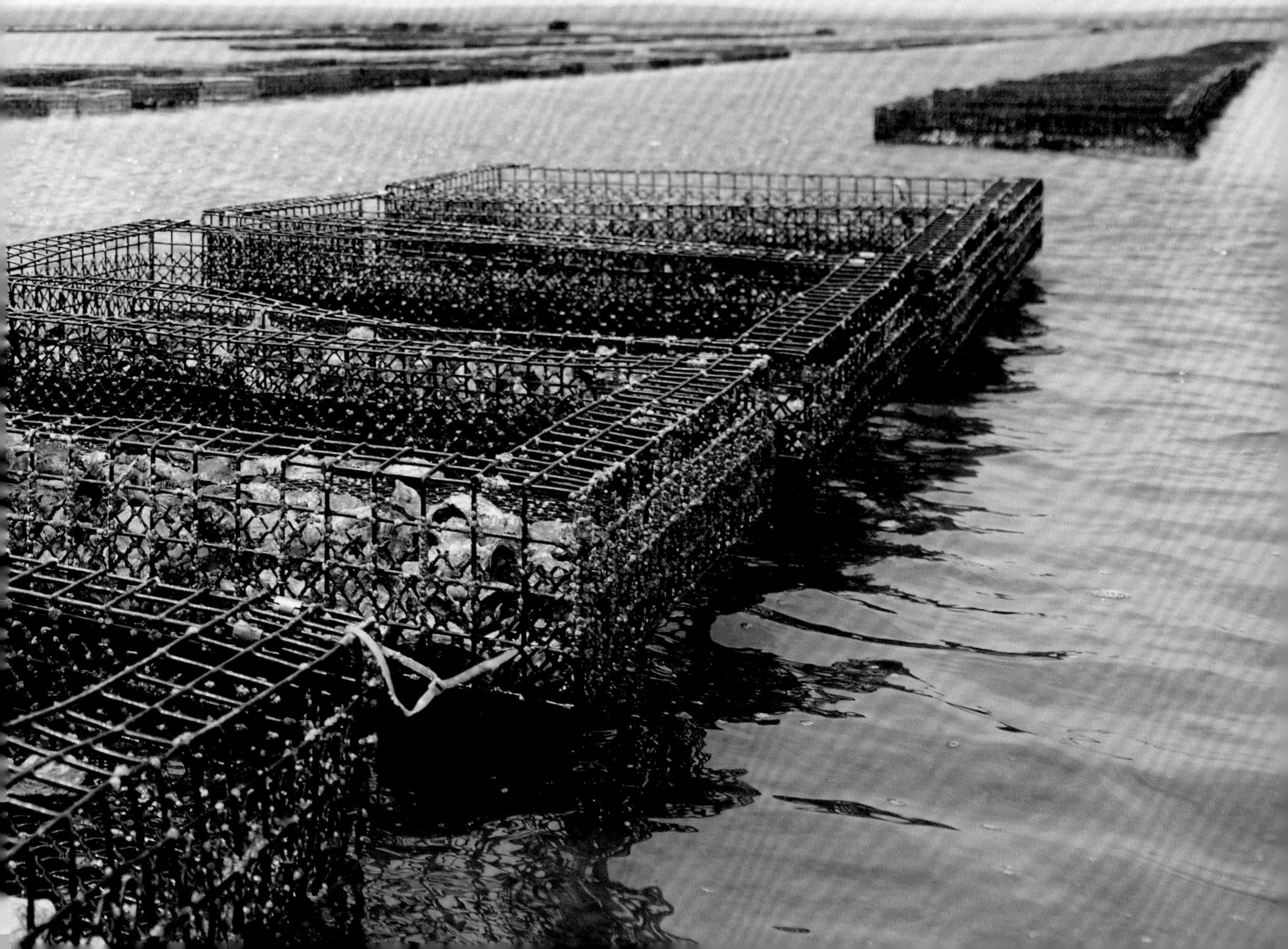

CAPE COD BAY

Have you ever had a lousy oyster from Cape Cod Bay? I haven't. In a region where new oyster farmers take hold like tunicates, somehow the Cape's particular blend of sand and cold and tide seems to ensure that, at worst, the oysters will be simple and salty.

With a little care, they become the epiphanies of the raw bar—the ones that make newbies discover, mid-gulp, that they adore oysters and didn't know it. Cape Cod Bay is the surest bet in oysters—yet still, strangely, unrecognized. People may know that they love Wellfleets or Island Creeks, but they haven't put in the cartographic work to realize that these two standouts are just the endpoints of a coastline that is one big happy smile of oystering.

The little curled arm of Cape Cod, shaking its fist at the Atlantic, has an outsized effect on the waters around it, and thus on the oysters. That sounds like a big claim for a skinny sand dune, but that's because we pay attention to only the part of it above the waterline. Georges Bank extends from the edges of Cape Cod hundreds of miles into the Atlantic, curling around nearly to Nova Scotia, staying close to the surface and walling off the Gulf of Maine, of which Cape Cod Bay is the southernmost extension. The Gulf Stream curls under Florida and carries waters up the Atlantic coast, bringing warm Gulf of Mexico temperatures to bathers desperately in need, but it gets stiff-armed by Cape Cod and Georges Bank and sent

across the Atlantic to keep the North Sea from turning into a slushie. Meanwhile, frigid waters from the Arctic slip past Nova Scotia into the Gulf of Maine and get trapped there, circulating in a counterclockwise direction.

That's true for Maine as well as Cape Cod Bay, of course, but Cape Cod offers something you don't find so much in Maine: sand. Cape Cod and Georges Bank are a giant pile of sand dumped by the melting glaciers as they retreated fifteen thousand years ago. (Back then, Cape Cod Bay was a giant lake many miles from the sea. It drained into the lake that was Buzzards Bay through a low river valley that was the obvious spot to dig the Cape Cod Canal.) Over the ages, the waves have smoothed this sand into wide, firm, gradually sloping tidal flats. Combined with Cape Cod Bay's ten-foot tides—a result of so much water sloshing into a small cul-de-sac every twelve hours—this has created the premier place on the East Coast for intertidal oyster farming.

Most oyster farmers on Cape Cod Bay—from Duxbury and Plymouth to the Dennis sand flats, where the Pilgrims discovered a beached pilot whale being butchered by the natives on their initial scouting of the bay in December of 1620, to Wellfleet Harbor—farm intertidally, which has huge advantages. You can set up your trays of oysters on the firm flats, and harvesting is as simple as walking out at low tide and tossing the market-sized oysters in your basket. A few hours of air and sun exposure also keeps seaweed and other fouling organisms from clogging your cages, discourages marine predators, and tones the oysters by forcing them to clamp shut each day. It's a system that won't work with the three-foot tides you find farther south.

It's such a good way to grow oysters, in fact, that it leads to a certain sameness. Although there are some differences in technique—some use free-swinging baskets, some finish their oysters on the bottom— you can pretty much count on a Cape Cod Bay oyster having a strong white shell shaded black or brown on top, a firm texture, and a very briny, chicken stock flavor. In late fall, when the cold Gulf of Maine waters cue the oysters to plump up in preparation for hibernation, this chicken stock can become the richest lobster bisque. And that's why, to me, the sameness is no great shame. When you're in Champagne, make Champagne.

The other thing Cape Cod Bay has going for it, of course, is the city

of Boston. No matter how many oysters Cape Cod Bay ever makes, the city of Boston will eat them—preferentially. This makes it the antithesis of New York, where the populace wants to sample oysters from every corner of the planet. (And if Mars produced oysters, they'd be curious about those, too.) But Boston has always had a more provincial outlook. Sox, Pats, and Cape Cod oysters. Boston has one of the strongest oyster scenes in the country, and its oyster bars are more likely to know everything about the farms they source from; it's just that most of those farms will be in Massachusetts, with maybe a Rhode Island or a Maine oyster thrown in for exotic appeal. That same dynamic is even more acute on the Cape itself, where you'll find oyster bars selling only their town's oyster—and sometimes growing it as well. It's the right kind of provincialism, the kind that says: *What we need is here. Why go anywhere else?*

ISLAND CREEK

DUXBURY BAY, MASSACHUSETTS

SPECIES Eastern

CULTIVATION In spring, hatchery seed (some from Island Creek's own hatchery) is started in upwellers beneath the dock of the Duxbury Bay Maritime School, then transferred to bags and cages in the bay's mudflats until they are about two inches long, then broadcast on the bay bottom in fall. Harvested the following August (eighteen months total, on average) by dredge (mostly) or hand-picking (during minus tides).

PRESENCE Classy, ridged shells of white, black, and golden brown, holding a mid-sized nugget of creamy white meat.

FLAVOR A New England clambake in a shell: quahog, lobster and sweet corn steamed in rockweed.

OBTAINABILITY Ubiquitous. One of the most carried oysters in the United States, thanks to Island Creek's masterful consistency, distribution, and chutzpah. Keep your eyes peeled for **Sweet Sounds**, John Brawley's flock from near the Back River marshes.

SKIP BENNETT GREW UP ON DUXBURY BAY clamming, hunting, and fishing. His dad was a lobsterman, so he did some of that, too. Skip, who can trace sixteen different lines of his family back to the Mayflower, learned how to live off the bay when he was still a child, and by the time he was in his twenties he was making his living off it, too, gathering clams and mussels. In the late 1980s, he became one of the first clam farmers in Massachusetts. A hurricane had wiped out the bay's mussel population, and Skip had this sense that farming could support a more stable lifestyle. Ha! After three years, all his clams died of a parasite. He was all set to quit the bay and take a finance job in Manhattan when he decided to give oysters a shot, using his clam equipment. He became the first oyster farmer on Duxbury Bay, now much celebrated as one of the jewels of New England aquaculture, and his oysters took off. Fed twice daily by the cold, plankton-rich tides ripping in from Cape Cod Bay, one pound of oyster seed turned into more than one hundred thousand pounds of briny, three-inch oysters in a year and a half.

Having no distribution, Skip simply drove his oysters around to various restaurants. When the market softened after 9/11, he began cold-calling. He wandered in the back door of Le Bernardin and won over Eric Ripert. Farm-to-table was just getting rolling, and chefs were thrilled to skip the middlemen. Thomas Keller adopted Island Creeks at Per Se. Soon the French Laundry piled on. The little Island Creek oyster truck became an iconic sight on Boston streets, as did C. J. Husk, the Thor stand-in who drives it and has become a celebrity in his own right.

Today, Island Creek is a cooperative of ten farms in Duxbury Bay that use similar techniques and distribute their oysters together under the Island Creek banner. Island Creeks have supplanted Wellfleets as the definitive New England oyster, always clean, deep-cupped, and full of salt, always making that ale taste that much better. It actually annoys me how often Island Creeks are the best-tasting oyster in any mixed platter. It would be nice if more boutique options bested them, but no: Like Hellmann's mayo, Island Creeks are kind of perfect. The company has now expanded to include a distribution arm, its own hatchery, a foundation that supports aquaculture initiatives in developing countries, and two celebrated Boston restaurants: Island Creek Oyster Bar and Row 34.

MOON SHOAL

BARNSTABLE HARBOR, MASSACHUSETTS

SPECIES Eastern

CULTIVATION 2.5-millimeter seed is started in spring in cylindrical "windowscreen" cages in the intertidal zone, then transferred to mesh bags for the summer and fall, then wintered over for four months in an insulated shed at 34 degrees. The following spring it's returned to the bay and grown to market size in open-topped cages on the bay bottom, tumbled periodically in a cement mixer to remove barnacles and strengthen shells.

PRESENCE Understated. In size, shape, and color, Moon Shoals feel like your basic New England oyster. Only after you've eaten a dozen do you realize that you are in the presence of greatness.

FLAVOR Chicken stock in summer, lobster bisque in fall.

OBTAINABILITY Produced in small quantities (a couple of hundred thousand or so per year), Moon Shoals are a highly coveted boutique oyster. Jon Martin sells everything he grows to Island Creek, which sells them at its own oyster bars. If you can't find Moon Shoals, look for the other excellent oysters coming out of Barnstable Harbor, such as **Beach Points**, **Scorton Creeks**, and **Thatch Islands**. The Naked Oyster bistro in Hyannis sells their own Barnstable oysters.

IN 1606, THE EXPLORER SAMUEL DE CHAMPLAIN became the first European to scope out the secrets of Cape Cod Bay. In the southern reaches of the bay, he wrote in his *Voyages*, he discovered a harbor so thick with oysters that he named it Port aux Huistres. Most observers have assumed that this was Wellfleet Harbor, and certainly spotlight-hogging Wellfleet oyster folks have been quick to promote this origin story. But Champlain actually described the harbor as falling five leagues (fifteen nautical miles) south and slightly west of the tip of Cape Cod, which would put him right in Barnstable Harbor. Might that be the true Port aux Huistres? Thoreau thought so, and so do I. Champlain had visited Wellfleet the year before; you'd think he'd have recognized it. In addition, the water depths and land features he describes match Barnstable perfectly. Either way, quite a few of the best oysters in New England are now coming out of Barnstable Harbor.

Moon Shoal is a perfect example of the breed. Snappy white shells flecked with purple, and a rich, salty tarragon-chicken flavor that holds up even in summer. Although Moon Shoals are exceptionally sweet and full, all Barnstable oysters have some variation of this. It's a function of the harbor, which funnels cold, briny Cape Cod Bay water into a chute that feeds deep into one of New England's best salt marshes. Water pours into the marsh on the neap tide, grows thick with marshy plankton, and then pours back out over the oysters on the ebb tide, providing a different mix of nutrients in each direction. The result: fat oysters brimming with umami and complexity.

Shellfish leases here are in high demand, and for years full-time fireman and oyster lover Jon Martin was unable to acquire one. Then his wife developed a close friendship with a man she was caring for in a hospice. After the man passed away, his family surprised the Martins with a gift of a two-acre shellfish lease they would no longer be using. Jon immediately began learning the ins and outs of oyster farming in the Barnstable marsh, which is notoriously difficult to navigate in the ten-foot tides. After running his boat aground several times on Moon Shoal, a beautiful oyster was born (and named). Martin still works as a Barnstable fireman, squeezing his oystering into his off days, and his fellow firefighters often lend a hand on the farm.

ROCKY NOOK

KINGSTON BAY, MASSACHUSETTS

SPECIES Eastern

CULTIVATION Seed is grown in upwellers in spring until large enough to be transferred to bags in off-bottom cages on the tideflats. In October, the oysters are planted on the bottom, where they ride out the winter, and harvested by hand-picking the following fall and winter.

PRESENCE Looks like a runty Island Creek, with the same twisted-teardrop swoop and the Duxbury stamp of white bottom shell and brown top. The cups are surprisingly shallow.

FLAVOR With less salt, the root-soup base note of Eastern oysters comes to the fore.

OBTAINABILITY These are regulars at Island Creek Oyster Bar and Row 34, and they are often sighted as far south as New York.

THE DUXBURY BAY OYSTER JUGGERNAUT built its reputation on brine. The shallow bay with the big tides gets a complete transfusion of seawater twice a day, keeping its Island Creeks, Standish Shores, and the rest near-oceanic in their salinity. From Duxbury Bay over to Plymouth Bay—Duxbury's other half, protected by its own barrier beach—the oysters are cold, firm, salty classics, and you'd be forgiven for assuming that's just how they roll.

But hiding in the western corner of the bay, tucked behind Rocky Nook Point, lies Kingston Bay and the mouth of the Jones River, named by the Pilgrims for the captain of the *Mayflower*. The river is not exactly the Nile—it runs all of seven miles down from Silver Lake—but it's still the largest freshwater river feeding into Cape Cod Bay, and, combined with the trickle of water contributed by nearby Island Creek itself, it manages to noticeably sweeten up Kingston Bay. The impact became apparent when Rocky Nook oysters came on the scene in 2011. It was the first oyster in Kingston Bay in sixty years, and immediately became a standout. It had the same clean look as its neighboring bivalves, with rays of color fanning across the bottom shell, but it was no brine bomb, replacing the salt with a mild sweetness. It remains an insider's favorite among the crowd that sloshes around Duxbury Bay for a living.

STANDISH SHORE

DUXBURY BAY, MASSACHUSETTS

SPECIES Eastern

CULTIVATION Seed is started in upwellers beneath the dock in Duxbury, then transferred to bags and placed in cages for the summer and fall. In winter, the bags are strapped to the flats of Duxbury Bay to ride out the ice, and the cages are removed. In spring, the oysters are broadcast on the bay floor, harvested by dredge six months later, and purged before shipment.

PRESENCE A strong, long, deep-cupped oyster with gorgeous black and purple streaks on the elegantly ridged shells. You won't find a prettier Eastern oyster. Comes in two generous sizes: Selects push four inches, while Petites are just under three.

FLAVOR Toothy and rich, like white asparagus in cultured cream sauce. Balanced between sweet and salty.

OBTAINABILITY Excellent. Harvested year-round. Pangea Shellfish distributes throughout North America, and Standish Shore is its flagship oyster.

BEN LLOYD FOUNDED the exemplary distributor Pangea Shellfish in 2001, but he always longed to get his feet wet, so in 2010 he bought a small shellfish farm in Duxbury Bay, a stone's throw from the Island Creek farm, and began growing his own premium oyster. He named it for the nearby high peninsula with the perfect cove where Captain Myles Standish made his home in Plymouth Colony. Spring and fall evenings on the farm, the sun sets behind the tall Standish monument, a reminder that we've been thriving on this bay's bounty for centuries. In the case of oysters, that thriving has a lot to do with Duxbury Bay's location on Cape Cod Bay's western flank. In summer, prevailing winds blow out of the southwest, pushing warmed surface water out of the bay as fast as it enters. That can keep Duxbury a good 15 degrees cooler than Wellfleet Harbor, facing Duxbury across Cape Cod Bay, where water can back up in the harbor and cook on a summer day. In addition to cool water, what makes Standish Shores stand out is a tremendous amount of hand labor. Every oyster has been graded, tumbled, and pampered for a couple of years before it finds its way onto a plate.

WELLFLEET

WELLFLEET HARBOR,
CAPE COD

SPECIES Eastern

CULTIVATION Seed is grown in off-bottom bags and cages in the intertidal flats of Wellfleet Harbor for two to three years until market-sized. A few growers bottom plant.

PRESENCE Coyote-colored and craggy, Wellfleets always feel serious and strong. Table chatter dies when they appear.

FLAVOR Salty, nutty, buttered popcorn with a few shakes of brewer's yeast.

OBTAINABILITY Very good along the Northeast Corridor; spotty elsewhere.

THE FIRST EUROPEANS TO SETTLE Wellfleet in the 1600s found the natural harbor to be so thick with seafood that they named it Billingsgate, after the famed London fish market, the largest in the world. The stars of the harbor were the oysters. Guarded by the arm of Great Island, never more than a few feet deep, and diluted by just enough freshwater seeps to reduce its salinity to a lip-smacking 28 ppt, Wellfleet Harbor grew millions of savory oysters, and it instantly became Boston's favorite supplier. Even back then, the little harbor couldn't keep up with the city's notorious oyster mania, and it was nearly depopulated by 1775, when some disease seems to have finished them off. In *Cape Cod*, Thoreau quotes an aged Wellfleet oysterman telling him what happened to those oysters: "When Wellfleet began to quarrel with the neighboring towns about the right to gather them, yellow specks appeared in them, and Providence caused them to disappear." After that, the resourceful Wellfleet oystermen began relaying the less savory oysters from Buzzards Bay and Narragansett Bay in the spring, planting them on the beds at Wellfleet—"where they obtain the proper relish of Billingsgate," a local explained in 1793—and shipping them to Boston in the fall, by which time they'd tripled in size. In the 1800s, Wellfleet switched to the bargain-basement supplies coming out of the Chesapeake. By 1850, 150,000 bushels a year of Chesapeake oysters were marinating in Wellfleet Harbor before their denouement in Boston.

Today, most Wellfleet oysters begin in New England hatcheries and are raised in bags, with the best being finished in the harbor's shallow flats. Because those flats are intertidal, a real Wellfleet will have a tough shell and a well-developed muscle with plenty of sweetness. (The town even stocks oysters at Indian Neck for visitors who want to gather their own Wellfleets. Just make sure you get a license and don't gather oysters from anywhere marked with yellow buoys, or you'll get a sense what those old quarrelers were like.) About one hundred Wellfleetians farm oysters in the town, though their overall production (about a million oysters) is less than 2 percent of those heady nineteenth-century days, making a true Wellfleet a coveted item. As with other public-domain oyster brands, cultivation techniques and standards vary widely; from different people, in different seasons, you can get scraggly snotballs or stately classics (like our little fleet of Wellfleetians here). Look for those from Barbara Austin, thirty-year oyster grower and three-time champion of the Wellfleet OysterFest Annual Oyster Shuck-Off; from Irving and Jake Puffer of Wellfleet Oyster & Clam (who capture their own seed on "Chinese hats"); or Chopper's Choice from four-time Wellfleet champ and former world champion William "Chopper" Young. Most prized of all are the robust Deepwater Wellfleets, which grow farther offshore in thirty feet of water and are harvested with dredges.

GULF *of* MAINE

The Gulf of Maine's defining quality, readily apparent to any summer visitor naive enough to take a leap off some cobbly Downeast beach, is COLD. The coast of Maine is not really a part of the Northeast; it's a different beast altogether. And so are its oysters.

Most of America's East Coast benefits from the Gulf Stream, but the same submarine ridge that walls off Cape Cod Bay turns the Gulf of Maine into a semi-contained basin fed by arctic water from Labrador. The result is that water temperatures in Maine can be 10 degrees colder than southern New England, and sometimes in summer even colder than Prince Edward Island, which is warmed by the Saint Lawrence River. And, everything else being equal, cold water produces a more substantial oyster, though it takes longer to do so. Just as a slow-growing wild tree has a density to it that can't be matched by a tree-farm tree (as evidenced by the tight growth rings in the wild tree), so a slow-grown oyster will have more heft to it—more stuff per cubic centimeter—than a weedy, fast-grown oyster. There, too, you can see it in the growth rings. Slow food, indeed. Cold climates also produce sweeter oysters in late fall as oysters gird themselves for the long months of hibernation by plumping up with sugary compounds that function as both energy reserves and natural antifreeze. The longer the hibernation, the sweeter the oyster. And Maine takes hibernation pretty seriously.

The other force imbuing Maine's oysters with their special character is its crazy coastline. As the glaciers advanced southward with the falling temperatures one hundred thousand years ago, they scoured Maine's soft sand and sediment and pushed it deep into the Atlantic, carving long troughs in the bedrock that became river valleys when the glaciers then retreated ninety thousand years later. As sea levels rose along with the temperature, those river valleys became long tidal rivers, leaving the state with its tattered shreds of coastline dangling into the sea. That's a very different habitat from the shallow salt marsh estuaries and barrier beaches farther south.

One unique oyster community thrived high on the Damariscotta River from 2,500 years ago until 1,000 years ago. The bathymetry of the Damariscotta includes several underwater sills that form a series of skinny tidal "lakes," almost like steps. Fed by the sea to the south and freshwater rivers to the north, each step down forms an increasingly salty finger lake.

Although wild oysters can thrive in salinities ranging from a nearly fresh 6 ppt salt to a fully oceanic 34 ppt, they do best in a brackish 10 to 20 ppt, because most of the things that love to eat baby oysters can't survive there. About 2,500 years ago, sea levels rose high enough to flood the step above the current towns of Newcastle and Damariscotta with enough salt water to turn it brackish year-round. Oyster spat from reefs farther downstream—reefs now salty enough to be decimated by predators—colonized the new lake, marine predators couldn't follow, and the result was a full flowering of one of the healthiest oyster colonies New England has ever known.

We know this because one predator soon discovered these abundant and delicious reefs, and left clear evidence of a 1,500-year feast. Not sea stars, crabs, or oyster drills, but *Homo sapiens*, which stumbled upon the spectacular reefs in the Damariscotta's Salt Bay and settled down for happy hour. By last call, those natives had produced two massive shell middens, and many smaller ones, made up of hundreds of millions of shells—many a foot in length—that rose thirty feet high and stretched for half a mile along the river's shoreline. One of those middens, known as Whaleback, was mined into oblivion in the late 1800s for chicken feed (literally), but the other, the Glidden Midden, is now protected. It's an easy boat ride from the docks in Damariscotta, and it lets you into another world. You can't miss it: All of a sudden, the western bank of the river changes from dirt and rock to pure-white shell hash. From the beach, the white cliff rises above you, and your mind struggles with numbers. Unfathomable abundance. This was clearly a processing operation—the pile is virtually identical to those at modern shucking houses—and the people who made it must have been smoking or curing oysters for their winter needs. (The Maine coast was a seasonal hunting and fishing ground for natives.) Over the

Preceding pages: Pemaquid oyster boat hard at work; Smokey McKeen lifts a tray of market-sized Pemaquids out of the Damariscotta River. Right: Abigail Carroll checks her bags of young oysters on the Scarborough River.

course of those 1,500 years, something ran out—either the oysters or the natives—a couple of times. Two striations of detritus run through the middle of the mound, indicating a few hundred years of abandonment each time, allowing the reefs to replenish.

But eventually luck ran out. As sea levels continued to rise, Salt Bay crossed the "drill line," a point around 20 ppt where oyster drills (voracious marine snails) can survive. Drills swarmed the reefs, and the combination of predation and overharvesting finished the oysters off. Shells in the top, most recent layers, which date back to around one thousand years ago, are significantly smaller.

By the time Europeans arrived in Maine, no native oysters could be found. In the 1950s, the state tried to grow European Flats, which thrived in the equally frigid North Sea, but the Flats weren't commercially viable, and it wasn't until the advent of hatcheries in the 1970s that Maine's oysters were reborn. With hatcheries producing the seed, and with aquaculture gear to protect the babies from drills, crabs, and other baddies, Maine was suddenly an oyster frontier: thousands of miles of coastline filigreed with coves and washed by clean, icy, very briny seawater free of the diseases that harried oysters farther south.

Maine became the ultimate cold-water oyster region, and most of the action centered on the Damariscotta River, source of those ancient shell middens. Once lined with shipyards, then brickyards, the Damariscotta enjoyed a third act as a wide river with a small watershed and little surviving industry, meaning lease sites were abundant and water quality always high.

For a long time, most Maine oysters came from the Damariscotta River, which to this day is a who's who of renowned oysters: Wawenauk, Wiley Point, Dodge Cove, Norumbega, Colonial Select, Glidden Point, Pemaquid, and others can be found amidst the one hundred acres of leases that parallel its pine-lined banks. Some leases almost touch each other, all producing hard-shelled oysters with powerful brine and lingering sweetness, yet unique character, which is why I

think of the Damariscotta as the Côte d'Or of shellfish: Nowhere else produces such consistently high quality that reflects the subtle differences a change in terrain or technique can impart.

But Maine also has one of the fastest-expanding aquaculture programs in the country. In the 1980s, when the Damariscotta first rose to fame, there were four oyster farms in Maine; in 2015 there were sixty-five. Too many newcomers have taken shortcuts, confining their oysters in floating bags on the relatively warm surface, where they grow faster but develop thin shells and thinner flavor. But in the past few years, new growers from Biddeford to Bar Harbor have emerged with oysters that can give the grand crus of the Damariscotta a run for their money, taking the steps necessary to grow the kind of slow, sweet, hard-shelled oyster that is once again as integral a part of the Maine landscape as the lobsters, the rock, and the fog.

BAR HARBOR SELECT

SPECIES Eastern

CULTIVATION Grown in upwellers in Mount Dessert Island's Somes Sound (the only *fjard*—not fjord—on the East Coast) until they are one inch long, then planted on top of predator netting in the intertidal zone of Goose Cove, on the mainland side of Western Bay. Harvested by hand at three inches, about a year later.

PRESENCE One of the prettiest shells on the East Coast, striped tan and purple and often garnished with a sprig of bright-green seaweed. The meats are deep-cupped and ivory with a thick muscle and a mustard-brown belly. The oyster feels heavy for its size.

FLAVOR Comes on powerfully briny, as you'd expect from the open-sea location, and then yields to a rich, sweet, cod-chowder finish.

OBTAINABILITY Very rare. Legal Seafoods in Boston was the first account to carry Bar Harbor Selects, which began selling on a commercial level in 2015. As production ramps up, they should become more available, but for now they are a sweet find.

MARINE SCIENTIST TOM ATHERTON became enamored of oysters during his thirty-five years of work on shellfish for the University of Maine and the state's department of natural resources, and he identified a perfect place to grow them: Goose Cove, on the bay that separates the mainland from Mount Desert Island and Acadia National Park. Few people, pristine water quality, the kind of icy water temperatures that make fabulously firm oysters, and those famously huge Downeast tides, ensuring a twice-daily infusion of fresh nutrients. The only problem: No aquaculture equipment was allowed in Goose Cove except for predator netting—plastic mesh that is spread over bay bottoms to protect the clams underneath from green crabs, an invasive species that has decimated Maine's shellfish populations in recent years. Without bags, Atherton's young oysters would be popcorn for the crabs. So, after some "soul-searching," Atherton and his partners hit upon a new strategy: They would keep their oysters in upwellers until they were an inch in size—much longer than oysters are normally kept in upwellers, because you need *a lot* of upwellers to hold a million inch-long oysters—then plant them in Goose Cove on top of the predator netting and see how they fared. "Lo and behold, the oysters grew great!" says Atherton. "Nice cups, good shell density, and some really good meat weight." The netting kept the oysters from sinking into the soft bottom of Goose Cove while still giving them the characteristics of a bottom-planted oyster: deep cup, thick shell, firm meat.

Bar Harbor Selects are one of the only oysters grown in this manner, but—judging from the results—others might want to give it a try. The shells have the depth and strength of bottom-cultured oysters, but the beautiful purple swirls of bag-coddled bivalves, and the harvesting is a breeze. In the fall, the oysters receive regular exposure to the cold at low tide, and they respond by bulking up with sugary antifreeze compounds, with which they can even survive brief slushy phases. They get crazy sweet. Still, the depths of a Maine winter would freeze even the most glycogen-pumped oyster, so when the bad stuff hits, they're moved deeper into the water.

BELON
(Maine)

MAINE COAST

SPECIES European Flat

CULTIVATION Wild-harvested
by divers.

PRESENCE Compared to other
oysters, Belons feel like the luxury model.
Scalloped shell in Cartier colors and
handsomely two-toned interior, with
creamy belly and ochre mantle.

FLAVOR Hazelnuts and anchovies
fried in seal fat, with a squishy crunch
like jellyfish salad. Is this good? Is it
bad? I don't know; it's like a nineteenth-
century Russian novel. The experience is
profound, and you'll be proud to check
it off your life list, though you may never
have the fortitude to do it again.

OBTAINABILITY Belons are plentiful
in Maine; the issue is getting them to
your plate. They must be hand-harvested
by divers, hand-banded with rubber
bands to keep their shells shut during
transport, and hand-packed cups down
so they can survive a few days out of
the water. Only a few distributors and
restaurants want to deal with them.

IN 1949, WHEN MAINE WAS OYSTER-FREE, a few
dreamers in the Department of Sea and Shore Fisheries noted that,
while Maine's water might be too cold to spawn the American
oyster, it was right in line with the temperature of Northern
Europe's waters, home to the European Flat. Since the Flat was
the connoisseur's oyster (this was back in the day when everything
European was ipso facto better), it would give Maine a unique
high-end product. Oysters were imported from the Netherlands
and planted in Harpswell, Boothbay Harbor, and a few other
sites. Unfortunately, the Flats grew and reproduced slowly, proved
virtually impossible to cultivate in aquaculture equipment, and
were soon abandoned. Forsaken and forgotten, a few went native,
breeding survivor stock. They laid low for several decades, then had
their coming-out party in the 1980s, when a diver harvesting sea
urchins near Harpswell blundered into a mother lode of Belons in
rocky, subtidal habitat. Soon divers started finding them in similar
spots all over the Maine coast. Like truffles, they have continued to
resist cultivation efforts while flourishing in the wild. And they have
become one of the most prized seafoods in America.

Yet, not one of the easiest. If the Flats from Brittany's famed
Belon River (the only ones with the proper right to the name) have
a hint of metallic twang, Maine's are copper-plated monsters.
Watch a newbie slurp one and you'll see what we mean when we
talk about "Belon face." I once volunteered on a NOAA research
vessel in the Gulf of Maine, hauling up fish from hundreds of feet
down; Belons always remind me of the smell of the net when it
hit the deck. When you finally succeed in prying one open, it feels
like you've unlocked the maw to some gaping underworld, freeing
something imprisoned for centuries.

Here's a secret: Belons make the best fried oysters. With less
water content and more firmness, they don't shrink as much and
they crisp up beautifully.

GLIDDEN POINT

DAMARISCOTTA
RIVER, MAINE

SPECIES Eastern

CULTIVATION Seed is raised in floating mesh bags high upriver, taking advantage of the nutrient-rich waters below the towns of Newcastle and Damariscotta. Bottom-planted when an inch long at one of three sites downriver and harvested by divers three to four years later.

PRESENCE Glidden Points feel older and wiser than other oysters. They have fashioned thick-walled houses in which to live, and those houses are maxed out in a way that any of us who have held down the same dwelling for years can sympathize with.

FLAVOR The well-developed muscle provides a lot of scallopy sweetness and texture. The Damariscotta River supplies the salt and the crisp, short finish.

OBTAINABILITY Glidden Points are some of the most famous oysters in the country, but Barb Scully has to allocate them carefully. You're guaranteed to succeed at Mine Oyster, in Boothbay Harbor, just a few miles downstream, but they are highlighted at oyster bars across the country. Not available in winter (*you* dive in that water!), but a particularly good choice in summer, when many oysters can taste funky.

BARB SCULLY IS THE ULTIMATE proponent of slow oysters. She bottom plants everything in cold water, believing there's no substitute for the impact of clay and rock on an oyster's development. For this reason she's watched with dismay as the oyster renaissance has swept America, bringing with it a wave of fair-weather oyster eaters who prefer immature bivalves, and a wave of new growers happy to supply them. But Barb sticks to her guns, because it has never been about the money.

What it has been about, since the moment in 1987 when her job with the Department of Marine Resources led her to the banks of the Damariscotta River, is growing the perfect oyster. Clean, cold, briny seawater surges up the narrow channel every tide, warming in the lakelike shallows of Salt Bay above the town of Damariscotta and cooking the day's plankton soup, then sending dinner downstream on the falling tide. The bottom is firm and the flavor of the oysters mysteriously fine. Barb bought a gray-clapboard house on the river, put in a dock, and began her quest.

That quest often involves strapping on a thick wetsuit and plunging into the Damariscotta. Thirty feet down in silty 40-degree water, she'll gather by feel alone, trying not to let the current sweep her to the sea. "No one else in the world is doing this," she says, "nor in their right mind would even try." In fact, for most people it would be impossible, but Barb, a lifelong diver built of bundles of corded muscle, can make an hour of air last two and a half. It's an insane amount of work, but it keeps the ecosystem intact.

Like single-vineyard wines, each of the three Glidden Point sites develop differently. **Newcastle Shores**, planted in just a few feet of water near the Salt Bay, grow the fastest and tend to be white-shelled from winter ice pushing them down into the silt, where algae can't colonize them. **Bristol Shores** grow forty feet deep in extremely cold water, taking four to five years to reach maturity, and boast the strongest shells of all. **Ledges** (pictured here) grow on certain shallow, current-blasted rocky sills in mid-river, leading to epic diving adventures but unparalleled oysters with sculpted cups, green-tinted shells, and sweet, firm meat. "By far the most beautiful oyster I have learned to produce," Barb says of the Ledges. "My pride and joy."

NONESUCH

SCARBOROUGH RIVER, MAINE

SPECIES Eastern

CULTIVATION Seed is raised in floating bags in the Scarborough River, across from Nonesuch Point. In late fall, when an inch in size, it is bottom planted in the firm clay of the river, where it overwinters. Harvest is on foot or by snorkel about a year later.

PRESENCE Shells the brilliant green of forest moss. When small, Nonesuches have adorable spiky frills. Abigail calls them "Maggie Simpsons." As they grow up, they round out into Betty Boop.

FLAVOR Clean, crisp, very briny. After the salt comes a sweet, malty, grassy tang, like a good saison beer (hint, hint).

OBTAINABILITY Still a boutique operation, Nonesuch's production is mostly scarfed up by Mainers at places like Portland's Eventide Oyster Bar. Abigail Carroll also offers boat tours of her farm all summer, which include, of course, a few oysters and a glass of something French. Look for the cheerful teal Nonesuch truck on the docks at the Pine Point Fisherman's Co-op.

ABIGAIL CARROLL CALLS HERSELF the Accidental Oyster Farmer. If you'd told her, circa 2008, that she'd one day be schlepping bags of bivalves in her native Maine, she'd have chuckled from the terrace of her Parisian pied-à-terre and gone back to her Champagne. She'd been living in Paris for years, you see, trading stocks, and she was engaged to a French count. She was thoroughly urban. Urbane, even. Then things changed.

Abigail's story in a nutshell: Grew up in Maine. Got degrees in French literature and international affairs. Moved to Paris. Hooked up with count. Got to know count's extended family. Got an increasingly clear picture of what life would be like as a countess. Flew the coop. Returned to Biddeford. Hooked up with oyster farmer wannabe. Wrote business plan for wannabe. Fronted money to buy farm equipment and oyster seed while wannabe waited for his "check to arrive." Discovered wannabe's check was never going to arrive. Dumped wannabe. Had *crise existentielle*. Decided to cowboy up. Became an oyster farmer, despite dearth of experience and tendency toward seasickness. Discovered learning French by immersion was actually pretty good training for learning oyster farming by immersion. Winged it. Discovered the site she'd leased grew especially delicious oysters. Discovered she really likes getting her hands dirty. Discovered the immense satisfaction of handing over a sack of oysters she'd grown to a beaming customer.

As Abigail will be the first to admit, she got some lucky breaks during her unorthodox journey into oystering, one of which was the fine site she stumbled onto, which is part of a local nature preserve. The Nonesuch River meets the Scarborough River and the sea in a wide fan of sandy shallows. Abigail is able to grow her oysters in just a few feet of water, walking distance from shore, between Maine's largest salt marsh and a sandbar. At high tide, the salinity is 32 ppt, and even at low tide it's 28 ppt, so Nonesuches are always mouthwatering. Salt marshes are some of the most productive habitat on the planet, and the spartina of the Scarborough Marsh is steadily infusing the waters of the estuary with tannins and phytonutrients as it breaks down. That terrific food supply produces the fastest-growing clams in Maine, and it's also what's responsible for the grassy, olive notes of a classic Nonesuch (which it shares with oysters from other grassy neighborhoods). Abigail also figured out that she has the perfect site for bottom planting, which makes all the difference in shape, strength, and pizzazz. Connected to the bottom, Nonesuches develop a stunning green patina on their shells—at least, the parts not scrubbed clean by periwinkles. More important, they slow down a little, which is necessary in what is one of the warmest sites in Maine. Those wide, shallow, sandy flats bake the water every incoming tide, making it less conducive to producing typically slow-grown Maine oysters, but extremely conducive to both snorkel harvesting and the post-harvest dip—something both Abigail and her visitors have been known to indulge in.

NORTH HAVEN

HIGHTIE'S POND,
NORTH HAVEN ISLAND

SPECIES Eastern

CULTIVATION In April, seed is started in upwellers, then transferred in July to plastic bags floating on the surface of Hightie's Pond, then broadcast on the bottom of the pond in fall and harvested by diving two to three years later.

PRESENCE Midsized, nicely cupped, white and green, and strong.

FLAVOR The complexity that comes with age hits you right away: firm muscle, brine balanced by sweet-cream richness, and a mouth-filling hit of Atlantic umami.

OBTAINABILITY Islanders consume a significant supply of North Havens, either directly in their homes or at local restaurants. The Grand Central Oyster Bar, Eventide Oyster Company, and other heavy hitters also serve them regularly.

WHEN OYSTER FARMERS DREAM AT NIGHT, here's what they see: some magical island miles away from the mainland's pollution where clean, cold ocean water surges up a channel at high tide and pours into some sort of pool that's dammed to keep it from draining at low tide. It would be a mill pond, basically, protected from the elements and predators, and in it the saline ocean would mix with a fresh spring to create a brackish oyster paradise. The bottom would be a firm mix of rock and clay, so the crop could be planted directly on it. Oh, yeah: And the oyster farmer would live on the mill pond, for easy access.

That's what Adam Campbell had in Hightie's Pond, a brackish pool on the island of North Haven created by his wife's ancestor Hiram "Hightie" Beverage; but, being a lobsterman, Campbell didn't realize it. In 1995, a marine biologist came to the island to investigate reviving its smelt runs and noted in passing that the pond at the top of Pulpit Harbor was extraordinarily well suited for oysters. That got Campbell's attention, so the full-time lobsterman treated himself to three hundred thousand seed oysters ($3,500) for his thirty-sixth birthday. Many years, trials, and tribulations later, Campbell has the sweetest oyster farm you'll ever see. North Havens steep in pure Atlantic brine for several years, developing sweet-salty meat and strong, noticeably round shells, a nice reflection of their pond. At low tide they can be plucked from the bottom by anyone in hip waders; at high tide some free-diving is necessary. Either way, it's one of the most elegant oyster operations you'll find. Campbell's five children help him on the farm, and with any luck at least one of them will be taking North Haven Oysters deep into the twenty-first century.

PEMAQUID

DAMARISCOTTA RIVER, MAINE

SPECIES Eastern

CULTIVATION Hatchery seed is started in upwellers beneath the dock in the town of Damariscotta until it's fingernail-sized, then moved a mile downstream and grown in floating bags until "predator-resistant"—about two inches, which usually happens in late summer. Then, it is bottom-planted on deepwater leases, harvested by dredge a year or two later, and wet-stored near the river's mouth, at Clark's Cove, to purge and salt up before market.

PRESENCE Absolutely ripped. Big, thick brown shells, deep cups, and burly muscles. These are the manliest oysters in America, and they somehow make even other large oysters look like underachievers. Think LeBron James. Pemaquids never have an off night.

FLAVOR A mouthwatering blast of salt, followed by waves of surimi-like sweetness and satisfying crunch. Keep that ale handy.

OBTAINABILITY After thirty years, Pemaquids are one of the best-known bivalves in the country. You'll find them featured at serious raw bars coast to coast, but they are practically a religion in midcoast Maine, which eats half of everything produced. Don't overlook the Pemaquid Oyster Festival, in which approximately eighteen thousand Pemaquid oysters are consumed in one long afternoon at Schooner Landing, right on the docks in Damariscotta.

THE PEMAQUID OYSTER TRIUMVIRATE—Carter Newell, Chris Davis, and Smokey McKeen—began messing about with oysters around 1980 after a professor at the University of Maine suggested to the college buddies that the Damariscotta River might be a fine place to raise oysters, since the shell middens upstream made it clear they had thrived there for millennia. He was right. In a state that had been struggling to farm European Flats, the trio got in early on the native shell game, and Pemaquids are now the type specimen for brawny, briny East Coast oysters. The three friends began experimenting with various techniques in Carter's twenty-foot lobster boat "instead of playing golf on Sundays," and after much trial and error they hit upon the system that pretty much defines Maine oyster farming. Part of the key was finding a great site—in this case Goose Ledges, where the river constricts through some underwater sills and blasts the oyster beds with tremendous flow, allowing them to grow three times as many oysters per square meter as sites just a few hundred yards away. Another trick they borrowed from French growers, who have always favored growing beds (for the young oysters) and fattening beds (for final flavor). Oysters grow wonderfully at Goose Ledges, which sits above the Glidden Ledge, which divides the river into an oceanic lower section where summer temperatures hover in the mid-sixties, and a brackish upper section where they can rise into the low seventies but the salinity is much lower. To turn up the brine to 11, market-sized Pemaquids are moved a few miles downriver, closer to the open ocean, and left in specially designed purge baskets long enough to salt up, purge any grit, and plump up in response to the cold seawater. That's why the finish of a Pemaquid screams North Atlantic.

And speaking of the North Atlantic, Smokey and Carter have played in a Celtic band called Old Grey Goose since the 1970s (Smokey: banjo, guitar; Carter: fiddle), and there's something about the whole Pemaquid gestalt—the shellfish, the chanteys, the shellfish-themed chanteys, the small boats working the coves, Smokey's Dude-like penumbra of hair, Carter's dancing shoes, the nineteenth-century brickwork of Damariscotta—that can make you forget you aren't in the British Isles. Best time to experience it: Free Oyster Fridays, when Smokey and Carter drop off a couple of sacks of oysters at Schooner Landing and sidle over to the mike to fire up the tunes.

WINTER POINT

MILL COVE, MAINE

SPECIES Eastern

CULTIVATION Seed is started in upwellers, then dropped into Mill Cove in trays for about six months, until large enough to be planted on the cove's clay bed and left alone for a couple of years. Harvested by barge three seasons, and in winter by cutting holes in the ice on Mill Cove. It looks just like ice fishing.

PRESENCE Famously deep cups, classy brown-and-white shells, green accents. Feels as stuffed with goodness as a pierogi.

FLAVOR Big and brothy, it packs a bowl of sweet-salty bisque into a single bite.

OBTAINABILITY Demand greatly exceeds supply. Per Se, Le Bernardin, and other top dogs get first dibs.

MILL COVE IS AN INQUISITIVE FINGER of the Atlantic that pokes its way deep into the craggy Maine landscape at the northeast corner of Casco Bay, catty-corner from Portland. There, a pine-studded peninsula called Winter Point meets the cove just off of Hennessey Road. John Hennessey's family has called the spot home for more than three centuries—since the king of England deeded the land to them—and John has raised his oysters here since the 1990s. He's a maniac about culling: He goes through every oyster by hand, and most don't meet his specs, so they go back in the drink to cup up. Supply is limited, and many of America's top chefs are hooked on Winter Points, thanks to the work of Portland's famous Browne Trading Company, so Winter Points are at times allocated like Screaming Eagle cabernet.

GULF *of* SAINT LAWRENCE

When the Jesuit priest Pierre François Xavier de Charlevoix visited the Atlantic coast of Canada in the early 1700s, he was impressed at the lengths locals would go to get their oysters.

"Oysters are very plentiful in winter on the coasts of Acadia," he wrote, "and the manner of fishing for them is something singular. They make a hole in the ice, and they thrust in two poles in such a manner that they have the effect of a pair of pincers, and they seldom draw them up without an oyster."

Amazingly, were Pierre François to tread the red sandstone cliffs of Acadia today, he'd still recognize the scene. The bays of the Gulf of Saint Lawrence are still full of wild oysters, they are still often harvested with wood-handled tongs, and boring through the ice to get to your stock is not considered unreasonable. The style suits the geology and climate of the region. Prince Edward Island and the New Brunswick coast may be nature's best attempt at a golf course: rolling green meadows bordered by sand dunes and laced with clever water hazards. The overall effect is as if somebody turned up the RGB knobs on an old color television, oversaturating the reds, greens, and blues to unreal levels.

The "rivers" you see as you drive are actually long capillaries of seawater that probe deep into the pastoral landscape, gnawing away at the soft red cliffs. These rivers and bays are "nowhere deep," as oyster expert Ernest Ingersoll noted enthusiastically in the 1800s, and sheltered enough to embolden both the oysters and the fishermen. Ingersoll estimated the cost of entry as a $10 skiff and a $2.50 set of tongs.

Today, $10 won't even fill your outboard, and a nice set of pliant, ten-foot, spruce-handled tongs will run you $140, but the lifestyle has barely budged. Many oystermen still work "dark to dark," and most still can't swim, but if you put your back into it, you can still make a decent living tonging oysters in PEI. What you do, a thousand times a day, is stand on the side of your boat, lower your tongs to the bottom of the bay (tongs range in length from six to eighteen feet; most oystermen have several), sweep the ends together a few times while lifting slightly as if you were tossing salad, then close on what you hope is a handful of oysters and not rocks and haul it to the surface. You dump the whole mess on your running board, hook your tongs onto the "sissy bar" so they don't fall over, and toss everything that isn't a market-sized oyster back over the side. Then you strip any living spat from the market "fish," toss it back overboard, and throw the "fish" in a cooler. Then you do it again. And again.

Or you can farm oysters, which has become increasingly popular in the Maritimes. But here at the northern limit of *Crassostrea virginica*, you run into certain problems. The Saint Lawrence River, which forms the largest estuary in the world, produces a generous summer environment of temperate, nutrient-rich waters. Late spring through fall, the food web springs to life with the urgent intensity of the north. From phytoplankton to whales, everything that respires works long hours in a sort of ecstatic trance tinged with boreal desperation.

Then winter hits. Early. Storms shellac this far northern land in a breastplate of ice (four feet thick in 2015, a record), and everything shuts down until May. That leaves a very short season for oysters to grow, so it takes them a lot longer to reach market size. That's of no concern if you're fishing wild oysters, but if you're a farmer buying

Left: Racks of Colville Bay oysters. Above: Tonging on the Souris River

seed, you have to deal with cash-flow timelines that would cause your banker in Virginia or California to hurl himself out of his office window. Yet, somehow they make it work, and thank goodness, because a three-inch Maritime oyster is entirely different from a three-inch American oyster. It can be five years old, six, even seven. That gives it a shell density, a look, and a flavor that is unique to the Maritimes. You'll see it in the fine stratigraphy of the shell layers, encrusted with their red dirt, and you'll taste it in the lean meat. If the South and Pacific Northwest are cranking out the fatted calves of the oyster world, these are the grass-fed steaks. They require a patient and understanding farmer, and they can be an acquired taste, but those who acquire it rarely go back.

BEAUSOLEIL

NEGUAC BAY,
NEW BRUNSWICK

SPECIES Eastern

CULTIVATION Wild spat is collected and transferred to floating bags, where they grow for three to five years. In winter, the oysters are dropped into deep water to wait out the ice.

PRESENCE As clean and inoffensive as a Jehovah's Witness. Their smallness is misleading: These oysters punch above their weight class.

FLAVOR Light, yeasty, and gently balanced, like an off-dry Champagne. The owners detect a hint of hazelnut.

OBTAINABILITY Common everywhere people enjoy dinky oysters (which means pretty much everywhere outside of the South)—even in winter (see text). Look for the rarer **French Kiss**, a **Beausoleil** grown for an additional two years to a more substantial size.

MAISON BEAUSOLEIL FOUNDERS Amédée Savoie and Maurice Daigle were the geniuses who put the cocktail oyster on the map. In those icy New Brunswick waters, it takes an oyster a good six years to reach three inches, so why not sell it in four years at two inches? Old-timers may have scoffed, but the nouveau oyster eaters of America scarfed them up. And why not? You get the same naughty thrill no matter the size. These are extremely popular oysters, and they have a place on any raw bar list, serving as a kind of gateway drug. *Hey, kid, c'mere. Ever try an oyster? Here. First one's free. Oh, yeah. In a coupla minutes you're gonna start feeling really good.*

As tonic as a sip of Champagne, Beausoleils are likely to leave the oyster skeptic in a swoon of reassessment. They are mild, yes; unintimidating, certainly; but not wimpy. There's some *there* there. They can be quite addictive.

Daigle and Savoie named their company after Joseph Broussard, aka Beausoleil, leader of the Acadian resistance against British occupation in the 1740s and 1750s, and there's a definite element of Acadian independence to their operation. Here, near the northern limit of *Crassostrea virginica*'s range, they have turned the coldness of New Brunswick into an asset. They have spent fifteen years refining their system of floating trays, and they now have a facility where in winter they can store oysters indoors in constantly pumping seawater, negating the need for spirit-killing forays onto the sea ice at 30 below, and giving Beausoleils some of the best winter availability in the Gulf of Saint Lawrence. The oysters are also hand-packed in cute boxes made of scrap wood in the Maison Beausoleil workshop.

COLVILLE BAY

SOURIS RIVER,
PRINCE EDWARD ISLAND

SPECIES Eastern

CULTIVATION Wild seed is collected on lime-encrusted "Chinese hats" near Vernon Bridge and grown out in bags attached to "French tables"—metal racks raised a foot off the bottom. After two years, they are bottom planted on the hard clay finishing beds of the mouth of the Souris River, where they spend an additional two years.

PRESENCE Every perfectly paisley shell looks like it's made of jade. Four years of slow growth makes for superb strength and shuckability.

FLAVOR Potato chips in clam dip.

OBTAINABILITY Excellent in Canada, which gobbles everything Johnny Flynn can grow. In the U.S., you're out of luck: Johnny stopped dealing with the hassle years ago. I rely on a friend with a cabin in PEI who smuggles a box back into Vermont every trip. Don't tell.

IN 1992, WITH CANADA'S COD population in a nosedive from which it would never recover, fisherman Johnny Flynn began playing around with oysters. His house bordered the Souris River where it opens onto Colville Bay, an ancient fishing port far removed from PEI's oystering hot spots. (The nearby town of Souris, or "mouse," was named for the teeming rodents that nearly drove out the first settlers.) PEI's south shore has much larger tides than the north shore, meaning more refills of water and fresh phytoplankton, and over the eons the river had built up a lovely, firm bed of Martian-red sand, as well as an extensive intertidal bar that protected the spot from swells and storms. Taking inspiration from his Old World precursors, Johnny began growing his oysters on French tables, then broadcast them on that nice firm bottom. To his surprise, the shells turned kelly green, standing out like jewels on the red velvet sands. To everyone else's surprise, that green—which shows up in just a few other oysters on the island—correlates with an amazingly rich and mouth-filling flavor. Today, Colville Bays are the most coveted oyster in Canada, and cod fishing is ancient history for Johnny, though he does lobster every spring—"two months paid vacation," as he calls it. David McMillan of Joe Beef fame, a longtime supplicant at the Colville Bay altar, describes a window each fall when the khaki meat on Colville Bays turns firm and pinkish, and develops what McMillan calls "clam-like tendencies": sweeter, chewier, with a satisfying iron bite. Colville Bays are regularly cited as the classic case of the oyster miracle. Why are they so screamingly good? There are some obvious factors—the ten-foot moon tides, the feeder streams that keep the salinity perfect, Johnny Flynn's unhurried cultivation—but honestly, it's a mystery. When asked, Johnny just shrugs. "Wish I could take credit," he says. "Our biggest contribution is keeping them alive so they can grow. It's just a great place!"

RASPBERRY POINT
SHINY SEA
PICKLE POINT

NEW LONDON BAY,
PRINCE EDWARD ISLAND

DAISY BAY
IRISH POINT

RUSTICO BAY,
PRINCE EDWARD ISLAND

SPECIES Eastern

CULTIVATION Wild seed from elsewhere on PEI is planted in New London Bay for finishing. Shiny Seas are raked from the bottom at an age of four years and a size of 2.5 inches, while Raspberry Points are given six to seven years to reach a size of 3 inches. Pickle Points are raised in cages instead of bottom planting. Harvest is by rake, tong, and machine. In winter, chain saws are essential.

PRESENCE Raspberry Points and Shiny Seas are small and pointy, with thick, heavy shells for their size, lined with bold growth grooves and often washed a mossy green. They feel old and content. Pickle Points grow faster and have more delicate, russet shells.

FLAVOR Very clean, moderately briny, quite crunchy. The finish turns bright.

OBTAINABILITY Widely distributed throughout Canada and the eastern U.S.

SPECIES Eastern

CULTIVATION Wild seed is raised in floating cages in Rustico Bay.

PRESENCE Rustico Bay oysters stay as black-and-white as a woodcut. A study in texture and grain. Irish Points are cocktail size, Daisy Bays three inches.

FLAVOR Muddier Rustico Bay produces an oyster with more earthy, vegetal notes than New London Bay. Salinity is medium high, sweetness is good in fall and winter.

OBTAINABILITY These newer members of the Raspberry Point gang are less known than the Raspberries and Pickles, but they share the same distribution network. Once you start looking for them, you see them everywhere.

LUCKY LIME

NEW LONDON BAY,
PRINCE EDWARD ISLAND

SPECIES Eastern

CULTIVATION The choicest seed is planted in the shallows of New London Bay just south of the sand dunes that wall off the bay from the Gulf of Saint Lawrence. Hand-manicured and rigorously culled, these can be seven or eight years old when they come to market.

PRESENCE Elfin, shamrock-green, and cutely named, these open up the oxytocin floodgates in your brain. It's crush at first sight. Rounder shells than other Maritime oysters and textbook cups.

FLAVOR The purest expression of Prince Edward Island National Park and New London Bay. Lean and clean.

OBTAINABILITY These are produced in smaller quantities than the other members of the Linkletter clan. If you find one, it's your lucky day.

SCOTT LINKLETTER IS THE SERIAL entrepreneur behind Cows Creamery (a Ben & Jerry's–style ice cream maker), BOOMburger, and so many other PEI enterprises it's hard to keep track. There's Avonlea Village, an *Anne of Green Gables*–themed tourist destination, and Avonlea Clothbound Cheddar, one of North America's great cheeses. There are houses and hotels. With his handlebar mustache, he bears some resemblance to Rich Uncle Pennybags, the Monopoly mascot. Scott's oyster empire arose in 1992, when he began selling Malpeques. He would acquire oysters from islanders and finish them in New London Bay, where a couple of years on the sandy bottom would give them much-improved shape and flavor. In 1999, to distinguish his oysters from less manicured Malpeques, he dubbed them Raspberry Points, after the spruce-capped promontory that overlooked his oystering grounds. It was marketing genius; Raspberry Points became a sensation. They were crisp and delicious, they developed a vivacious green patina from algae that thrived on the sandy bottom, and the name was unforgettable. (If the Linkletter group photo were the United States, Raspberry Points would be Washington State.) Shameless imitators soon appeared. Today you can find Blackberry Points, Gooseberry Points, and Sunberry Points coming from PEI; they are all basically Malpeques.

A few years later, Scott and his business partner, James Powers, began raising a faster-growing cage oyster. To differentiate it, they named it Pickle Point (Texas in photo), after New London Bay's Pickering Point, which, if you squint hard, looks pickle-shaped. Since then, to meet demand, they've added a cocktail-sized Raspberry, knows as Shiny Sea (California), as well as two oysters from Rustico Bay, a few miles east: regular-sized Daisy Bays (Maine) and smaller Irish Points (Florida). Rustico Bay has a muddy bottom that would suck oysters to their doom, so grow-out happens in floating OysterGro cages. The oysters grow faster, but they don't develop the green patina or the super-thick shells. Still, growth is so slow in the Maritimes that shell strength is never an issue.

Recently, the Linkletter gang decided to outdo Raspberry Point with an ultra-premium New London Bay oyster, the Lucky Lime (Wisconsin in photo). It spends its whole life nestled in the shallow, behind the dunes of Prince Edward Island National Park. It's a super-clean, super-firm environment, and the oysters grow incredibly slowly. These can be eight years old at harvest, with remarkably sculpted cups. They aren't huge by any means, but they do have that incredible depth that comes with slow growth. They are also remarkably clean on the finish, something all New London Bay oysters seem to share. James Powers describes the cultivation process as "high-grade, high-grade, high-grade." Grab them if you see them.

No matter how you grow your oysters on the rough north side of PEI, you have to deal with winter. At the mercy of the Gulf of Saint Lawrence and the prevailing winds, the Raspberry Point sites get hammered. Floating oysters must be sunk to the bottoms of the bays if they are to survive. In 2015, even that wasn't necessarily enough. Four feet of ice formed on New London Bay, more than anyone had ever seen. The guys had to swap out their regular chain saws for ones with cartoonishly long bars. Some alarming pictures made the rounds on Facebook. ("Ice? No problem! We're harvesting fresh oysters all winter long!") I'd always appreciated Raspberry Points. But now I *really* appreciate them.

MALPEQUE

PRINCE EDWARD ISLAND

SPECIES Eastern

CULTIVATION Wild-harvested with tongs by men in dories, usually in less than ten feet of water. The province enhances its Malpeque production by dragging "Chinese hat" spat collectors through the waters during the summer spawn, then transferring this spat to the wild beds. It takes five to seven years for oysters to reach market size.

PRESENCE Long, skinny, brown shells often tinged with brick dust where the shells meet (which you can chalk up to PEI's rusty sandstone). You almost never see flutes or ridges in wild Maritime oysters— just smooth bills. Inside, more often than not, the oyster is a translucent gray.

FLAVOR Moderately salty with a tannic tea finish.

OBTAINABILITY They're everywhere in the U.S. and Canada. Pretty cheap, too. Increasingly, the best Malpeques are marketed under a branded name. **Cooke's Cove, Sand Dunes,** and **Indian Points** are all choice Malpeques. **Summersides** (pictured here) are representative of the paisley shape and brothy depth that all Malpeques aspire to. On PEI itself, look for **Hardy's Malpeques,** or head for Stanley Bridge, where Carr's Oyster Bar harvests from its own beds.

THE GOOD NEWS ABOUT MALPEQUES: On any given day from May 1 to July 15 and from September 15 to November 30, you can still see men in small dories tonging wild oysters throughout PEI. There may be no prettier sight in oysterdom. The crenellated blue water limned by the garden island's green fields and red sandstone cliffs. The patchwork dories stippled across the bays. The bob of tongs. The clack of shells dumped onto the running boards of the boats. PEI has done a better job than any state in the U.S. at maintaining its wild oyster fishery, which still supports seven hundred fishermen. Harvests are stable, and there's as many newbies as old-timers in the trade. And everyone seems to be smiling.

Now the bad news: If you live in the States, it may well have been years since you had a decent Malpeque. This is partly the nature of a wild fishery. The oysters are left to their own devices, and they don't even have to come from Malpeque Bay; the name simply designates any wild oyster from PEI. In fact, few of them come from the cold, iconic north-facing bay. About three-quarters of Malpeques are fished from Bedeque Bay, whose richer, warmer waters face south toward the Northumberland Straits. On opening day, Bedeque will be packed with four hundred dories tonging with abandon. After that, the action spreads out across the island.

Depending on their locale, Malpeques can vary tremendously. Oysters that luck into hard-packed areas with lots of water flow are going to develop a great shape and flavor, while oysters stuck in the mud are going to grow long and curved ("bananas" is the term of art) in a desperate reach for food. With so many different spots on PEI and so many different fishermen, you're gonna get some beefy oysters and some scraggly ones. But in the States, at least, the ratio of scraggle to beef has been climbing for years. Malpeques are sold in two grades: Choice (nicely shaped shells with deeper cups) and Standard (everybody else). The Standards are cheaper, and so if you are plowing through Malpeques during $1 Oyster Happy Hour, you're probably experiencing the Standard.

As charming as the wild Malpeque fishery is, the trend on PEI, as elsewhere, is toward private leases. These are where you'll find the kind of beautiful bivalves that local islanders have appreciated for thousands of years, beginning with the Mi'kmaq. People with leases will still collect wild seed, but they'll raise that seed in bags or baskets, sometimes bottom planting it for the final year or two. Whatever the method, a good Malpeque should have a bit of sweetness and brine offset by a distinctive iron finish.

SAINT SIMON

SPECIES Eastern

CULTIVATION Wild spat is collected on "Chinese hats," then transferred to upwellers until large enough to be moved to floating mesh bags on the surface of La Saint Simon Bay. After about four years, they are finished on intertidal racks.

PRESENCE Small, smooth, dense, white with black flecks, these are Beausoleil look-alikes. They feel solid and stony in your hand.

FLAVOR Simple, modest brine, with a glutamate finish. An honest, non-showy flavor.

OBTAINABILITY Good in Acadia, and almost as good in the Northeast.

THE NORTHERN TIP of New Brunswick fractures into a hash of extraordinary bays and inlets that bring on fantasies of messing about in boats. Chief among them is Chaleur Bay, home to Shippagan, New Brunswick's fishing capital. Starfish-shaped Chaleur branches off into several prime oystering arms. Lameque and Saint Simon oysters are found here, and the famed Caraquets are just around the corner. Of these, the Saint Simons are noteworthy for their beautiful shells and full meats. Although they are grown primarily in floating bags, which would make a Pacific oyster thin and brittle, New Brunswick oysters grow so slowly that even at their shrimpy size (Saint Simons are about 2.5 inches long) they feel heavy and solid, and their meat has some nice tooth. There's actually a lot of essence packed into a small package; despite their size, these don't feel immature. They have some of the best shelf life of any oysters I know, thanks to some combination of the small size, thick shells, and tight seal. That combination is definitively Acadian, as is the shucking board these chaps are posing on. You'll find this style—carved from a single piece of wood, with a groove for holding the oyster and a pedestal to brace it against—all over the Maritimes, but it's only beginning to make inroads in the United States. This one was carved by Quebec artisan Tom Littledeer, famed for his canoe paddles, and had been well and roughly loved by the gang at La Mer, Montreal's oyster palace, by the time we borrowed it.

WALLACE BAY

WALLACE BAY,
NOVA SCOTIA

SPECIES Eastern

CULTIVATION These grow wild for five years or so in the icy depths of Wallace Bay and are harvested by desperate men in masks and snorkels looking to make beer money.

PRESENCE Lots of lumpiness in the shells, befitting wild oysters, but they are always strong and shuckable. Many have a light green or pearlescent white patina on the outside and a yellow-purple nacre inside.

FLAVOR Hits you with a one-two punch of salt and fish sauce, in that order. Can be gamy and tongue-coating, like intertidal mutton.

OBTAINABILITY You're at the whim of the underemployed fishermen of rural Nova Scotia.

THE SEASIDE TOWN OF WALLACE, Nova Scotia, is named for William Wallace, the thirteenth-century Scottish hero of independence who managed to thoroughly piss off the English for a few years before being captured, disemboweled, emasculated, beheaded, and quartered. Despite—or perhaps because of—the rough end, Wallace has been canonized as a Scottish hero of resistance, and I like to think the Wallace Bay oyster captures something of that never-say-die quality. One can almost hear it screaming "Freedom!" as it is shucked, eviscerated, dismembered, and displayed on ice.

The toughness comes from the wildness. These are oysters that have fended for themselves for years amidst the crushing ice of Wallace Bay. Their ancestors were almost certainly there before the British laid claim to New Scotland. Wallace Bay is a shallow finger of the Northumberland Strait that pokes eight miles into the red-soiled grasslands and spruce forests of Nova Scotia, ending in a National Wildlife Area. Well protected and sandy bottomed, it has always served up nice beds of bivalves, first for the Mi'kmaq, then the Acadians, then the Brits.

The flavor is positively gamy, like no farmed oyster I know. Why these should be so much stronger in flavor than PEI oysters, grown right across the straits, I have no idea, but something gets a bit more savage when you cross over to Nova Scotia. In the case of Wallace Bay oysters, think peat and lamb. And no, you wouldn't be *aff yer heid* to pair them with Scotch.

OVERSEAS

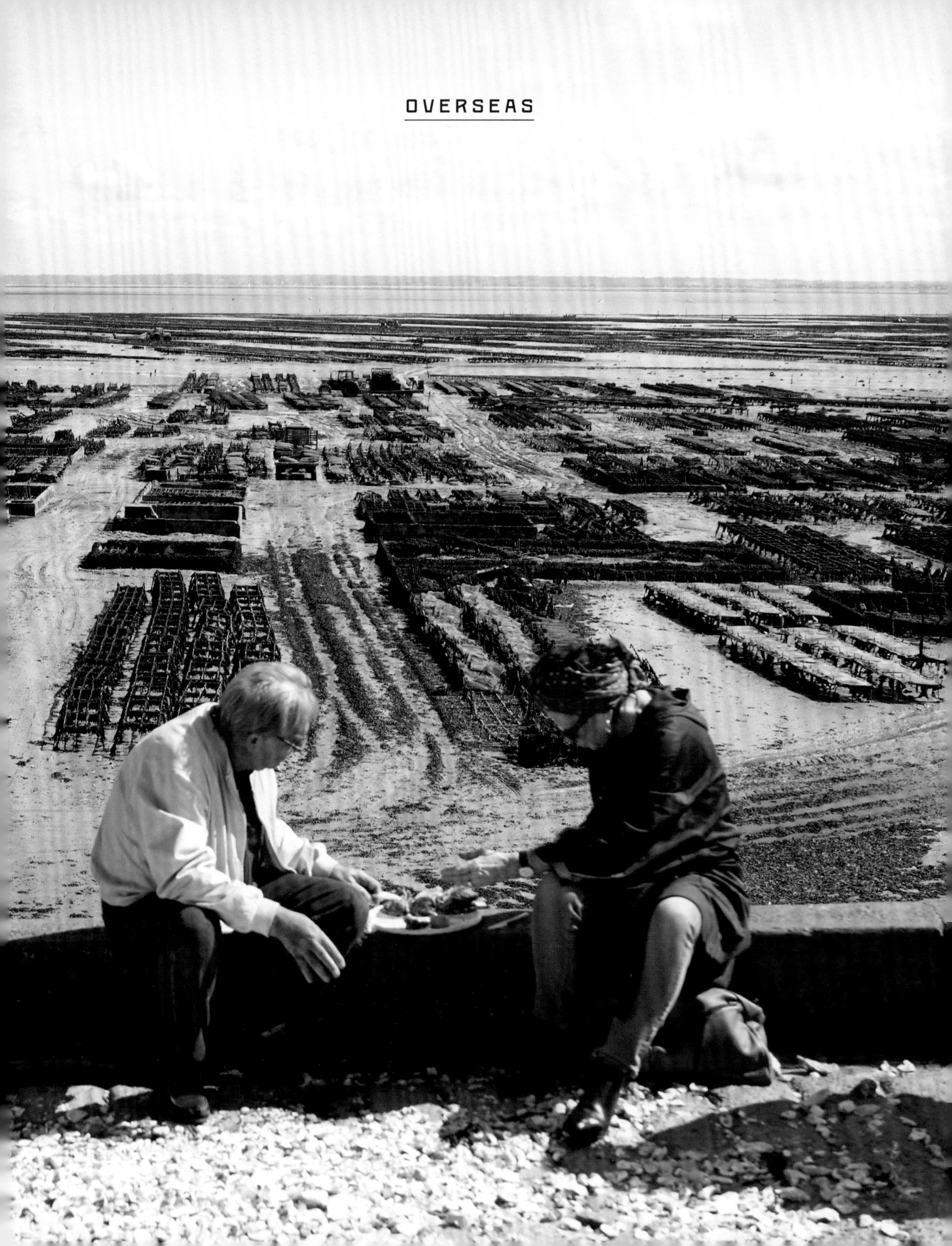

OVERSEAS

Sitting in your cute little American oyster bar, scanning the chalkboard of varieties and place names, quizzing your earnest waiter and sipping your even more earnest beer, you'd be forgiven for thinking that North America is the gravitational center of the oysterverse. It all seems so fresh here, so energized. So centripetal.

But zap yourself over to Cancale at low tide and you'd be disabused of the notion. There on the gray Brittany coast, the huge tides pull back twice a day to unveil a vast, gradually sloping flat of firm bottomland covered in orderly rows of racks and bags. It looks like an intertidal cemetery. And it cranks out twenty-five thousand tons of oysters every year. Tractors glide through the rows, hauling flats of oysters behind them. Most get shipped into Paris, but an impressive percentage gets slurped right there on the Cancale seawall as reverent tourists suck them down off plastic plates and hurl the shells back from whence they came.

  France produces an astonishing one hundred thousand tons of oysters per year (seven times that of the United States) and eats almost all of them domestically. To accomplish that, French citizens need to wolf down 4.5 pounds of oysters each per year, which is about eighteen times what their American counterparts are capable of. Half of those oysters get consumed during the winter holidays.

And 95 percent of them are Pacific oysters, the same beast you'd find in Japan or China or Australia or Ireland or California. France dominates oyster culture, but its producers aren't all that curious. They grow Pacific oysters, they grow them as they have always grown them, and nobody complains. Sure, regional terroir is important, those clay finishing ponds are cute, and the occasional European Flat still shows up, but that's about as adventurous as it gets over there. They aren't into new techniques or varieties. They don't know from Kumamoto.

France may be the center of the oyster solar system, sucking shells into its burning orb like meteors, but it is a pretty one-dimensional body. North America spins in its orbit like a bright jewel, Terra, the junior partner in the arrangement, but we are the fine-textured place where all the colorful stuff happens. The golf-ball Kusshis. The diver-down Glidden Points. The killer Capers Blades.

Still, like the farm boy in his Iowa cornfield, staring at the stars and wondering what's out there, you can't get serious about oysters in America and not wonder what you're missing, because most of the stuff that's missing you can't get. Only four countries have jumped through the necessary hoops to be allowed to ship live shellfish into the United States, and it's a weird club: Canada, Mexico, Chile, and New Zealand. The great oysters of Europe are verboten, as are the exotic delights of Australia, Asia, and Brazil.

But the short answer is that you've got things pretty good. Sure, there's no Sydney Rock Oyster, that buttery Antipodal treat; and no Caribbean Mangrove Oyster, served at room temp on the beach and likely to lay you low for twenty-four hours; but most of the bucket-list experiences to be had can be had right in the States—or at least in Canada, which welcomes Irish and French oysters with open arms. Still, to do justice to that bucket list, you really should feast beyond the comfortable confines of U.S. and Canadian waters. While the species may be familiar (with the exception of that unicorn of oysters, the New Zealand Kiwa), the waters are not. You have the merroir of entire new oceans to explore. You can be the Bering of bivalves, poking your nose into Brittany's Belon River, savoring the salty burn of Baja, noodling around New Zealand. Ultimately, it may leave you with a newfound fondness for home and hearth. But you won't get that by staying in Iowa and shucking corn.

Preceding pages: The seawall at Cancale at low tide, with the massive oyster farms exposed; Gallic oyster farmer. Right: Pacific oysters, the workhorse of the French industry.

BELON
(France)

SPECIES European Flat

CULTIVATION Young Flat oysters are relayed from various locations in France to be finished in the Belon River in rectangular, walled finishing beds known as claires.

PRESENCE Although Belons come in a variety of sizes, most you see are flat disks the size of pocket watches, each holding a generous tablespoon of amber bivalve. The scaly brown shells feel prehistoric.

FLAVOR Comes on with the cedary tang of pine-needle tea, then sideswipes you like fermented tuna, then finishes with astringent walnut-skin notes.

OBTAINABILITY Even in France, Flats account for less than 2 percent of oyster production, and few of those have any right to call themselves Belon (though many do, especially in Brittany). Illegal to import into the United States (like all French oysters) and seldom seen in Canada. Get on your horse and start riding, Galahad. If you are into extreme thrills, go for a wild **Pied de Cheval**, as wide as a horse's hoof (well, maybe a pony's) and ten to twenty years old.

FOR MANY, THIS IS THE HOLY GRAIL OF OYSTERS, gleaming like a chalice over some far-off point of oyster enlightenment. Thus it has been for centuries, when French bon vivants began celebrating the extraordinary noisette flavors of oysters that bathed in the sacred waters of the Belon River, particularly the shallow coves that lap the stony shores of Riec-sur-Belon. Belons soon developed a reputation as the crème de la crème of oysters and, like Champagne, quickly became the most name-abused. Other French oyster regions are scandalous in their eagerness to call their Flats Belons, and even Maine has gotten in on the game. But a true Belon must undergo an *affinage* period in the Belon River, a skinny little estuary on the underside of the Brittany peninsula.

The Belon experience is unique. Wade onto a mudflat and stand there until your waders sink into the muck and you fear you will never escape the iodine suck of the salt marsh. That's Belon. The lasting impression is of touching your tongue to a battery terminal. Your taste buds can feel tingly for an hour. A few drops of lemon or mignonette help.

This is Europe's only native oyster, growing in its home waters, which is something very difficult to find nowadays, and it should be experienced for that alone, so that you can mind-meld with Roman emperors and Louis XIV and Casanova and all the other famous oysterheads. So go, pilgrim. Experience Belon. And when you get there, if you snoop around and follow the hand-drawn sign, you will reach the shore and, if you're lucky, before you will rise a blonde vision in a wool fisherman's hat. Her name is Anne de Belon, and she'd make a good stand-in for Joan of Arc. She is utterly devoted to the Belon oyster, as were her parents and grandparents before her, and if she deems you worthy she will sell you some, maybe even shuck them for you. And you will take them from her hand, and tilt the wild brine into your mouth, and then you will lie down at her feet on the cold, wet cement floor of her packinghouse, and your quest will be at an end.

CLEVEDON COAST

KAWAKAWA BAY,
NEW ZEALAND

SPECIES Pacific

CULTIVATION Wild spat is collected on wooden batons, which are nailed to long racks in the intertidal zone. Oysters are harvested at about one year of age.

PRESENCE So random and chunky in shape that it feels more like a rock than an oyster. Roller-coaster shells and gray-green accents mimic the New Zealand landscape.

FLAVOR Mild and musky, like salted Tibetan butter tea.

OBTAINABILITY Your window of space and time is summer in San Francisco or New York. In addition to Clevedon Coasts, New Zealand's **Coromandels** and **Kaiparas** are excellent summer options.

NEW ZEALAND SEEMS LIKE A HELL OF A LONG way to go to source your oysters, but when it's August and the local Pacifics are off-gassing like a cargo hold of dogfish, New Zealand starts to seem like an increasingly reasonable option. Summer here equals winter there, so the Kiwis come into their prime just as ours are going off. July through November is good for New Zealand oysters, but the first half of that period is when they are going to outshine the American stuff. They can be very good. Water temps that hover around 50 degrees and abundant phytoplankton make them very fat and very fruity.

Clevedon Coasts were started in the 1980s by the wonderfully named Callum McCallum, whose family had farmed sheep and cattle on Kawakawa Bay, an hour outside Auckland, for generations. McCallum hatched a unique cultivation system that has served him well ever since, taking advantage of New Zealand's abundant natural set of Pacific oysters.

Pacifics are not native to New Zealand. But in the 1950s, as barges left Japan carrying sections of Auckland's new Harbour Bridge, the local spat flattened itself against the barge hulls like ninjas and rode across the Pacific, deploying in New Zealand's bays. By the 1970s, Pacifics were well established on the North Island.

Kaipara Harbour, on the northern tip of the North Island, is their stronghold. Before the wild oysters spawn there, McCallum sets thousands of four-foot wooden batons in the water. The spat set on the batons, which are then transported to Kawakawa Bay and nailed directly onto racks in the intertidal zone, just a few feet offshore. A few hours out of the water each day reduces predation and fouling and levels out the oysters' growth rates. McCallum keeps many of the batons in tight bundles for months, to reduce the young oysters' access to food and stunt their growth. These replace the batons of market-sized oysters as they are ready, ensuring a steady supply of marketable oysters throughout the year. A mature rack makes a remarkable sight, a raised carpet of jagged green shell four feet wide and hundreds of feet long, with the occasional oystercatcher blissfully grazing the top.

From the stool side of the oyster bar, what matters most is that these oysters, with their natural genetics and noninterventionist upbringing, feel completely wild. The shells are full of dips and curves, much like the New Zealand road system, and the flavor has the same charm, unpredictable but full of happy surprises.

SUR-BÉLON

loise

GAULOISE

SPECIES Pacific

CULTIVATION Six-month-old seed is grown for six months in bags staked to French tables in the vast flats surrounding the town of Cancale, then finished in the Belon River for a minimum of two months.

PRESENCE Very plain-looking Pacific oysters with a nice golden tinge to the shells and a healthy barnacle set. Sometimes there is a touch of dusty purple on the bottom shell. The meats have contrasting white flesh and black rims.

FLAVOR An intensely saline seawater-up-the-nose burn quickly fades to the mild flavor of salted hazelnuts.

OBTAINABILITY Good in France and the UK; occasionally make their way to Canada. Contraband in the United States.

I ALWAYS THOUGHT THE NOISETTE flavor of Belon oysters had more to do with nature than nurture, but danged if some of that nutty thing doesn't get into La Gauloise, which is something you rarely find in a North American *gigas*. I prefer the chic, retro taste of Gauloises to Belons, and I find that their non-fruity, non-cucumbery profile makes them a particularly good match for European wines, which are more austere than their New World counterparts. What I'm saying is I surrender to this Gaul, and so should you.

GLACIER POINT

HALIBUT COVE,
ALASKA

SPECIES Pacific

CULTIVATION Suspended in trays from rafts in the deep, icy waters of Halibut Cove, and tumbled periodically to strengthen the shells.

PRESENCE Small and light but firm inside. Khaki meats, almost like Eastern oysters.

FLAVOR Full brine yields to a flowery, salmon-like finish reminiscent of popcorn.

OBTAINABILITY The great challenge of growing oysters in Alaska is, of course, getting those suckers to market. If you happen to be in Homer, Alaska, you'll find Glacier Points in most good restaurants. Better still, take the free ferry over to Halibut Cove for dinner at The Saltry, Alaska's best restaurant. Outside of Alaska, things are tougher but not hopeless: Boston's Pangea Shellfish distributes Glacier Points in the Northeast, and Hog Island occasionally features them in its Bay Area oyster bars.

ANYONE WHO'S SPENT TIME IN ALASKA KNOWS that the place is truly its own country, whatever the political map may say. As with its geography and populace, its oysters are outlandish enough to put it firmly in the "Overseas" chapter. I used to describe the finish of Alaska salmon as "oystery," but when I tasted my first Glacier Point, I realized that I had it backward. The finish of Glacier Points is salmony, which makes you wonder if the sweet, savory sea essence that defines Alaska gets into all its foods. Perhaps one can simply describe the flavor of both king salmon and Glacier Point oysters as "Alasky." Alasky is light and graceful, which goes against the burly frontier image Alaska likes to present to the world, but if you've ever knocked around the forty-ninth state in midsummer, you know there is a shimmery, dreamlike quality to the place, as if it were made of light instead of matter. Every Alaska oyster bottles a spoonful of this.

Glacier Points are farmed by Greg and Weatherly Bates in Halibut Cove (pop. 15, more in summer), a storybook hamlet a half hour's boat ride from the Homer Spit. They used to farm oysters in Maine, until they decided that was too tame. Now they farm amidst glaciers and bears that amble through their yard. For fun, they wrestle sharks in the shallows and get towed around the cove in their skiff by giant salmon. They had a semi-tame sea otter named Fat Rat who always hung around the oyster rafts, until he got eaten by a killer whale in 2014. Their daily adventure is simply farming oysters in this supersized environment. Sometimes glacial ice plows their rafts out to sea. Sometimes they're working by headlamp in suicidal winter gales. Bodies burn out fast in that environment, but the reward is an oyster like no other, a cocktail of arctic sweetness and glacial minerals animated by a single, plankton-mediated spark of the midnight sun.

KELLY GIGAS

GALWAY BAY, IRELAND

SPECIES Pacific

CULTIVATION Hatchery seed is grown out in mesh bags attached to racks placed low in the intertidal zone, where the tides of Galway Bay will cover them most of the time. Shaken regularly to promote shell strength and cup depth (or "train" them, as they say in Ireland), these are harvested at two to three years of age.

PRESENCE Stunning purple-striped shells with cups as long and deep as curraghs. The meats are downright porcelain, with swank black mantles. Surprisingly easy to shuck for a non-tumbled Pacific.

FLAVOR A clean wave of Jolly Rancher green apple candy fades into a dry white-tea finish.

OBTAINABILITY In Ireland, excellent. Canada is its second home. Try Boîte aux Huîtres in Montreal. Irish oysters are also all the rage in Asia. About the only place you won't find them is the good old U.S. of A.

KELLY NATIVE

GALWAY BAY, IRELAND

SPECIES European Flat

CULTIVATION Wild oysters are collected up and down Ireland's west coast and fattened in the Kelly family's finishing beds in Galway Bay's Killeenaran Inlet, where the Atlantic mixes with the fresh, mineral-rich waters of two rivers. At harvest these are a sobering five to six years of age. Savor slowly.

PRESENCE Dressed in humble earth tones, of unmemorable size, and not especially juicy, Kelly Natives, like Aran Island monks, give no hint of their fortitude.

FLAVOR Like a tomato rolled in turmeric, these are as volatile as curry. They'll have you thinking about them for some time.

OBTAINABILITY This is the best reason to attend the Galway Oyster Festival, where for two days this otherwise exceedingly rare oyster becomes as ubiquitous as Guinness. Thousands of Kelly Natives are slurped at the festival, and they are the official oyster for the world's premier shucking contest, which throws off contestants who cut their teeth on Pacifics and Easterns. Outside of Galway, your best bet is Patrick McMurray's Céilí Cottage in Toronto.

THE WORST-KEPT SECRET OF THE FRENCH OYSTER INDUSTRY is that many of its finest oysters are about as French as James Joyce was Parisian. They may have been finished on the French coast, but they are Irish through and through. Water quality is so much better on the west coast of the Emerald Isle, populations so much smaller, that it only makes sense to grow them there. But why ship to France at all? Are they somehow lacking some *je ne sais quoi* that only Gallic waters can impart? After tasting Kelly Gigas (left half of photo), you will say *non*, for these rival anything coming out of France. To me, they are like Kumamotos on steroids: same sweet, appley good nature, four times the size. Win, win. What they don't have are the cucumbery, vegetal, or fishy notes typical of most *gigas*; somehow Galway Bay strips it out of them. The Kelly family has been on to this secret for sixty years. For most of that time it was a local secret, best enjoyed at Moran's Oyster Cottage, or maybe Paddy Burkes, but now the world is on to them.

David McMillan, the pull-no-punches palate who has made Montreal's Joe Beef a requisite stop on the *huîtres* circuit, will tell you without hesitation that Kelly oysters are the Best. Ever. Period. I'll go so far as to say that their Flats (right half of photo) are the best of that audacious breed. Separated-at-birth twins to Nick Jones's Shoal Bay Flats, grown five thousand miles away, they are perhaps a tad more refined in flavor. But "refined" is a strange word to use with any Flat, and these are no exception. They are aggressively mineral, full of piss and iodine, with a hearty chew and a haunting tang. Still, though they will prickle your palate, they are the only Flats I know that won't leave it feeling like it just received shock therapy. Like their *gigas* neighbors, the lasting impression they leave is of *clarity*—something seekers have been prizing in Galway Bay since the first monastery was built on the Aran Islands in the fifth century. Those monks may well have fished a few of these out of the sea from time to time, and one can imagine the religious experience that ensued.

KIWA

SPECIES Bluff Oyster; aka Chilean Oyster; aka New Zealand Flat; aka *Ostrea chilensis*

CULTIVATION Hatched in Kono's own hatchery, these are grown out in unique lantern nets submerged in thirty feet of water in Port Underwood, reaching market size at about a year and a half of age—incredibly fast for a Flat.

PRESENCE Flat as a sand dollar. Feels like a Belon-Pacific cross, more saucer-shaped than a Pacific but more elongated than a Belon. Has the familiar scaly beige top of a Belon, and a mother-of-pearl bottom dabbed with rose.

FLAVOR As concentrated and strident as a mouthful of cartilaginous Worcestershire sauce.

OBTAINABILITY Very rare. First appeared at Waterbar, in San Francisco, in 2014. Rumor has it that Connie & Ted's in LA has also gotten in on the game.

THE NATIVE BLUFF OYSTER HAS ALWAYS been a huge deal in New Zealand. A Flat, like the Belon and Olympia, it was once found all over New Zealand's coastlines, but—stop me if you've heard this one before—was quickly overharvested after settlers arrived. It bounced back once harvests were limited, tanked in the 1980s when a parasite called *Bonamia* killed billions, then rebounded in the past decade, particularly around the nautical town of Bluff, on the southernmost tip of the South Island. Now harvests are pretty strong, and when Bluff Oyster Season (March to August) arrives, it makes the front page of the local papers. For years, people have told me that I hadn't lived if I hadn't experienced the Bluff oyster. Now, at last, I can begin my life, because a Maori-owned company called Kono has begun farming the Bluffies and exporting them to the States. The farming involves these funny circular trays that look like the kind of thing a waiter would use to deliver your Campari and soda, hanging nets, and a choice spot in the Marlborough Sounds, a fractal field of channels and islands where the tip of the South Island nearly touches the North Island. Sparse populations and deep, virtually infinite coves are a Flat oyster's dream. This is a very special treat, priced accordingly. Simply hack off your left hand and slide it over the bar to your server. In exchange, you will get to experience what is, pound for pound, the most ferocious Flat in the world. Think Floyd Mayweather Jr. with iodine on top.

Trivia for old-timers: You may remember an oyster called Chiloé, named for the island off the Chilean coast where it grows, that used to turn up at the Grand Central Oyster Bar and a few other places fifteen or twenty years ago. Same oyster. When the Chilean oyster industry collapsed, *Ostrea chilensis* disappeared from North American circles. The oyster is native to Chile, New Zealand, and nowhere else. It was probably a piece of driftwood that facilitated that first crossing, but I like to think it was some Pacific Islander with an outrigger and a culinary dream.

RECIPES

You know those amazing fund-raising dinners where a different celebrity chef sends out some extraordinary bite, course after course? That's the idea here.

I called on the rock stars of the oyster world, and they came through with their favorites. Think of it like a dinner party in bivalve heaven. Chef Andrew is pouring really dirty martinis, Chef Ryan brings his fried oysters, Chef Sandy turns up with his pan roast, Chef James is doing something dangerous with fire, Chef Renee comes in lugging a tureen of nettle soup with pickled oysters, and on it goes, and just when you think it's over, Chef Ryan comes *back* with his tartare. As host, I tried to fill in around the edges (drinks, mignonette). Bon app.

Eating very fresh raw oysters is the kind of intense, primordial, in-the-moment experience you remember forever. The subtleties of oyster flavor and the whole grappling-with-nature vibe don't

survive the heat. But cooked oysters do have great culinary appeal. As meltingly tender balls of protein, they take well to smoking and frying, and their uniquely marine brand of salt and umami enlivens and deepens anything it touches. As you'll see on the following pages, the trick is to cook them quickly. Like scallops and squid, a few minutes too many will cause the muscle proteins to link up into a virtually indestructible matrix. At that point, there's nothing for it but to cook them a lot longer to relax those matrices.

We haven't specified particular oysters in these recipes. The key is to use big ones. Oysters are mostly water, so they shrink significantly when cooked. An oyster that is way too large to eat raw is perfect for cooking. Pacific and Eastern oysters both work well. Using Kumamotos or Olympias would be insane. European Flats, so firm and flavorful, are my favorite culinary oysters of all. But don't go down that road lightly: They're an expensive habit.

ICED ROSÉ MIGNONETTE

ROWAN JACOBSEN, #10 POND, CALAIS

A mignonette sauce is simply acid, shallots, and pepper. Many recipes mix in a bit of white wine to round out the acid. I've never understood why they don't use rosé. So dry, so pretty. I use Eric Sussman's County Line rosé, knighted by the *New York Times* as California's go-to rosé, and, as it says on the label, "oyster-inspired," which means Eric wanted to craft the perfect wine to accompany his oyster habit. County Line is bone-dry but wonderfully aromatic, and a mystical shade of pink. It's all pinot noir. If you can't find County Line, look for another pinot-based rosé. You can combine these ingredients for a great room-temp mignonette, but to me granita-style makes all the difference. The ice crystals stay in the saddle all the way into your mouth, and then they burst like Pop Rocks.

Zest and juice from 1 lemon
1 cup dry rosé
1 shallot, peeled and finely minced
A few grinds of fresh pepper

1. Combine all ingredients in a bowl, then pour into a small, flat pan just wide enough that the liquid is about 1 inch deep.

2. Place the pan in a freezer. Every half hour until it freezes, scrape a fork through the liquid to break up the ice and prevent it from forming as a solid sheet. When it eventually freezes, it should look like shaved ice. Cover with plastic wrap.

3. To serve, ladle a small spoonful onto each oyster, or place a small bowl of the iced mignonette in the middle of the shucked oysters. Serve immediately.

Makes enough for several dozen oysters

ICE QUARTET

ANDREW TAYLOR, EVENTIDE OYSTER COMPANY, PORTLAND

When you order oysters at Eventide, they come with this snazzy quartet of accoutrements—further support for my theory that all oyster sauces are best served iced. The Kim Chi Ice is made with juice from Eventide's amazing house-made kim chi, but to keep this simple, we've gone with prepared kim chi here. Koreans have a tradition of adding raw oysters to kim chi brine to kick-start the fermentation process, so this even has historical/philosophical precedent.

Kim Chi Ice

1 package prepared or homemade kim chi

Strain off the kim chi liquid into a wide and shallow container and freeze. When thoroughly frozen, scrape with a fork to create a shaved ice.

Pickled Red Onion Ice

1 red onion, peeled
4 cups water
1 cup sugar
2 cups rice wine vinegar
1 tablespoon kosher salt

1. Shave the red onion thinly on a Japanese mandolin and place it in a container large enough to hold all ingredients.

2. Combine water, sugar, vinegar and salt in a pan and heat to boiling. Pour over the shaved red onion. Press the onion below the surface of the liquid and let cool at room temperature. Once at room temperature, place in the refrigerator to cool completely.

3. Strain off the liquid from the pickled red onions. (The onions can be used for the Oyster Slider recipe on page 276.) Put the liquid in a wide and shallow container and freeze. When thoroughly frozen, scrape with a fork to create a shaved ice.

Horseradish Ice

1¼ cups prepared horseradish
½ cup champagne vinegar
⅓ cup simple syrup
1¼ cups water

Combine all ingredients in a blender
and blend thoroughly. Strain into
a wide and shallow container
and freeze. When thoroughly frozen,
scrape with a fork to create a
shaved ice.

Tabasco Ice

1 standard 5-ounce bottle Tabasco
¼ cup simple syrup
1 cup water

Combine all ingredients in a bowl
and mix well. Pour into a wide and
shallow container and freeze.
When thoroughly frozen, scrape
with a fork to create a shaved ice.

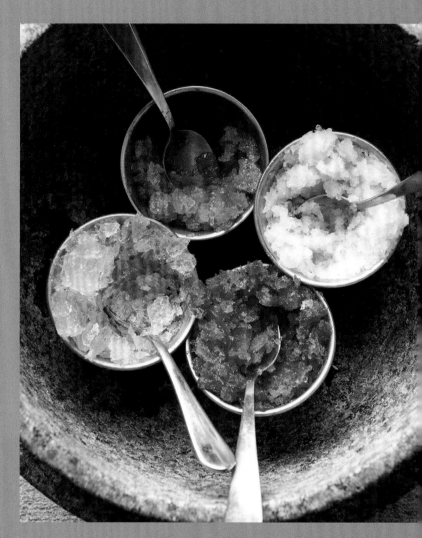

FIDDLEHEAD MIGNONETTE

STEPHEN RICHARDS, MINE OYSTER, BOOTHBAY HARBOR

Mine Oyster is two floors of unpretentious joie de vivre with a pinch-me view of Boothbay Harbor and a strategic location where the Damariscotta River meets the sea. This puts it just downriver from some of the planet's best bivalves. Chef Stephen Richards serves this mignonette only in spring, when the fiddleheads are up. It's his ode to that moment when winter's grip breaks, the oysters are starting to feed and fatten after their long nap, and Mainers start to believe that, against all signs to the contrary, life might go on. He recommends Maine sea salt, Maine fiddleheads, Cold River Maine vodka, and, of course, Damariscotta oysters.

10 fiddleheads, blanched and minced
¼ cup vodka
½ cup champagne vinegar
1 shallot, peeled and finely minced
2 tablespoons honey
A few grinds fresh pink peppercorns
1 drop harissa
1 pinch sea salt
Zest and juice from ½ lemon

Whisk together all ingredients in a small, nonreactive stainless-steel bowl.

Makes enough for dozens of oysters

FRIED OYSTERS
with Cucumbers and Pickled-Pepper Mayonnaise

RYAN PREWITT, PÊCHE, NEW ORLEANS

Pêche has been a Miracle on Magazine Street since it opened its doors in 2013, reinventing the Gulf Coast approach to seafood and quickly getting the nods from the James Beard Foundation for Best Chef in the South and Best New Restaurant in the country. This is where you go in New Orleans to eat a whole fish that was just dropped off at the back door by the fisherman, and to discover oysters from the new wave of Gulf Coast visionaries. This dish rings all the dopamine receptors: sweet, sour, salty, savory, spicy, crunchy, juicy, pretty. If you don't have a deep fryer, you can fry the oysters in a heavy pot in oil deep enough to submerge them.

For Pickled Peppers
1 pound hot banana peppers, sliced into rings
1 yellow onion, thinly sliced
2 cups cider vinegar
2 cups white vinegar
¾ cup sugar
1 tablespoon salt

For Cucumbers
2 small cucumbers, or enough to make about 2 cups,
    cut into ¼-inch-thick rounds
1 small red onion, thinly sliced
½ cup mint leaves, torn
2 tablespoons lemon juice
1 teaspoon salt
1 teaspoon sugar

For Pickled-Pepper Mayonnaise
1 cup mayonnaise
½ cup pickled peppers (above), chopped
2 garlic cloves, minced
4 tablespoons chili vinegar

For Oysters
Oil for frying
24 oysters, shucked, held in their liquor
2 cups cornmeal
4 cups white flour
Salt
Finely ground black pepper

1. Make the pickled peppers ahead of time. Heat the vinegars, sugar, and salt to a rolling boil. Pour over peppers and onions. Allow to sit at room temperature for a few hours or overnight.

2. Combine the cucumbers, onion, mint leaves, lemon juice, salt, and sugar in a bowl and allow to sit at room temperature for about 10 minutes.

3. Combine the ingredients for the pickled-pepper mayonnaise. (You will have some pickled peppers left over for another purpose.) The mayonnaise should be pourable.

4. Heat a deep fryer to 350 degrees. Combine the cornmeal and flour in a large bowl. Remove oysters from their liquor and toss them around in the flour mixture so they are totally covered.

5. Fry the oysters, in batches if necessary, until lightly golden brown and crispy, about 2 to 3 minutes. Remove to a towel-lined tray and season with salt and black pepper.

6. Cover the bottom of a large platter with the cucumber mixture, then place the hot fried oysters on top. Drizzle mayonnaise on top and serve.

Makes 4 servings

FRIED OYSTERS, *James Gang-Style*

LISSA JAMES MONBERG,
HAMA HAMA OYSTER SALOON, HOOD CANAL

Someday, if you are very lucky, you will spend a night in the Hama Hama cabin. And if you are really, really fortunate, Lissa James will fry oysters for you while you are there. It happened to me once, and I watched Lissa break all my rules. Cook as lightly as possible? The James Gang parboils first, then fries the hell out of them. Lissa also favors premade breading and a healthy dollop of tartar sauce at the end. And they are utterly delicious. It could have been the soaring evergreens around us or the thundering Hamma Hamma River beside us, but I'm pretty sure these would be delicious in Detroit, too.

Shucked Oysters
Flour-based breading (Lissa recommends Willabay Breading, available online)
High-heat oil, such as canola, for frying
Lemon wedges, tartar sauce, and hot sauce for serving

1. Put the oysters in a pot of water and bring to a boil. Once it boils, turn off the heat and drain the oysters in a colander. Rinse them with water just so they're cool to the touch. Do not pat them dry, as a little moisture is necessary for the breading to stick.

2. Roll the oysters in your favorite flour-based seafood breading. If you're using a panko or other crusty breading, you'll need to be a little more careful with how you bread the oysters, and should probably roll them in flour and then dunk them in an egg wash (beaten egg plus a tablespoon of water or milk) before rolling them in the panko. Or you can add wheat flour and cornmeal to the panko until it looks like something that will stick without a wash.

3. Put the breaded oysters on a plate and let them sit in a refrigerator for at least 20 minutes. Then pan fry them in a high-heat oil until they're crispy and hot. Serve with lemon wedges, tartar, and hot sauce.

Plan on 6 oysters per person

SMOKED OYSTERS
with Crème Fraîche and Saltines

MIKE LATA, THE ORDINARY, CHARLESTON

This sets a new bar for smoked oysters, as the southern foodways maven John T. Edge made clear when he named it to his Top Ten Dishes of 2014 in *Garden & Gun* magazine. "Those oysters are sophisticated and understated," he said. "They are haute and unfettered. They are bliss." You can smoke these on an outdoor smoker instead of a stovetop, but you'll obviously need more hickory chips.

12 saltine crackers
1 tablespoon unsalted butter, melted
¼ teaspoon Old Bay seasoning
2 teaspoons toasted whole
    coriander seeds
½ cup crème fraîche
¼ teaspoon finely grated
    lemon zest
1½ tablespoons hickory chips
1 dozen oysters on the half shell,
    liquor reserved
1 tablespoon finely chopped heart
    of celery, leaves included
2 teaspoons minced shallots
1 teaspoon finely chopped chives
1 tablespoon fresh lemon juice
1 tablespoon extra-virgin olive oil
Fresh hot sauce for serving (adjacent)

1. Preheat the oven to 375 degrees.

2. Place the saltine crackers on a parchment-lined baking sheet. Brush both sides with melted butter and bake until golden brown, about 5 minutes. Remove from the oven and immediately sprinkle with Old Bay seasoning. Let cool.

3. Grind the coriander seeds and combine them with the crème fraîche and lemon zest. Whisk gently to incorporate. Refrigerate.

4. Place the hickory chips in a small pile in the center of the base of a stovetop smoker. Place a perforated pan on top of the wood chips. Place a wire rack on top of the perforated pan. Place the oysters, still in their shells, on the wire rack. Place the smoker, with the lid slightly open, on a burner set to medium heat. When the first sign of smoke rises, close the lid and smoke the oysters for 10 minutes.

5. Remove the oysters and shuck into a bowl, taking care to include as much of the "liquor" or juice as possible. Add the celery, shallots, chives, lemon juice, and olive oil and mix gently.

6. Serve with the saltines, crème fraîche, and fresh hot sauce.

Makes 4 servings

Fresh Hot Sauce
1 pound cayenne or jalapeno peppers, chopped
2 tablespoons kosher salt
½ cup white wine vinegar

Place all of the ingredients in a blender and purée. Strain.

BBQ BOURBON CHIPOTLE OYSTERS

GARRET HAMNER, HOG ISLAND OYSTER BAR, TOMALES BAY

This is a specialty of Hog Island's retail farm manager, Garret Hamner. The rich/sweet/salty/spicy combo is a knockout, especially with Hog Island Sweetwaters or another meaty Pacific oyster. Best enjoyed on the shores of Tomales Bay with a Lagunitas Pils in hand, but pretty damn good in any kitchen anywhere.

½ cup brown sugar
½ cup bourbon
½ pound (two sticks) unsalted butter, softened to room temperature
¾ cup garlic, minced
Half a 10-ounce can of chopped chipotle chilies in adobo sauce
50 oysters in the shell

1. In a medium bowl, dissolve the brown sugar into the bourbon. Add the butter, garlic, and chipotles and mix well, though it will remain a bit lumpy in texture. (You can use a food processor if you prefer.)

2. Lay out a piece of parchment paper and pile the bourbon-chipotle butter along the center, forming a "log" the dimensions of a foot-long stick of butter. Wrap the butter, folding it into a log shape, and refrigerate for at least an hour. (Note: You can skip the log step and scoop the butter mixture straight out of the bowl onto the oysters, but the log makes for ease of use when cooking.)

3. Shuck the oysters, keeping them in their bottom shells.

4. When ready to barbecue, fire up your grill to medium. Shuck the oysters. Remove the bourbon-chipotle butter from the fridge and cut it into thin pats, about ¼-inch. Place a pat of butter on each shucked oyster and place the oysters on the grill. Open a cold one and wait for the butter to melt and start to bubble. Let the oysters sizzle and bubble for about one minute, then remove them from the grill, let cool for a brief moment, and enjoy!

Serves 5 to 10 friends

DRIFTWOOD-GRILLED OYSTERS
with Lardo Crudo

DAN MEISER AND JAMES WAYMAN, OYSTER CLUB, MYSTIC

This recipe sprang into the universe in 2015 when Dan Meiser and James Wayman of Connecticut's Oyster Club were visiting Steve and Sarah Malinowski of Fishers Island oysters. They found themselves on the beautiful, bony beachside of Fishers Island. Dried wood everywhere. They had oysters, of course. And somebody found a hunk of lardo crudo in his pocket. Presto. The lardo recipe comes via Dario Cecchini, the Tuscan butcher immortalized by Bill Buford in *Heat*. When you walk into Cecchini's Panzano shop, he will hand you a glass of Chianti and a piece of bread slathered with lardo crudo—raw back fat seasoned with rosemary and pepper and slightly cured with salt and vinegar. "On a piece of toast it blows butter out of the water," says Dan Meiser. "It's the stuff of gods." If you don't want to make your own lardo crudo, you can probably score some from your local hipster butcher. If you don't have driftwood, any hardwood will do. If you don't have a beach, you can substitute your backyard. If you don't have an ocean, use a kiddie pool, but it's not the same.

For lardo crudo
1 pound high quality pork back fat, cut into one-inch cubes
1 tablespoon fine sea salt
1 tablespoon freshly ground black pepper
2 tablespoons fresh rosemary leaves
½ teaspoon high-quality wine vinegar

For oysters
6 oysters per person, in shell
1 armful driftwood or other dry hardwood
1 beach
1 ocean
Lemon wedges or hot sauce for serving (optional)

1. Make the lardo. In a large bowl, toss together the back fat, salt, pepper, rosemary, and vinegar until evenly coated. Place in a refrigerator for at least two hours, or even better overnight.

2. Grind through a ¹⁄₁₆-inch die on a meat grinder. Then massage the mix vigorously with your bare hands for at least 5 minutes, until the heat from your hands begins to melt the fat.

3. Pack into a glass jar and store in the refrigerator for up to one month.

4. When you're ready to make the oysters, build a roaring fire, preferably near the ocean, with driftwood or hardwood. A mix of oak and cherry or another fruit wood is nice. Let the fire subside to coals and cover with a grate.

5. Put the oysters on the grate for approximately 2 minutes or until you see a little steam escape from the shells. Using tongs, pull them aside and open immediately. Top with a generous dollop of the lardo crudo and place back on the fire until it melts over the top of the oysters. Serve immediately, finished with a splash of lemon juice or hot sauce if you want. Eat on the beach, tossing the shells back into the waves, until it's too dark to see.

Makes enough for dozens of oysters

NETTLE SOUP *with* PICKLED OYSTERS

RENEE ERICKSON AND BOBBY PALMQUIST,
THE WALRUS AND THE CARPENTER, SEATTLE

The banks of the Hamma Hamma River are lined with stinging nettles, and the delta is lined with fat oysters (which the Hama Hama Company has been known to pickle); this recipe channels those Olympic Peninsula energies into a single dish. Nettles are the greatest of wild greens, and there's no perfect substitute for their deep yet mild flavor and brilliant color, but Swiss chard or spinach would certainly get the job done. Renee, who seems to always get life's small details just right, sometimes serves this with fried oysters or fried mussels, but I like how the pickled oysters give a homey touch and a sharp counterpoint to the gentle soup.

1 tablespoon canola oil
1 tablespoon butter
1 pound onion, peeled and chopped
½ pound carrot, peeled and chopped
½ pound celery root, peeled and chopped
1 pound potatoes, peeled and chopped
1 quart of fish stock
¼ pound nettles, stalks removed
Salt
Pickled oysters (recipe adjacent)

1. Heat the oil and butter in a pot over medium heat. Add the onion, carrots, celery root, and potatoes and sweat them until soft but not browned, about 5–10 minutes.

2. Add the stock and simmer until the veggies are really soft, about 30 minutes, adding the nettles toward the end of the cooking time.

3. Purée in batches in a food processor or using an immersion blender. Strain and season with salt.

4. Garnish with pickled oysters.

Makes 8 servings

Pickled Oysters

2 dozen shucked Olympia
  or Kumamoto oysters in
  their liquor
1 cup champagne vinegar
½ cup water
6 peppercorns
1 bay leaf
2 tablespoons sugar
1 garlic clove, peeled
  and sliced in half
½ teaspoon salt
A few sprigs fresh dill

1. In a pan, cook the oysters in their
liquid over medium heat for 1–2
minutes, until their edges begin to
ruffle. Remove from heat and cool in
their liquid.

2. In a separate sauce pan, combine
all ingredients except the oysters
and the dill. Bring to a boil and simmer for 2–3 minutes. Turn off heat
and let cool.

3. When completely cool, add in the
fresh dill. Strain the oysters from
their liquid and place in the pickle
brine. Store them overnight and
then serve as a garnish with the
soup. Renee likes to dress the oysters
in olive oil and a pinch of fleur
de sel. Use any remaining oysters within a day or two,
before the pickling acid makes them mushy.

OYSTER PAN ROAST

SANDY INGBER, GRAND CENTRAL OYSTER BAR, NEW YORK

This dish was on the menu the day the Grand Central Oyster Bar first opened its subterranean doors in 1913. It's one of those buttoned-down, airtight, retro dishes that really can't be improved upon, and it's actually been canonized by *New York* magazine as the greatest NYC restaurant dish of all time. A big part of its success is the unique steam kettle it gets cooked in. If you've never seen these in action, you owe it to yourself to grab a seat at the bar on your next layover in Grand Central and watch the show. Don't blink: It takes a whopping 2.5 minutes. The double-jacketed steam kettles are on swivels and pipe bona fide New York City steam between their steel walls, so the heat transfer comes from every square inch. The best you can do at home is to get your pan very hot and to make espresso-machine noises for verisimilitude.

¼ cup clam juice
1 tablespoon unsalted butter
½ teaspoon Worcestershire sauce
¼ teaspoon celery salt
¼ teaspoon sweet Hungarian paprika,
   plus additional for garnish
6 large Eastern oysters, shucked, with their liquor
3 tablespoons Heinz chili sauce
2 cups half-and-half
1 slice white bread, toasted, crusts removed
Oyster crackers

1. Combine the clam juice, butter, Worcestershire sauce, celery salt, and paprika in a saucepan over high heat. When the butter melts, add the oysters and their liquor and cook, stirring, until the edges of the oysters begin to ruffle. Remove the oysters with a slotted spoon and keep warm. Stir in the chili sauce and half-and-half and cook, stirring often, until it is about to come to a boil. Return the oysters to the pan and turn off the heat.

2. Put the toast into a warmed soup plate and pour in the pan roast. Garnish with a shake of paprika and serve immediately, with oyster crackers.

Makes 1 decadent serving

WINTER OYSTER STEW

PERRY RASO, MATUNUCK OYSTER BAR, MATUNUCK

I first had this after a cold day on the water, and I'm sure the inspiration for it must have been similar. Nothing chills your marrow like working an oyster farm in winter. No dry suit yet invented can keep that 40-degree water and relentless wind from sucking the BTUs out of your soul. The Matunuck oyster farm is on the pond just outside the restaurant, and I guarantee more than once the crew has dragged themselves in from the barge and lifted their eyes in thanks when steaming bowls of this rich soul sustenance appeared before them. You can prep this in advance by doing the first three steps, then bringing the soup back to a simmer and adding the oysters just before service.

4 tablespoons unsalted butter, divided
2 small shallots, minced
1 bunch rosemary, roughly chopped
4 cups heavy cream
2 cups light cream
1 cup small diced parsnips
1 cup small diced sweet potatoes
2 tablespoons all-purpose flour
2 teaspoons Worcestershire sauce
1 teaspoon Tabasco
Salt and pepper to taste
2 dozen fresh shucked oysters, liquor reserved

1. Sauté 2 tablespoons of the butter with shallots and rosemary over medium to low heat in a small stock pot or pan for 10–15 minutes, until caramelized. Add the light and heavy cream and simmer for 10 more minutes. *Do not boil* even for a second. Remove from heat and strain through a fine mesh strainer.

2. In a 3 or 4-quart heavy pan, sauté the remaining 2 tablespoons of butter over low heat until melted. Add the parsnips and sweet potatoes and sauté until slightly soft. Add the flour and stir to combine. Slowly add the cream mixture to the pan and return to a simmer, stirring.

3. Add the oyster liquor and season with the Worcestershire, Tabasco, and salt and pepper. Simmer for 5 minutes and adjust the seasoning as desired. Turn off the heat.

4. Add the oysters and let them poach for about a minute. Serve immediately.

Makes 4 servings

OYSTER SLIDERS

JEREMY SEWALL, ISLAND CREEK OYSTER BAR, BOSTON

I always intend to order something new when I go to ICOB. I have grand visions of being less predictable, but then the table beside me gets a brace of sliders and I crumble. It's just hard to resist that perfect evening formula: raw oysters, beer, sliders, beer. If you ever get the chance to make these with European Flat oysters, do.

1 small red onion, peeled and sliced thin
¼ cup white wine vinegar
¼ cup sugar
¼ cup mayonnaise
2 tablespoons lime juice
1 teaspoon Tabasco sauce
8 large oysters, shucked
¼ cup flour
1 egg
¼ cup panko
1 cup canola oil
Salt and pepper to taste
8 mini-brioche or similar rolls
½ cup baby arugula

1. Mix the sliced red onion with the vinegar and sugar and let sit at room temperature for about two hours, mixing every 15 minutes. The onions will wilt and turn a pink color when ready. Drain from the liquid.

2. Meanwhile, mix the mayonnaise with lime juice and Tabasco sauce and chill until ready to use.

3. Dredge each oyster in flour, shaking off any excess, then dredge in egg and then panko. Put breaded oysters on a plate and refrigerate for 15 minutes.

4. In a heavy sauté pan, heat canola oil up over medium heat. Fry each breaded oyster on both sides until golden brown, about 1 minute per side. Carefully remove the oysters from the pan to a plate lined with a paper towel. Season with salt and pepper.

5. To assemble, slice open each roll. On the bottom half, spread 1 teaspoon of the mayonnaise, add a few slices of pickled onion and a few leaves of baby arugula, and top with the warm oyster. Serve as a bite-sized sandwich or appetizer.

Makes 8 sliders

STEAK TARTARE *with* SMOKED OYSTER MAYONNAISE

RYAN PREWITT, PÊCHE, NEW ORLEANS

My original plan to feature one recipe each from my favorite oyster chefs crumbled when Ryan sent this second recipe. No way this wasn't going in the book. If you don't want to deal with smoking your own oysters, you can use the canned kind, but be careful: The ones from China are dreck. Much better to order Hama Hamas or Willapas online.

For smoked oyster mayonnaise
6 oysters, on the half shell with liquor
   (or a tin of high-quality
   smoked oysters)
¾ cup mayonnaise

For tartare base
3 cloves garlic, minced
3 anchovy fillets, minced
2 tablespoon capers, rinsed
   and minced
3 tablespoons Dijon mustard
½ teaspoon Tabasco
¼ teaspoon Worcestershire sauce

1 pound top-quality sirloin, trimmed of any sinew
4 farm egg yolks
2 teaspoons salt
½ teaspoon black pepper
½ cup thin-sliced celery hearts
¼ cup thin-sliced parsley
1 tablespoon lemon juice
1 loaf ciabatta or other rustic bread

1. Heat a smoker to about 200 degrees. Build a very smoky fire, place the oyster in their shells inside, and close the lid tightly. Cook until the oysters are firm to the touch and have taken on the color of the smoke. Cool completely. (As an alternative, you can use commercial smoked oysters.)

2. In a food processor, purée the oysters and any remaining liquor with the mayonnaise. Scrape into a bowl.

3. Make the tartare base. In a food processor, purée the garlic, anchovies, capers, mustard, Tabasco, and Worcestershire.

4. Slice the sirloin very thinly, then dice it as small as you can. Combine it with 2 tablespoons of the tartare base (reserve the rest for another purpose), the egg yolks, and the salt and pepper. Adjust the seasoning.

5. Combine the celery, parsley, and lemon juice.

6. Slice the ciabatta ½-inch thick and toast on a grill or in the oven. When the bread is toasted and still hot, smear on a generous amount of the oyster mayonnaise. Top with a dollop of tartare and some of the celery mixture.

Serves 6 as an hors d'oeuvre

KAKI MESHI

ADRIENNE ANDERSON, COLUMBIA PRODUCTS STUDIO, BROOKLYN

I turn over this headnote to stylist and guest host Adrienne: "Most cooking relies on the senses of sight, smell, touch, and time. Great rice is all about sound. You must not peek under the lid: just listen to the water. There's even a Japanese nursery rhyme about it: *Hajime choro choro / Naka pappa / Akago naite mo / Futa toru na.* This roughly translates to *First it bubbles / Then it hisses / Even if the baby is crying / Don't remove the lid.* (An older, rarer, harsher version translates to *First a slow fire / Then a blazing fire / Don't remove the lid / Even if your parents are dying.*) Kaki Meshi is only two things: oysters and rice. Learning to prepare each one perfectly so that they meld to an even greater whole is probably a lifetime pursuit. This recipe is a good place to start. And if you listen closely enough while you're cooking, you'll hear the sound of the sea."

2 cups short-grain Japanese rice
24 oysters
¼ cup mirin
3 tablespoons soy sauce
3 tablespoons rice wine vinegar
1 tablespoon fresh grated ginger
1 tablespoon fresh grated horseradish
1½ cups dashi
1 bunch scallions, thinly sliced
1 cup grated daikon (optional)
Sansho pepper (optional)

1. Rinse the rice, place it in a bowl, and cover it in a few inches of water to soak for at least 30 minutes.

2. Meanwhile, prepare everything else. If using whole oysters, shuck them and reserve the liquor. If using pre-shucked oysters, drain them and reserve the liquor. If you are a traditionalist, you can rub the meats gently in grated daikon to freshen them.

3. In a medium bowl, mix the mirin, soy, rice wine vinegar, grated ginger, and grated horseradish.

4. Add the reserved oyster liquor to the dashi and bring to a gentle boil. Submerge the oysters and lower the heat. Poach just until their edges ruffle, about one minute. Remove the oysters with a slotted spoon and add them to the mirin/soy/vinegar/ginger/horseradish mixture. Set aside while preparing the rice.

5. Measure out 2 cups of the dashi poaching liquid into a medium saucepan with tall sides and a tight-fitting lid. (If you have less than 2 cups of liquid, add water.) Strain the rice and discard its soaking water. Add the strained rice to the dashi.

6. Cover the saucepan with its lid and place on a high flame. Sit. Listen. Do not remove the lid. After 5 minutes or so, you'll hear the bubbling. It sounds like a gentle rain beginning to fall. Reduce the flame to low. Do not remove the lid. Continue to listen. The rice will begin hissing like a winter wind. When it dies down, after about 15 minutes, turn the heat to high for a few moments to blast the remaining water from the bottom of the pan. Then shut off the heat completely and let the rice sit for 20 minutes. Do not remove the lid.

7. Remove the lid. Turn the rice with a wet wooden paddle and scoop it into bowls. Spoon the reserved oysters over the rice with however much of their soaking liquid you like. Top with sliced scallions (the more the better) and some sansho pepper if you happen to have it. Eat silently, like an oyster.

Makes 4 servings

CHUPACABRA'S DELIGHT

ROWAN JACOBSEN AND ADRIENNE ANDERSON, #10 POND, CALAIS

The Chupacabra is a much-feared cryptid of Latin American wastelands known for its proclivity for sucking goat blood. Hence the name: *chupar* (to suck) + cabra (*goat*). Less known is that the Chupacabra originally evolved to suck blood oranges in Sicily, where it was known as *strambino di sanguinello* ("little orange-sucking weirdo"). For this drink, all you really need to know is that the marriage of the Chupacabra's original quarry and the booze of its adopted homeland is dangerously good with oysters—especially when you add in Clamato, another Latin American staple. You can use tequila blanco, too, but it won't have the smokiness of an artisanal mezcal, which is cooked over open fires, and it won't taste like a murder victim (see Introduction). If not serving with oysters (or if your oysters aren't that briny), glaze the rims of the glasses with sea salt.

1 cup good mezcal (such as Del Maguey Vida)
2 cups Clamato
1½ cups blood orange juice
Juice of 2 lemons
2 teaspoons sriracha
Ice cubes
1 blood orange, sliced into wedges (for garnish)

1. Mix mezcal, Clamato, blood orange juice, lemon juice, and sriracha in a pitcher. Stir well.

2. Fill four tumblers with ice, pour in the evil brew, and garnish with a wedge of blood orange. Serve with raw, vulnerable oysters on the half shell before noon.

Makes 4 drinks

DIRTY DIRTY MARTINI

ANDREW TAYLOR, EVENTIDE OYSTER COMPANY, PORTLAND

So saline. So savory.
So dangerous.

3 ounces gin
½ ounce olive brine
½ ounce oyster brine
1 dash hot sauce

Combine all ingredients in mixing glass or cocktail shaker. Add ice. Shake vigorously and strain into chilled martini glass. Garnish with an olive. Or two.

THE OYSTER OASIS: MY GO-TO PLACES

WHAT MAKES A GREAT OYSTER BAR? WELL, THERE'S NO ONE MODEL. There are those that carry twenty-five varieties of oysters and allow you to be the ultimate barstool traveler. There are those with life-changing lists of obscure oyster wines. There are ones that make you feel like you're in Paris, and ones that make you feel like you're on an oyster farm. If it makes you feel like a Rat Packer, zinc bar and shiny ice and a martini in your hand, that's pretty nice; and if it makes you feel like the sketchiest sketchball that ever oozed along the boardwalk, that's kinda nice, too. Ultimately, the one thing the great ones have in common is that they know and love oysters: They serve them very fresh, shuck them very well, and have very strong opinions on the matter. There are lots of other great places in North America—and more every day—but these are the ones I know and love.

AQUAGRILL, NEW YORK CITY
The Sneetches have rushed off to have the star tattoos removed from their bellies in Bushwick, but Aquagrill continues to curate one of the best oyster collections in the city, as it has done without fail for twenty years.

B&G OYSTERS, BOSTON
Subterranean, as they all once were. Wicked wines.

BLUE PLATE OYSTERETTE, LOS ANGELES AND SANTA MONICA
A Yankee oasis in SoCal, from the lobsters to the *virginicas*.

LA BOITE AUX HUÎTRES, MONTREAL
Cozy oyster shop tucked into the corner of Jean Talon Market, run by a family with the sea in its veins. Spectacular selection of oysters from the U.S., Canada, and Ireland, including rare Maritime finds like Quebec's **Tresor du Large** and Nova Scotia's **Ruisseau**. Sit at the little counter, point, and they'll shuck on the spot and slide your little wooden box of oysters before you.

CLADDAGH OYSTER HOUSE, CHARLOTTETOWN, PEI
Lots of dark wood and bright oysters— PEI's best selection.

COASTAL PROVISIONS OYSTER BAR, SOUTHERN SHORES, NC
Dan Lewis's breakthrough oyster bar highlights the great new oysters being produced in North Carolina, along with classics from far and near.

CULL & PISTOL, NEW YORK CITY
A spot of Zen amidst Chelsea Market's bedlam. Cull & Pistol is the restaurant claw of The Lobster Place, the seafood shop that seems to costar in every show ever filmed for the Food Network, whose studios occupy the floors above. Make your way through the Guy Fieri–crazed throngs, turn right at the glowing waterfall, and melt into polished service, perfect oysters, and a meaningful moment.

ELLIOTT'S OYSTER HOUSE, SEATTLE
Long before the hipsters discovered oysters or farm-to-table, Elliott's was lining its waterfront bar with boxes of squeaky-clean oysters, each labeled

by provenance and cultivation technique. Way, way ahead of the curve. For twenty-five years, the premier oyster event in America has been their Oyster New Year, held every November (please take note, all you misguided summer oyster festivals). Thirty-plus varieties of Washington oysters, often shucked by the farmers, plus a flood of Northwest beer and wine, and the Most Beautiful Oyster competition. All proceeds benefit the fab Puget Sound Restoration Fund.

EVENTIDE, PORTLAND, ME
Everything an oyster bar should be, and nothing an oyster bar shouldn't.

GRAND CENTRAL OYSTER BAR, NEW YORK
The granddaddy of them all. Please don't change a thing. Ever.

HAMA HAMA OYSTER SALOON, ELDON, WA
Sit at the open-air bar, watching the guys haul crates of oysters off the Hamma Hamma Delta, with the Olympic Peninsula at your back and an afternoon of beer and brine before you.

HANK'S OYSTER BAR, WASHINGTON, DC
Jamie Leeds named her pitch-perfect oyster bar for her dad, Hank Wolfe Leeds, who's also honored in the naming of the Salty Wolfe, a Chincoteague-style salt bomb from the Eastern Shore. The bar's other proprietary oyster, Hayden's Reef (named for Jamie's son), is a big, sweet Chesapeake-style oyster grown to her specs (high in the water column, so it won't be salty) in Virginia's Nomini Creek.

HOG ISLAND OYSTER COMPANY, MARSHALL, CA
When Hog Island began selling oysters out its back door in 1988, it had no idea it was on its way to "destination location" status. It turned out (retrospect: duh!) that the combo of fresh oysters, picnic tables, grills, and a seaside spot was pretty much exactly what everybody in the world was looking for, and the place has been mobbed ever since. Not half as mobbed, however, as Hog Island Oyster Bar in San Francisco's Ferry Building, which must do more business than any oyster bar in the country not named Grand Central. Funny story: When Hog Island first agreed to be an anchor tenant in the revived Ferry Building in the late 1990s, they and the other anchor tenants were so skeptical of the area's commercial potential that they added special opt-out clauses to their leases. (Retrospect: duh!)

ISLAND CREEK OYSTER BAR, BOSTON
A revelation when it appeared in 2010, ICOB did a few things that had never been done before. It was owned by a grower, it worked directly with growers all over New England, it listed information about growers and locations directly on its menu, and it trained a staff that could act as oyster sommeliers, finding the right molluscan match for every customer. Now with two branches—plus two Row 34s, its beer-centric sister spot—the world has become Island Creek's oyster.

JOE BEEF, MONTREAL
Dangerously addictive. At first, you just stop in for tiny doses. A plate of Sawmill Bays here, a bottle of Chablis there. Then, pretty soon, your wallet always seems to be empty, you can't remember the last time you didn't come here, and you're wondering if you really just saw a bison in the bathroom. Look for Vanya, who teleports between Joe Beef and Vin Papillon next door, and who knows all the things about oysters, wine, and life that you wish you did.

L&E OYSTER BAR, LOS ANGELES
Actually feels like a cozy neighborhood place, because it is. Airy, friendly, smart. Love the light boxes.

LITTLE CREEK OYSTERS, GREENPORT, NY
No better place to take the pulse of the Long Island oyster scene than on the front porch of this waterfront shack, shucking your own.

MAISON PREMIERE, BROOKLYN
The dollar oysters at happy hour get all the attention, but to me, the real draws are the dizzying selection and the garden out back, where the escape to the fin de siècle French Quarter feels complete, and wise. More absinthe, please.

MATUNUCK OYSTER BAR, SOUTH KINGSTOWN, RI
What a spot. Matunuck hangs over a churning aquamarine inlet where the Atlantic Ocean pours into Potter Pond. Matunuck Oyster Farm glints on the pond, and a barge goes back and forth, ferrying fresh oysters. Owner Perry Raso lives in a cove around the corner in Captain John Potter's 1740 Cape masterpiece and grows all the vegetables for the restaurant in his backyard. Matunucks are always on the menu, usually accompanied by a handful of their Rhode Island buddies.

MINE OYSTER, BOOTHBAY HARBOR, ME
Owner Ralph Smith, an oyster fanatic, has made Glidden Points his house oyster, which is kind of like pouring Château Latour by the carafe. Yet, so far away from the power centers of civilization, it remains a well-kept secret.

OLD EBBITT GRILL, WASHINGTON, DC
Power spot next to the White House. Half the country's business is decided in the interstices of their weekend-long Oyster Riot in late November, when a thousand people a night schmooze amidst limitless oysters, wine, and tunes, proving that there is no lobbyist like a *virginica*. This is the only place I know that tests every batch of oysters it receives for bacterial count.

THE ORDINARY, CHARLESTON
Actually fulfills the fantasy that you're going to walk into an oyster bar and discover something totally new. Capers Blades, Phat Ladies—it's a whole different lexicon. New England native Mike Lata has been Charleston's oyster point man for years; he

knows what's notable up and down the coast, and works closely with oystermen to keep it coming.

OYSTER CLUB, MYSTIC, CT
Club indeed: local oysters only, no outsiders allowed. Out back there's The Treehouse, a deck perched high over the restaurant, where Chef James Wayman grills seafood over a wood fire during summer. Smoke + sea breeze = ecstasy.

THE OYSTER GIRLS, MARIN COUNTY
Traveling raw bar crewed by sisters Aluxa and Jaz Lalicker and their loyal femmes. Top Tomales Bay oysters and chic shucking. They pop up throughout the Bay Area and have a standing Sunday afternoon gig at Iron Horse Vineyards in Sebastopol.

PASCAL'S MANALE, NEW ORLEANS
Buy a token that's worth a dozen oysters, then walk over to the stand-alone oyster bar, hand it to Thomas "Uptown T" Stewart, and let the show begin. (It's been running for twenty-five years.) The oysters will be Louisianans and he'll keep piling them up on the bar and razzing you until you wave your hands in surrender.

PÊCHE, NEW ORLEANS
Best oysters in New Orleans. Need I say more? Ask the shuckers about their highly unorthodox knife-sharpening technique.

SALTWATER OYSTER DEPOT, INVERNESS, CA

Proprietor Luc Chamberland is the Lorax of Tomales Bay. For years, as the oyster guru at Nick's Cove and Hog Island, the founder of Pickleweed Point Community Oyster Farm, and the tireless promoter of bay ecology (human and wild), Luc has kept the bay's spirit strong. Now at Saltwater, a tidy paean to the beautiful bivalve on the road to Point Reyes National Seashore, he dishes the most eclectic mix in the Bay Area: Scotty's Coves, Tomasini Points, Drake's Little Bajas . . . It's a whole different world out there on the peninsula.

SHAW'S CRAB HOUSE, CHICAGO

Art deco masterpiece displaying perfect equanimity for East Coast and West Coast for more than thirty years. Steadfast custodians of the Oyster Hall of Fame.

SWAN OYSTER DEPOT, SAN FRANCISCO

A true lunch counter, as it has been since 1912. (No breakfast or dinner service.) Have your lunch at 10:30 a.m. to avoid the two-hour lines of tourists fighting to snag one of the barstools.

THE WALRUS AND THE CARPENTER, SEATTLE

A tiny space that has remained smokingly hot for an unprecedentedly long time. What's Renee Erickson's secret? The tucked-away speakeasy vibe? The crazy chandelier (snagged at an LA flea market and reimagined)? The perfectly curated and shucked oysters? It's just instinct, man. If you don't get it, you never will.

WATERBAR, SAN FRANCISCO

One of the most eclectic and adventurous oyster programs in the country. Nowhere else do you find Kumamoto flights (Baja, Humboldt, Puget Sound), New Zealand Flats, and other exotic fare. The view of the Bay Bridge doesn't hurt, either.

THE WISH LIST
Haven't been, but I hear great things.

Carr's Oyster Bar, Stanley Bridge, PEI
The Céilí Cottage, Toronto
Curious Oyster Company, New Orleans
Eat the Rich, Washington, DC
Fishing with Dynamite, Manhattan Beach, CA
GT Fish & Oyster, Chicago
John Dory Oyster Bar, New York City
Kimball House, Decatur, GA
Maestro S.V.P., Montreal
Merroir, Topping, VA
Mignonette, Miami
Naked Oyster, Hyannis, MA
Notkin's, Montreal
Rappahannock, Richmond, VA
Rocksalt, Charlotte, NC, and Charlottesville, VA
Rodney's Oyster House, Vancouver, Calgary, and Toronto
Saltine, Jackson, MS
Seither's Seafood, Harahan, LA
Select Oyster Bar, Boston
Taylor Shellfish Oyster Bar, Seattle

ACKNOWLEDGMENTS

THIS BOOK WOULD NOT EXIST if Adrienne Anderson hadn't walked into the Black Trumpet Bistro in Portsmouth, New Hampshire, where I sat brooding over the impossible logistics of shooting scads of oysters across an entire continent, and waved her magic wand and made all my troubles go away. As it turned out, we got stuck at the same table, and as it turned out, she was a food stylist, and as it turned out, her studio partner, David Malosh, loved oysters and had a few insights about how to photograph them. Sure, she said, they'd do the studio shots and the location shots, too. No problem.

Just like that, we had a book.

Adrienne, David, and I have now spent months on the road together, coordinating oyster shipments and shoots, standing in bays in the rain at 6:00 a.m., and crashing in an extraordinarily strange variety of pads, and it's all gone down like a charm. This book puts their talents on full display, but what it doesn't show is what idyllic companions they are. They can laugh off plane cancellations, charm strangers, and produce unforgettable meals out of random kitchen scraps. Their palates are far more acute than mine will ever be. Many of the best flavor descriptions in here are theirs. Anything having to do with hot dogs or mac and cheese is definitely David's.

But David and Adrienne were just the start. This book would also not exist if a dream team of oyster farmers, distributors, scientists, chefs, bookish types, and just flat-out great people hadn't donated their time, expertise, shellfish, extra bedrooms, and hip waders to the cause. Roll 'em:

DEPT. OF MODEL WRANGLING

Jim Arnoux, Tom Atherton, Jackie Baird, Weatherly Bates, Matt Behan, Sam Bennett, Skip Bennett, John Bertino, Graham Brawley, Abigail Carroll, Luc Chamberland, Steve Crockett, Deema Crockett, Ryan Croxton, Travis Croxton, Crystal Cun, Joey Daniels, Caleb Davis, Jolie Davis, Renee Erickson, John Finger, Johnny Flynn, Mary Edna Fraser, Chris Gargiulo, Luciano Gentile, Jim Gossen, Shore Gregory, Anita Grove, Garrett Hamner, Brian Harvey, George Hill, Jason Hulse, CJ Husk, Eric Hyman, Sandy Ingber, Adam James, Jennifer Jenkins, Nick Jones, Matt Ketcham, Anthony Kinik, Aluxa Lalicker, Jazmine Lalicker, Mike Lata, Dan Lewis, Dan Light, Scott Linkletter, Sharon Littledeer, Ben Lloyd, Connie Lu, Kevin Lunny, Nancy Lunny, Heather Lusk, Pete Macandrew, Steve Malinowski, Michelle Marek, Jon Martin, Kathy McLaggan, Victor McLaggan, Smokey McKeen, Annie McNamara, Dan Meiser, Carter Newell, Kathleen Nisbet-Moncy, Sean O'Brien, Jules Opton-Himmel, Danielle Orcutt, Jeff Orcutt, Pete Orcutt, Nick Papa, Pig, Marco Pinchot, Steve Plant, James Powers, Ryan Prewitt, Paula Quigley, Tim Rapine, Perry Raso, Keith Reid, Christa Relyea, Dave Relyea, Karen Rivara, Frank Roberts, Rosalie Rung, Richard Rush, Terry Sawyer, Brenna Schlagenhauf, Erik Schlagenhauf, Barb Scully, Ben Scully, Morgan Scully, David Seigel, Jeremy Sewall, Chris Sherman, Bill Silkes, Billy Smith, Ralph Smith, Thomas "Uptown T" Stewart, Andrew Taylor, John Martin Taylor, Malindi Taylor, Karen Underwood, Boris Vega, Tommy Ward, Matt Welling, Ian Wile, Molly Woodhouse, Greg Woods, Tracy Woody, Brian Yip, Jordan Zirlott, Lane Zirlott, Krystof Zizka

DAVID MALOSH
is a Brooklyn-based photographer
who shoots food and then eats it.
He has shot for *Martha Stewart Living*,
Food & Wine, the *Wall Street Journal*,
and many others.

ADRIENNE ANDERSON
is a Maine-based stylist who makes
food and then looks at it.
Her pottery studio, Factory Island,
turns old oyster shells into ceramics.

ROWAN JACOBSEN
is a Vermont-based writer who eats
food and then thinks about it.
He is the author of *A Geography
of Oysters*, *American Terroir*,
Apples of Uncommon Character,
and other books.

DEPT. OF SLEEP Erik Anderson, Linda Landry Anderson, Heather Blackie, Danae Blythe, Andy Bromage, Annie Christopher, Matt Clery, Pipes Cove, Jock Crothers, Davida Ebner, Johnny Flynn, Maryellen Hanley, Paige Hicks, Sarah Jones, Tim Jones, Sharon Kitchens, Liz LeBleu, David McMillan, Alison Moncrief, Karen Rivara, Greg Rivara, Sarah Malinowski, Lissa James Monberg, Steve Pocock (for preventing an untimely death by bear), Eric Sussman, Mick Unti, Brent Zirlott, Rosa Zirlott

DEPT. OF CONSULTATION John Brawley, Jessica Burkins, Patrick Canton-Gayton, Clammerhead, Joth Davis, Helen Labun Jordan, Brian Kingzett, Don Lindgren, David McMillan, Patrick McMurray, Ian McNulty, Daniel Notkin, Ilene Polansky, Julie Qiu, Stephanie Richards, Charlie Robertson, Jon Rowley, Carter Stowell, Al Sunseri, Bill Walton, Beth Walton

DEPT. OF MUSTARD PICKLES Catherine Baird

DEPT. OF SCRIVENING Kathy Belden, Rachel Mannheimer, Nancy Miller, Patti Ratchford, Laura Phillips. This book smolders thanks to Ben Tousley.

DEPT. OF HOMELAND SECURITY Special thanks to Mary Elder Jacobsen for classing up the joint with her perfect poem, and to Eric Jacobsen for eating the Belon.

GLOSSARY

ADDUCTOR. The muscle an oyster uses to hold its shell closed. The adductor is clearly visible in an opened oyster as a white disk in the center of the meat, and it's responsible for a lot of the sweetness and chew in an oyster. Note that it isn't *abductor*, though you will find it listed as such in lots of sloppy books and websites that should know better.

AQUACULTURE. Farming the sea.

BIOFOULING. See *Fouling*.

BIVALVE. A mollusk having two hinged shells (bi-valve) that open and close. Oysters, clams, mussels, scallops. Not snails.

BOTTOM PLANT. A method of oyster cultivation where oysters are broadcast into the water once their shells are large and strong enough to withstand predators. The oysters drift to the bay bottom. Connected to the mud (as opposed to living out their golden years in bags or other gear) they develop stronger, rounder shells and more intense flavor.

BRINE. Saltwater. Flavorwise, seawater has a lot more body than mere salty water; there are rich mineral and umami elements. The bane of my writing life is that there are no real synonyms for "briny."

CHINESE HAT. A spat-collection device made of stacks of conical, lime-encrusted plastic disks. The disks are dipped in a concrete-lime slurry to simulate shell (baby oysters' favorite target) and are positioned in the water near wild oyster beds in summer, just before spawn. The larvae "set" on the Chinese hats and then the spat are scraped off and grown in protected environments. Some styles really do look like Asian paddy hats, while others look more like the flowerpots the band Devo used to wear on their heads.

COCKTAIL OYSTER. A shrimpy one (under three inches). Like a cocktail napkin.

COCKTAIL SAUCE. A red amalgamation for-merly used to mask the flavor of feeble oysters.

CULTCH. Empty shell used as a setting surface for oyster larvae. (Oyster sperm and eggs fertilize in the water column, and the resulting free-swimming larvae have about two weeks to find something hard and slightly rough to attach to. They like shell best, followed by concrete, ceramics, and rock.)

DREDGE. A toothed metal basket dragged behind a boat that scoops up oysters from the sea floor. Also a verb.

FINISHING. The practice of moving market-sized oysters to different waters for a short period to give them the flavors of that place.

FLUPSY. FLoating UPweller SYstem. It's how most people raise their seed oysters these days. You float a raft in a bay, or you use a dock, and you grow the oysters in open barrels beneath the decking, with motorized upwellers constantly pumping water through them.

FOULING. All the crap that grows on oysters and oyster gear while it's underwater. Seaweed, algae, sponges, barnacles, tunicates, and god knows what else. It can pretty quickly choke off the flow of water through a cage or bag, so most growers expose their gear to air and sunlight regularly to kill the slime. Also known as biofouling.

GIGAS. The Pacific oyster, *Crassostrea gigas*. Native to Japan, now farmed on six continents. Its fast growth rates and flexible requirements have made it the main oyster farmed worldwide.

GLYCOGEN. The animal form of starch. Animals combine glucose (sugar) molecules to form tightly packed glycogen molecules that make excellent long-term energy stores. An oyster in late fall is packed with glycogen in preparation for hard times. A glycogen-stuffed oyster looks plump and opaque. Glycogen is usually cited as the source of an oyster's sweetness, but there's no reason it should taste sweet any more than starch does. I sometimes wonder if glycine or other amino acids are responsible for an oyster's sweetness (as they are in shrimp and lobster).

GRADE. The act of sorting oysters by size and cup depth. A surprisingly important part of what sepa-rates the top oyster growers, who "high-grade" their oysters to extremely exacting specs. Oysters that don't make the cut get returned to the water for additional growth or sold under a second name.

HATCHERY. A facility for producing baby oysters (seed). Particularly godlike male and female oysters are "conditioned" in warm saltwater tanks to make them think the summer breeding season is nigh. They convert their energy stores into sperm and eggs. Then they get the full hot-tub treatment and they shoot their wads. Males look like they're shooting a thin stream of milk into the water; females clap their shells to pump out a gray cloud of fine particles. After fertilization, the larvae hatch, and they are put in a new tank containing fine grains of sand or ground-up shell. Once the larvae set on these grains, they are ready to be shipped to farms.

KUMIE. Nickname for a Kumamoto oyster. Also known as Kumo.

LONGLINES. Lines of rope strung on poles off the ground in the intertidal zone. Some growers string spat-covered shells directly onto the lines, others attach bags of oysters to the lines.

MANTLE. The outer "lip" of the oyster, which it uses to both build new shell and to sweep food across its gills. Generally dark on a Pacific oyster and pale on an Eastern oyster.

MERROIR. The taste of place, sea-style. The terroir of *La Mer*.

MIGNONETTE. Classic French sauce for oysters. Traditionally, just red wine vinegar, shallots, and ground pepper. Today, all sorts of vinegars and citrus juices can supply the acid, wines and booze sometimes play a role, herbs pop up, sweeteners crash the party, and the whole thing is sometimes iced. Don't tell France.

MINUS TIDE. An extreme low tide that exposes more of the intertidal zone than usual. Minus tides are predictable and very handy for oyster farmers growing intertidally, because they can harvest by simply walking out on the flats.

OLY. Nickname for an Olympia oyster. Rhymes with "holy."

OSTREAPHILE. Oyster lover.

OYSTER DRILL. A sea snail and ostreaphile. Drills relentlessly stalk oysters, drilling a hole through the shells with file-like tongues and devouring them inside their own shells.

PHYTOPLANKTON. Single-celled pseudo-plants. Algae. Photosynthesizers par excellence. The base of the marine food chain. And oysters' favorite food. Oysters feed by pumping seawater across their gills and straining out the plankton— the microscopic organisms.

PLUFF MUD. The distinctive muck of the South Carolina Lowcountry. As described by Lowcountry native Cathy Miller on her *Charleston Audubon* blog: "The slippery, shiny brown-gray, sucky mud, with a distinctive smell like none other, of the tidal flats and spartina grass salt marshes . . . It is a sweet, pungent, distinctive odor that emanates and combines with the damp, salt air."

PPT. Parts per thousand. (See Salinity.)

PURGE. The practice of placing bottom-grown oysters in an off-bottom location so they can spit out any sediment that has accumulated inside their shells.

SALINITY. The salt content of water, measured in parts per thousand (ppt). Nothing affects the flavor of an oyster more, because an oyster's saltiness directly corresponds to that of the water it grew in. The open ocean has a salinity of about 34 ppt, with a few hot, dry places, which get a lot of evaporation, going even higher. (The Red Sea pushes 40 ppt.) Most bays are brackish, mixing freshwater from rivers with seawater. The top of Chesapeake Bay has a salinity of less than 10 ppt, while the mouth is closer to 25 ppt. Most people prefer an oyster from waters having 20 to 30 ppt salt, though tastes run the gamut.

SEED. Baby oysters. At first, when they're just a few weeks old, they really do look like seed—quinoa in particular. But they double in size every day over the summer. In one to two years (longer in a few cold places), a pound of oyster seed will balloon into more than 100,000 pounds of market-sized oysters. Crazy, Silicon Valley numbers. Some oyster farmers buy seed from hatcheries at the quinoa stage and raise it in flupsies (see above), while others prefer to buy it when it's thumbnail sized and get it right into bags.

SHUCK. To open an oyster shell, generally using a specialized knife.

SINGLES. Oysters being grown for half-shell service instead of shucking houses. Singles should have a nice shape and cup depth and shouldn't be attached to other oysters, as opposed to "clusters," which come clumped together in all sorts of shapes and are traditionally shucked and sold by the gallon.

SPAT. A dot-sized new oyster that has just settled onto a hard surface. So called because they were just "spat" from the adults. Somewhat interchangeable with "seed," except seed generally refers to baby oysters bought by the millions from hatcheries, while "spat" refers to wild babies that spatter existing shells, rocks, concrete, and any other hard surface in an estuary.

SPAWNY. Description of an oyster that is getting ready to reproduce. It has converted most of its energy reserves into gonad. It will tend to look milky and lumpy, with translucent gills, and will not taste very good.

SUSPENSION CULTURE. A method of growing oysters in which they are suspended from a floating raft in trays or nets. Popular in places with little beach and very deep basins, like British Columbia. Tends to producer an oyster with a lighter flavor and thinner, more elegant shell.

TONGS. Traditional tools used for harvesting oysters from skiffs in shallow water. Basically, twelve-foot salad tongs with toothed baskets on the end. Not for the faint of back. Still used in the Gulf Coast, the Maritimes, and a few other places.

TUMBLING. A relatively new method of raising oysters, which like to grow long and flat and turn into "potato chips" if they can. Tumbling—originally in mechanical barrel tumblers, now also by growing the oysters in bags attached to floats that go up and down with the tides—keeps chipping off the thin growing lip of the potato chip, forcing it to "cup up" and strengthen its shell. Tumbled oysters look polished and deep-cupped.

UMAMI. The "fifth taste." Umami is the savory, meaty sensation you get from anchovies, soy sauce, and prosciutto. MSG is pure umami. We have taste buds specifically for detecting umami, just as we do for sweet, salty, sour, and bitter. Oysters are incredibly high in umami, and that's a big part of their appeal. You can shake as much salt as you want on a cod filet, but it's still not going to have the mouth-filling flavor of an oyster; the difference is umami. Umami is the taste of amino acids, and oysters produce amino acids to keep their osmotic pressure in balance; without those amino acids in their cells, the salt in seawater would suck all the water out of them. So the saltier an oyster's environment, the more umami it will produce, and the more savory it will taste.

UPWELLER. A tank or tube that holds baby oysters and pumps fresh seawater over them, ensuring a constant supply of food. Baby oysters feed like velociraptors, so an upweller allows you to grow many more in a confined space than would be true under natural conditions.

UPWELLINGS. Plumes of deep water that rise to the surface. This often happens where deep ocean currents collide with the coast, forcing deep water to the surface and providing extra nutrients for algae growth, since key nutrients tend to sink. Upwellings are thus key drivers of marine productivity.

VIBRIO. A naturally occurring bacteria in oysters. It doesn't harm the oysters, but it can make people sick. Most cases of vibrio involve garden-variety food poisoning, but a strain called *Vibrio vulnificus* that occurs primarily in the Gulf of Mexico can be lethal to people with compromised immune systems. Vibrio is only active during the warm summer months, and it is killed by cooking. Stay strong, avoid raw oysters in August, and you're golden.

VIRGINICA. The Eastern oyster, *Crassostrea virginica*, native from the Gulf of Saint Lawrence to the Gulf of Mexico.

INDEX OF OYSTERS

So many oysters, so little space. Every oyster mentioned in *The Essential Oyster* is listed below. But although we've spent the better part of a year combing the continent (yea, the globe) for bivalves, there are just too many brilliant oysters out there to fit them into anything as finite as a book. And new standouts appear constantly as more and more people get into the shell game. If you're seeking information on oysters you don't see here, try my websites: Oysterguide (for my opinions) and Oysterater (for everyone else's).

INDEX OF RECIPES

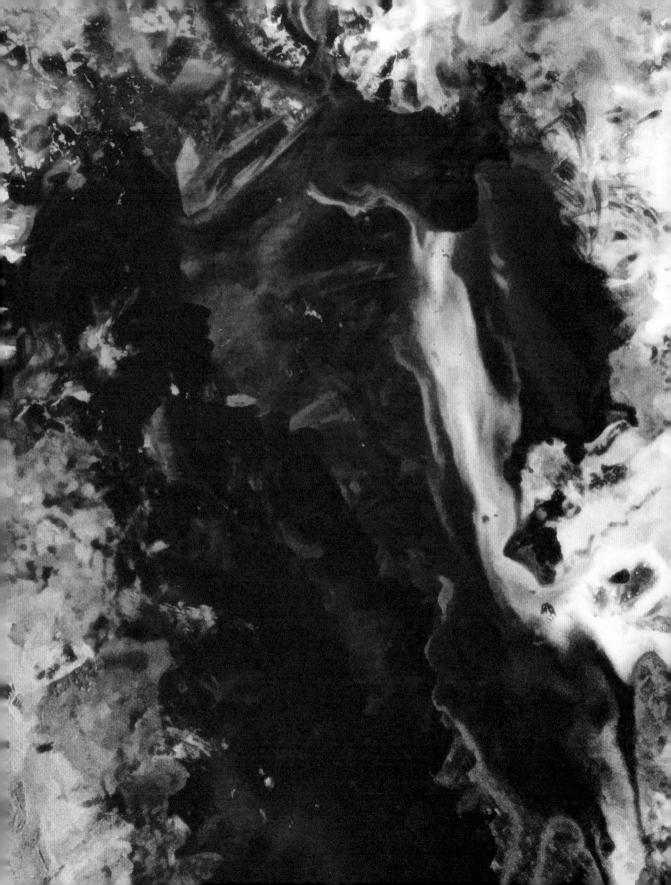

DATE DUE